Sequel to Acorn Publishing's
2016 *Memoir of Excellence* Award-Winner
Woman on the Verge of Paradise

In this refreshingly intimate search for the line between "sanity" and "insanity," a sassy seductress encounters human grit, benevolence, and one man who isn't weird.

"This gem of a story sews together personal reflections on trauma, unbearable loss, and survival. The author's wicked sense of humor makes for a page turner filled with colorful observations of therapists (she is one herself), relationship conundrums as a single woman, clergy, religion, politics, and troublesome neighbors. Although her comments are often tart, her essential vulnerability and courage shine through.

I highly recommend *InSanity*, especially if you appreciate an earthy, authentic, and witty style. It's Engel's best book, and I loved it."
—Silona Lynne Reyman, Ph.D., Author, *Musings of a Ghost Mother*

"I guzzled it. If you are after sunshine and roses, this book is NOT for you. If you can cope with suicide, pain, grief, frustration and anger with a generous helping of laughter and hope, come along for a dramatic, no holds barred ride . . ."
—Sue Goldberg, Blogger, Elephant's Child

I don't think I'm insane. I don't want to be. Am I merely in denial of my insanity? As we know, denial is its own form of insanity. So, I'm insane for believing that I'm sane and not insane. Right? If you're confirming my insanity and you're insane too, can we be normal together? Because if you're sane but I'm insane, I don't want your company. And if you're insane but I'm sane, feel free to drop by whenever I'm bored. You entertain me. Don't stick around too long, though. You exhaust me. *from page 61 of InSanity*

<u>Author's Note:</u>

While you need not have read *Woman on the Verge of Paradise* to follow the characters and events in this story, and while I'm biased on the matter, that would be ideal. Please note that *InSanity* is a heavier story. I go darker in this memoir, so you might even enjoy reversing the order and (re)reading that one next.

Regardless, I come out smiling in both, as will you (fingers crossed). Furthermore, I'll take good care of you by inciting laughter and nudging you towards a deepened sense of self-love and forgiveness, throughout our shared adventures.

InSanity draws the reader into my real-life events. I took creative liberties here and there. Names have been changed, excepting for those who generously granted me permission to use their actual names. All told, *InSanity*'s substance is as true as my desire for chocolate right now. (That's intensely "true". Excuse me while I scour my kitchen cabinets for chocolate remnants. Fingers crossed.)

Cover Graphic Designer, Steven Kistler
Galaxy background photographed and shared by NASA
Hubble Space Telescope Images / Hubble_ultra_deep_field
Image of the Earth from Wikipedia.com

Introduction: Is it Just Me?

"My mind is a bad neighborhood that I try not to go into alone."
—Anne Lamott

Musings swirl. Then twirl. And hurl. They contort into skilled, agile backflips across a sleek narrow balance beam, twisting gracefully to land with breasts pumped outwards. An enthused series of tens from all but the Russian judge ignites suspicion. What a piss ass. He probably needs to get laid. Oy. Why do I go there?

Popcorn. A popcorn ceiling. Not nearly as tasty as movie theatre style. Not that I tasted the off-white, bump-infested ceiling in my little bedroom in Chico, California where we have . . . ginormous spiders. I could practically ride that one. It's huge, unlike almost any penis I've seen.

Shit, is it just me or are everybody's brain cells mysteriously busy boogers, frenetically body-slamming against each other's elastic membranes, then rebounding full speed ahead like Martha Stewart at the mention of Chippendale's most girthy, barely-of-age hottie. Or am I merely jealous of anyone with money to burn? There's that too. But let's fixate on the former. It's more fun, and I'm weird that way.

He doesn't notice.

My right arm floats in slow motion towards my torso, as I keep sight of the spider. It's moving quickly to the doorway now. I bet he wants out.

Hey, how do I know it's a he? I'm not *that* close. I'll kill her later. Wait, why would I do that? She means no harm! No reason to go all homicidal psychopathic murderess on poor Charlotte. So sweet and innocent, best friends with a pig and all.

Am I crazy? Am I not crazy? If I'm crazy, am I crazy for thinking I'm not crazy? But if I'm not crazy, am I not crazy for thinking—my musings hurt. That's it; I'm not crazy. No? No, no?

Oh all right, yes. Yes, yes. Check box one, check box two. Cash? No, check. Check please.

I hate waiting for the check. You know? They're never quick to bring it. Bring the damn check! Twenty minutes later they act all

smiley, flip it under your nose, and say "Take your time." I already did, honey, waiting for you to bring the damn check! Oy.

Warmed bed sheets brush briskly against my right calf.

My face lowers itself hypnotically, as I sink into Jeff's thoughtful gray-blue irises. Oh, I forgot: I'm having sex. Like, now. And I'm not alone. Jeff and I. No joke. No dream. I'm sure it's not a dream. Dream sex proceeds flawlessly. Right?

I'm right, right? Wait a minute. You're awfully invested in my mental state. What's up with that? I'm a kind, caring person at times. Sure I'm a bitch too, but only when merited. Usually. Other times, I'm an accidental bitch who knows better. I mean, what's all the "You're crazy" stuff about, and what qualifies you to say it? Then again, perhaps you state it lovingly. Shall I thank you for the praise and return to shamelessly unfocused love-making?

Jeff's staring at me. Oops, I keep checking out—trying to protect my heart I suppose.

Doesn't bode well for a successful romance, does it?

Chapter 1: Strings

"If my heart could do my thinking, would my brain begin to feel?"—Van Morrison

Jeff's a good one, I remind myself. I'm sure. I always am. (In retrospect, he wasn't so good. Retrospectively, they never were.)

"He's too nice to give you any writing material," Brandi had told me. Jeff was honest about his desires for sex sans strings. I'd tossed Brandi a "Sign me up," and he called a few days later.

Now, with Charlotte still eying us from the door frame of the popcorn ceilinged bedroom in the house I share with Stephen, his house, I'm having sex. And I'm not alone. As in right now—the friends with benefits package I'd desperately craved for so long. Yes! Sex. Now. Me. And someone else too.

Um, oops. He's alongside me.

"You seem a million miles away." Jeff's voice, sad and somewhat irritated.

Oops. "I'm sorry." I feel bad. "I was lost in thought, I guess."

"What's wrong?"

"No, nothing. Sorry." I curl over to my side, now face-to-face with my lover. I reach out to stroke his stilled forearm.

Our arrangement involved weekly trysts. That's all he could afford—emotionally, practically. It worked for me. I had too many distractions as it was. It'd take the edge off, I figured. An ideal situation, I'd told myself, as if there's such a thing.

Let's face it, either there's an attraction or not. Sometimes it grows, but sparks can't be willed into existence. Thoughts don't make it so.

Yet once the hormones start dancing, the brain is nowhere to be found. Jeff and I had at attraction fresh out of the starting gate.

For that first date, I'd rushed into Starbucks two minutes behind schedule.

A slender, fair-skinned man strolled towards me. "You must be Robyn. I'm Jeff." He grinned and offered his hand.

"I am. I mean, I'm Robyn. Good to meet you." Nice warm handshake, and you're pretty cute, I thought.

"Nice to meet you too, Robyn."

Jeff treated me to coffee and a brownie. We sat at the nearest table, where easy conversation included talk of family, career, and my favorite comedic movie, *Airplane!* He knew all the best lines: the surely-Shirley banter, the cockpit and Turkish prison quips, the prim and proper little girl with a penchant for coffee that she takes Black like her men, etc.

I don't remember laughing so much during a date, except under my breath. This was a very good sign, so good, my mind drifted from the concept of "no strings attached" and into stringy steamy delight.

Pizza. Steamy hot pizza with long hearty stretches of cheese that get twisted around the tongue, generously entangled throughout the mouth in a flavorful feast that would sustain me for weeks, months, perhaps years to come.

I nibbled at the last of my brownie crumbs.

We noticed it was dark outside, so Jeff walked me to my car in the parking lot. Our date ended with a warm embrace, a quick peck, and an agreement to see each other again.

Anticipation simmered as we attempted to mesh schedules for several days. My birthday plans and Jeff's long work hours posed challenges.

At last: "I know it's last minute," he told me one evening, "but I have a birthday gift for you. I want to see your face when you open it. Are you free tonight?"

I tried to play it cool. "Ah, you shouldn't have. I'll be right over." We laughed.

"Actually, give me an hour or so."

Jeff welcomed me into his dimly lit apartment. I couldn't see beyond a glow from a cluster of candles on the coffee table. He took my hand and walked me to the sofa, where we sat side by side. Jeff reached for a small wrapped package. "Belated happy birthday, Robyn."

"You shouldn't have." I gushed and ripped off the paper. "*Airplane!* I love it!"

"Thanks," I whispered, leaning towards him. We then partook in nibbling, intense breathing, and disrobing.

His place felt like a sauna that had been set ablaze. Typical Chico summer. Add to that our broiling attraction, the formula equated with a hotter date than I could've imagined.

"Just to let you know . . . I don't usually have sex so fast. Actually, I don't usually have sex at all."

"Don't worry," he assured me. "I know you're not like that. I'm not either. I just really like you."

Jeff slipped a condom out of his pocket.

His heavy breathing and sweaty forehead aroused me until hefty droplets of his sweat hit my neck and chin. Yuck.

His efforts took a while. A long while.

Damnit, I thought. Another man with penile incompetence. Not again.

Finally, he worked it out.

Blissful sigh.

BBRRIING! BBRRIING! An alarm sounded, jolting us into vertical position. BBRRIING! "Shit," he said. "Sorry."

Jeff walked through the—BBRRIING!—darkness to shut off his fire—BBRRINN—alarm.

I giggled—humored, awkward, slightly embarrassed.

As he hovered over the slew of candles, I watched his silhouette banish the flames in one decisive breath. "I guess it was all too much," his tone more boastful than abrupt.

"Yeah, we are pretty hot."

Jeff eased back onto the sofa and wrapped himself around me. "We won't forget this night."

"No, we won't," I giggled.

Hours later and fully sated, I slowly collected myself.

"I'll call you tomorrow," he said, as we stood by my car.

I drove home in a giddy haze, that free-floating afterglow frame of mind.

As promised, he called the next day.

Our connection evolved into a salacious summer fling. Between romps, there were frequent "I'm here for you" phone calls. We'd stroll along the creek at Bidwell Park hand-in-hand and laugh about absurdities like a chihuahua chasing its own tail.

Wow, I thought, I wanted good "pizza" and that's what I got. Big chunks of sausage, thick bubbling stringy cheese, ingredients mixed together in ways I'd never thought possible, prepared and delivered with extra passion, just when my appetite peaked.

Meanwhile, feelings grew.

"I love you," he professed, three weeks (and approximately 5 inches) in.

The length, though not impressive, worked for me. The sentiment, however, did not.

I had decided, whether true or not, Jeff was simply using "love" in the same manner that I do with friends in this hippie slice of northern California. Still, my nonresponse must have hurt his ego.

But all's fair; he effectively took the lead in creating a different type of awkwardness.

See, Jeff was really good with his hands. I fully appreciated his heated palms massaging all stretches of my body. It felt really, really good, so good that I told him: "This is the best sex I've ever had."

"That's sweet," was my lover's only response.

Ouch. Um, did I mention how low the bar was set? It's not *that* sweet, dude.

Truthfully, as if I'm not prone to be truthful, Jeff grappled with penile issues.

Time and again, he gripped my lower back and butt in a somewhat agitated manner, then thrust and thrust and thrust into me. Jeff thought that if he shook my mid-section and bed forcefully and for long enough, he'd provide the precise degree of tension he needed to reach orgasm.

"Shh, shh, this is making too much noise," I'd say. "Stephen's home. He's asleep in his room and the walls are thin." And "I'm uncomfortable. Please stop."

Fortunately, he respected my limits. Yet Jeff was so nice, and determined to orgasm, I submitted to a moderate level of being shaken frenetically.

Approximately four weeks into our routine, I mustered the courage to ask him, "I'm the only one you're seeing, right? Do you see a possible long-term arrangement for us?"

Without hesitation, he answered: Yes, of course I was the only one. No, we have no future. Jeff wouldn't commit to an exclusive partnership with anyone, not now or later. If he met someone else he was interested in, though, he'd do the honorable thing and tell me.

<u>Note to self:</u> No strings, remember? What were you thinking?

<u>Note in response to note to self:</u> I wasn't. Lust led the way. You can't simultaneously have sex and be at your most thoughtful state.

As I continued to lose faith in our relationship, I slipped into a bout of depression. I didn't realize this then, but my brain was screaming for balance. I'd started taking antidepressants when mom died, close to 30 years earlier.

When I lost my healthcare before I moved to Chico, I went unmedicated. Several months passed, and I felt perfectly fine. Eventually the void of medication, though, caught up. At times, I couldn't control my tears.

At the heart of my sadness, I had to end things with Jeff.

On the morning of August 1st, we had the talk. "I wish you'd agree to monogamy. It's not as though there's anyone else in the picture," I told him.

"It's not for me, Robyn. I told you that from the beginning."

"I know. I guess I was hoping you'd change your mind." Damn tears. "It would hurt a lot more, Jeff, if we stayed together and down the road, you dumped me for someone else."

"I wouldn't do that. I wouldn't dump you if I met someone else." He looked at me and asked, by way of a seductive, curious expression, if I'd be open to a threesome. Or perhaps many threesomes.

"No." Hell no. "That's not for me." I sighed. "I need to end this. I hate to, but I need to."

"Okay. I mean, I don't want this, but I understand."

I leaned over and rested against Jeff's chest. He wrapped his arms around me and kissed the top of my head. Then, his lips were on my forehead. Then, on my lips. Soon, we were having breakup sex. And second servings.

"Maybe,"—I failed to deliberate with my brain—"maybe, if we need this again, can we be on call for each other?"

"You don't have to ask me that, Robyn. I'm always here for you."

After another round and hungry for real food, Jeff suggested a bite at In 'N Out. I'd never had a breakup lunch, or breakup sex, but I didn't want to say "goodbye."

So there we sat next to a sweet elderly couple who sipped milkshakes and grinned at us. I felt jealous of both their coupledom and the fact that I didn't order a milkshake.

<u>Note to self:</u> He paid; you should've ordered a chocolate milkshake.

<u>Note in response to note to self:</u> I know.

This is strange, I thought. They think we're another loving couple, yet we just broke up.

I put my burger down and looked into Jeff's eyes. "Do you see the irony in us having our last meal at In 'N Out?" He paused for a moment, before we burst into laughter.

"Let's not lose this, Robyn. I want to keep you in my life."

I didn't want to let go, but I knew it was best. Then again, I agreed to and even suggested an "as needed" arrangement. That doesn't coincide with "letting go."

"I'll try, Jeff. I'll try to be friends. I'm not sure if it can work for me."

The heart and hormones far outpower the brain in moments of weakness. Rather, in moments of humanity. Rather, maybe, all the time.

A lone tear trickled down my face. I watched it drop onto the darkened end of a French fry. Loosening my hand from Jeff's, I picked up the fry, pressed it between my lips, and slowly munched. It tasted extra salty.

Jeff and I talked by phone the next few evenings—friendly banter, nothing sexual. The calls stopped briefly after that.

I continued to slide into emotional darkness, so I broke down and called him. It'd been ten long days since the breakup.

"I just need a friend right now. Are you okay with that?"

In a concerned tone, Jeff asked what was going on.

"I'm okay. Well, no, not really. I'm really sad." I cried silently. "I'm just so tired of losing everything and everyone."

I heard Jeff's steady, caring breaths.

"I'm starting to regret everything. I've lost jobs, I lost you, I lost so many people before I moved here. And why did I move here? I gave up a great place by the beach in Alameda. I feel so stupid about everything. I was so stupid to marry Justin. It's so fucked up. I'm left with all this pain. How could I not see it coming? I should've just stayed in the Bay Area. At least I have a lot of friends there and much better job opp—"

"Robyn, listen," Jeff interrupted. "If you hadn't moved here, I would never have met you. And I don't regret anything. Not a minute of our time."

I sniffled, then asked, "You're not mad at me?"

"Why would I be? It was wonderful being with you. You're a beautiful woman and I'm grateful you're in my life."

"Thanks," my voice, calmer now. I ran the back of my arm across my face, wiping the tears.

"Do you feel any better now?"

"Yeah, I do," I told him. "I'm just going through a slump."

"Let me ask, Robyn. I have to ask." Jeff sounded hopeful. "Do you want me to come over? I'd love to make you feel better in person," he chuckled, "all night long."

"No!"

"Well, I had to ask."

"No, you didn't. I needed a friend, Jeff." Friends don't fuck. Besides you could've had me but you refused to be monogamous, as if scores of women are offering themselves to you. Or as if there's even one other female prospect. It feels more like you rejected me. And now, you don't really want a friendship either, just more sex.

Nearly two weeks of no contact elapsed.

I jumped out of bed when my phone rang amid deep sleep.

"Raw-bin!" Jeff sounded deranged. He chortled and snorted, "You woke me up, so I decided to wake you up. Bahahaha!"

Jeff's laughter was not unlike Jack Nicholson's in, well, any of his movies.

"What are you talking about? I was asleep in my bed alone. It's five a.m.! Why'd you call?"

"You woke me up, Raww-biin. Believe me. My dick's still hard. I figured it's only fair to wake you up! You broke up with me, remember! Ahaha!"

"Don't ever do this again!"

"Hahaha. Yeah, yeah, okay I won't."

Jeff didn't drink, smoke, or take drugs. The guy had an erection dreaming about me and thereby felt justified in waking me up at that hour? Must've been angry that I pulled the plug.

Admittedly, I gave mixed messages. But I was clear, I believed, that I only wanted friendship in the traditional sense. Maybe not so clear. Maybe not at all clear.

Does "no strings attached" mean, simply, "We'll fuck whenever and whomever we want. There'll be no rules, emotions, boundaries, or common courtesy?"

Even if it does, grown men don't make deranged phone calls like that. Grown, sane men don't.

That was a moment of mental illness in my book (this one), so much so that I visited T-Mobile later that morning. They gave me a new phone number, after which I proceeded to spend hours updating my contacts.

Does sex, love, or lust cause insanity?

People hide their genuine hurt, a hurt that's made exponential by the sex-love-lust thing. Men, even more, because Prince Charming oozes stoicism. That can't stick, though. A turbulent mass of emotions will free itself somehow. It occasionally explodes in the form of bitter, crazed rage.

Justin demonstrated this, time and again. But Jeff's a lot more stable, I thought. Did he have a moment of crazy due to a stiffy? Or love? Dream-state lust?

I don't understand. It makes no sense, and it makes no sense to attempt to make sense of nonsense. Still, we try. We want control and understanding. Err, we *need* control and understanding. We need to predict our futures.

Since we can't predict the greater world, we pretend to control our own little worlds. We deny our feelings. We ignore our thoughts regarding what's best for us.

Moreover, we deny our humanness. We say "I'm fine" when we aren't. We withhold tears that beg escape. We ignore the brain cells when hormones are activated. We make the same mistakes in relationships: repeatedly pursuing the same type that we know isn't good for us. We also avoid relationships and sex altogether to keep the heart intact.

We declare "No strings attached" as if this will safeguard the heart. It doesn't work that way.

We can neither control nor predict how we or others will act, or what life will pelt at us, or when we'll be taken from this world, or anything really.

The brain has no heart, and the heart has no brain. Of these things, I'm certain. Maybe.

Chapter 2: Dead Ends

"There is love in holding and there is love in letting go."
—Elizabeth Berg

A half step removed from the mucky despair of yet another breakup with yet another man who disappointed me, I merged closer to a monstrous symbolic road sign. Its letters in black bold Impact font instructed: "Keep going. No U-turn."

I did miss him. But I was relieved to have ceased contact after Jeff's crazed phone call.

Relatively speaking, I was doing all right. Then again, what's relative? Compared to my dead relatives, I set the standard for jubilant ecstasy. But compared to my living family members, I'd be considered morose.

<u>August 21, 2012.</u> I looked at my laptop screen, "Need to talk to you. Please call!" Colleen emailed.

Over the past several years, she and I had bonded over our love and worry for Justin. She'd been one of his closest friends.

I'd severed contact with him well before I moved to Chico. I was too spent to respond to his final "I'm sorry, please forgive me, I want you back and blah blah blah" letter. Actually, it evoked sincerity. He admitted to an angry temper, a troubled relationship with his father, the demolition of our wedding vows. He apologized profusely.

I withheld response, permanently. Anything I would've expressed, short of "I'm going back to you," would have angered him. Returning wasn't an option. My fears of his temper had only escalated.

It was far, far too late. I knew the pattern. Had I returned, he would've held me tight, told me I was his one and only, promised to never behave so terribly again. He'd have said and done all the right things for a full day or week.

Then he'd berate and rage at me, diminish me to nothingness. I'd cry, argue, attempt to soothe and care for him. He'd call me "a pain in the ass who needs to back the fuck off!"

The minute he ended us, I knew Justin was falling. No cushion primed for his landing.

Colleen said that Justin was terribly disappointed by my lack of response.

My ex-husband had another close friend, Ruthie. When he and I watched the news reports about the 2008 fires in Paradise, California, he dug up Ruthie's number and called her. They used to date years earlier, he'd told me. She'd since married and moved to Paradise.

Ruthie was unaffected by the fires. She ended that phone chat by promising to stay in Justin's life.

Last I heard, he was preparing to move to Ruthie's place in Paradise because he could no longer pay rent in the Bay Area.

Only ten miles from Chico, Justin would once again destroy my life. So I feared.

A stark vision got entangled in my angst: Justin's gun. That shiny metal silver-black Colt Revolver that slumbered in a glass case adjacent to Justin's precious rolltop desk. I feared his plan for its awakening.

I worried about Justin reading my book too—honest as my writing is. He'd sustained a raging paranoia regarding what I'd say to anyone about him or us. I was a "traitor," because I told Dawn about our marital problems. I was supposed to keep secrets, even from my own sister. As long as I continued to smile for the audience. That part, I mastered. Secrecy, I did not.

Worse yet, fret over Justin's suicide transformed into choking fright that he'd upgrade the level of trauma. An extremely dramatic dark fear lingered. "How dare you write all that trash about me! You, Robyn, you fuckin bitch, you were my biggest mistake. You've betrayed me for the last time!" He'd shoot me. Then he'd kill himself.

Incidentally, this murder-suicide, however incredibly devastating, would make for a box office smash. *Woman on the Verge of Paradise* would hit the big screen, starring Halle Berry and Barack Obama or Bruno Mars. In the event these celebrities were unavailable, Honey Boo Boo and Danny DeVito would work for less.

Despite the upsurge of posthumous fame and glory, it wouldn't be worth it. I'm not vain. (Not to sound vain.) Also, if someone's going to star in a movie with Barack Obama or Bruno Mars, it's going to be me. Damnit.

"Please call!" I refocused on Colleen's message on my laptop screen, then pulled my phone from my purse.

"Colleen. Hi. Is everything okay?"

"No, it's not, Robyn."

Crap. Is this it? Is he dead?

"Our friend, he . . . I hadn't spoken to him in a while so I called Ruthie. Justin never moved to Paradise. Ruthie said she couldn't find our contact information to tell us."

"Oh no." My body froze.

"Robyn, Justin's dead. He shot himself."

Relief, my first thought.

Numbness, my first emotion.

"Oh my God. When?"

"August 1st."

August 1st. Same day I ended things with Jeff. Same month our marriage ended. Same month the divorce finalized. Dad's birthday. Life cycles. Death cycles. Haunting, taunting cycles.

I'll get through this. It'll be much easier this time around. I'm fine. I'll be fine.

"Thanks for telling me, Colleen. You were a great friend to him. I was a good wife. Well, until his breakdown. I just wasn't going down with him. I knew he was suicidal, I still didn't really expect it, I'm still, I don't know, oh God. How are you?"

Colleen had survived three bouts of breast cancer. A strong, stoic woman, she'd be fine.

"I'll be okay, Robyn. We'll get each other through this. I was remembering our last conversation, and so many nice memories. Justin really made me laugh."

My brain flashed back to Thanksgiving at Colleen's house. Justin held up a turkey baster, said "Oh, *this* isn't phallic," then pretended to read aloud from it: "not endorsed by Planned Parenthood."

"Really?" I asked, insanely gullible.

"No, Robyn," Colleen gently replied, "he's kidding."

"Oh, oops. Of course."

Silly man, our Thanksgiving ham.

"I think it was a cumulation of so many years of disappointments," Colleen rationalized. "In the end, he was evicted from his apartment."

"Yeah, August 1ˢᵗ," I said, "Rent was due."

"Right. He was a stubborn man and hell bent on self-sabotage. But he was one"—tears muted her voice—"one of my closest friends. I'll really miss him."

I needed to go. I didn't know why or for what, but I needed to end the call. "We'll stay in touch, now more than ever." My voice cracked. "I love you."

"I love you too, Robyn."

I dropped the phone.

Tears torpedoed down my face.

Words raced from my mouth: "I choose life! I choose life! I choose life! I choose . . . ."

Justin's suicide released a floodgate of decades-old memories. The straitjacket. The gurney. The words, his words, "She hates me."

Mommy, God I miss you! Me. My brother, my innocent brother. The troubled middle children. The ones who ravaged breadcrumbs from Mom and Dad's best. Neglectful parenting. Inconsistently affectionate, mostly dismissive, absent, critical. She always loved me, though. Mom. My beautiful Mommy. Lousy daughter. Lousy sister. Lousy wife. "Pain in the ass."

Too much pain.

Too much fucking trauma.

Dead. The love of my life. My everything. No wonder I'd been feeling so depressed. He'd killed himself the day I broke up with Jeff. My body and soul somehow knew. We were one. He's in me, his spirit, his energy.

Justin shot himself. I predicted but didn't actually expect it. Should I have? How can we expect ourselves to expect the darkest shade of dark?

How do I keep living now?

My mind's crazy. I feel crazy. I believed so wholeheartedly in us.

My wedding vows, the promise of unflinching faith. We'd conquer any and everything in our path. My soul mate. My love. My bashert, my destiny.

Could it be possible that I'm completely sane and yet fell truly, madly, deeply in love with an insane man? Is that "mad love" in the most literal sense?

It'd be easier to bypass these questions. But denial isn't healthy. It is in fact, or possibly and under certain circumstances, crazy. Besides, I'm stable, sane, grounded. In comparison to most people. That means nothing, really. What's "norm" but an alcoholic character on Cheers?

Per www.Dictionary.com:
Normal 1. approximately average in any psychological trait, as intelligence, personality, or emotional adjustment. 2. free from any mental disorder; sane.

Accordingly, the average, "normal" person experiences no depression, no anxiety, no grief, no intellectual challenges, no repetitive concerns about finances, housing, health issues, global warming or World War; none of that. Only cheer. Perfection. Yippee.

The rest of us, all of us, "insane" and "abnormal." Wait. If "insane" is "normal," how can we be "abnormal"? If "abnormal" is "insane," there is no "sanity."

My musings hurt.

At my lowest lows, I muster the strength to reach out.

"I don't know how to deal with this," I told Shira.

"You're dealing with it, Robyn. You're dealing."

When I told Susan the details, her astute response included: "You dodged a bullet, Robyn, in more ways than one."

Kathryn reminded me of my strength, what I'd already been through.

Jonathan and Angela sent care packages and made regular phone calls to check on me. Josiah understood that Justin was "sick in his brain."

He didn't remember Justin. "You were the smart one," I told him. "You slept through the wedding, honey."

I called Dad. In part, I wanted his support. I also figured he should know. Dad had survived several heart attacks by now, in addition to many other tragedies. I needed to break the news gently. But there's no way to sugarcoat death. When someone's dead, they're dead. And suicide is not something to dance around.

"I'm sorry to say that Justin died," I told him.

"Oh no. What happened?"

"He . . . killed himself."

"Sorry to hear that, baby." Dad sighed heavily. "I never liked him much anyway."

Dad never liked him much anyway. Wow.

The local free clinic offered counseling. I knew this, because I'd volunteered to do counseling there.

"My ex-husband died. It was a suicide," I reported to the intake worker. "Can I see a counselor?"

Douglas, a senior therapist—that is, a 77 year old therapist—quoted the Bible. "'Precious in the sight of the Lord,'" Robyn, "'is the death of his saints.'"

Um, Justin wasn't a saint. I thought.

"I'm Jewish. This doesn't help. I just need to grieve." He struggled with that one. Most therapists do, it seems. Why do we have such a hard time being with people's pain? Just being with them? Just conferring safe acceptance? Even counselors are challenged by real, gritty, human emotion. Insane.

But Douglas imparted what no other therapists had. At the end of our sessions, he stood up and said, "I'm going to give you a warm hug."

I readily accepted. I needed physical comfort. In fact, my survival depended upon it.

Now, with Justin dead and Jeff gone from my life, I yearned for contact. Hell, I missed sex—that irrational, hurried, burning flesh-on-and-in-flesh intimacy.

Perhaps renewed celibacy had accentuated my desires.

"Can we talk about sex?" I asked Douglas.

He blushed but tried to appear cavalier. "It wouldn't be the first time, Robyn."

That didn't quite seem a welcoming invite. Rather than divulging details about, say, Jeff's inability to orgasm despite his repeated thrusting in missionary and then sideways positions while aggressively shaking me, my mattress, and wooden bedframe; or the indescribable sensation of his magical fingers stimulating my clitoris once he finally mastered the intensity of touch, optimal speed, and precise movement, which took weeks (and I use the term "mastered" loosely); or specifics of that nature, I instead described Jeff's maniacal phone call.

With an air of expertise, Douglas responded, "That's crazy."

"I know." Was it a justified crazy? Insanity due to stiffy?

What about me? Am I oversexed due to a lack of touch throughout my childhood? Or am I oversexed because I'm trying to make up for lost time—having been such a late bloomer? I've wondered about these things, though never out loud and certainly not in published format.

Perhaps trauma makes us all crazy. We know from large amounts of brain research (thanks to Dr. Bruce Perry, no thanks to Dr. Ben Carson) that trauma shifts the brain in such a way as to activate the "fight, flight, or freeze" response. In other words, we do whatever it takes to survive.

In the duration, our emotions shut down. They need to be freed once the crisis subsides. That part, the painstaking work of processing trauma, is key to successful healing.

Knowing this, I returned week after week for Douglas' hugs in exchange for "Jesus our Savior" sound bites. He also appropriately, astutely encouraged me to make closure some way, as much as "closure" is possible.

The mission was too easy.

Someone walked out of the main door on Montecito Avenue, so I slipped inside the building. No need to input a code. Our home in Oakland, California. I'd returned, now four years since our split and three since our divorce.

Here I am, I realized. The confining elevator in which I often rested my trusting cheek against Justin's chest.

I stepped out to face our former apartment door, a Notice of Eviction taped to it.

The halls we trekked daily.

The neighbors we were so close to, they came to our wedding. I wondered if they still live here.

A small, dark man carrying a paintbrush departed our former abode. "Hi. Looking for something?"

"Oh, um, yeah. I used to live here with Justin. My name's Robyn. I was his wife. We lived here for two years until we separated."

"I see. I'm Philip." He extended his free hand. "Justin. Yes, he wasn't good. Not good. He didn't seem right, when I tried to talk to him. What happened to him? They only told me to fix the place for new renters."

"He died. He"—it spooked me to say and hear the words—"shot himself."

"So sorry. He wasn't right. So sorry."

"Thank you. Are you okay if I look around one last time?"

"Yes, no problem. I'll let you in."

Philip swung the thick brown door wide open. Our former home smelled of a loud "vacancy" and fresh new paint fumes.

Our long hallway felt longer than ever.

The bathroom. Our, I mean my, pink bathroom. I beamed, enthusiastically appreciating its loud pink walls. I wanted to shout: "He painted it pink for me! It's still pink!"

The bedroom. Vast emptied space. I slept alone in it most nights.

A living room bereft of his numerous model planes and ships, countless books too.

The kitchen, where Justin cooked meals for me in happier times. Our routine exchange: "For you madam," he'd hand me a plate of tilapia, broccoli, and mashed potatoes. "Thank you, my babushka." Then he'd chide: "I am NOT your Russian grandmother!"

The office, still stuffy and gray toned.

One lonely chair, the only piece of furniture left. Justin's old dusty and faded cherrywood, black cushioned office chair.

After I thanked Philip, I drove downhill to Lake Merritt, a fraction of a mile away. I sat, stared up at the cloud-peppered sky, then focused on sparkly yet pollution-infested water—the area, a former haven. Time to say "goodbye" somehow.

I remembered the one walk around its perimeter we did together. Justin's sole fell off of his shoe. He was irate. I couldn't stop laughing. That piss ass. My Justin. My love. Stubborn, miserly man.

"I loved you with all my being, Mister Case. It wasn't enough. I knew that. You knew that. I'm sorry babe. I couldn't stay." Your rage and instability scared me too much. But "I'll always love you."

Nanette and Colleen planned a Memorial at Fort Point, along a small stretch of silent, inactive waters of the San Francisco Bay. Shira accompanied me for support. Fourteen folks gathered in a circle by the water on that Saturday in September of 2012.

"I'm handing out sage bundles," Nanette started. "This replaces the negative energy. We know how Justin died."

Nanette talked about how she and Betty had met Justin in law school. He complained about their giggling and "making too much noise" in the school library. Despite this, they became fast friends.

Betty would think of Justin whenever she saw or read about film noir.

Valerie remembered an abundance of sticky sweet loving moments between me and Justin.

I read the story on our wedding handout, "Little Tiny Cowboy Boots":

". . . a lakeside campsite in Ukiah, California during the summer of 2005 . . . . Robyn arrives as camp is closing, tired and disheveled. She grunts at her fellow campers and quickly hits her pillow. Robyn awakens in the middle of the night to catch a glimpse of a pair of little tiny cowboy boots at the foot of her sleeping bag."

They're not paying attention, I could tell. Cut the whispering, people! It's our story.

". . . she fades back to sleep realizing that Justin was the culprit. The next morning, while Justin is intently reading *Fabulous Small Jews* by Joseph Epstein, Robyn sneaks into his tent and places the pair of little tiny cowboy boots in Justin's travel bag. And the next day, while Robyn is semi-intently chatting with fabulous medium-sized Jews, Gentiles, and Agnostics, Justin places the pair of little tiny cowboy boots in the back seat of Robyn's car. Just as he is closing the door, Robyn peers his way. 'Justin, what are you doing?' she asks, as if she doesn't know. Caught red-handed, the lawyer is defenseless. . . The rest is history and her story and the story of a pair of little tiny cowboy boots that led to great big things!"

Shira relayed a lovingly proud "You did it" nod.

Colleen gave a touching tribute. I can't say more about it. I don't remember it. I was so focused on having delivered my, I mean, our Little Tiny Cowboy Boots story, but they weren't listening.

I realized then that the group had broken up into small clusters of folks, catching up on each other's lives.

Memories visited—Mom's memorial gathering after the funeral. It was all about the glorious, multicolored, delectable food on our kitchen table. So much cheer. In the end, Dad and I sat in shared silence.

"I'm Henry," a kind man, around 70, shook my hand. "I was Justin's Speech and Debate coach at Washington High. He was a star, the best on the team."

"Oh yeah, I have no doubts." Courtesy hid my snark. "Justin loved to argue."

A tall woman in platform shoes and casual attire approached. "Are you Robyn?"

Justin's sister. "Gayle!"

We hugged.

Ruthie wasn't there.

Susanne, his first ex-wife, blatantly absent. "She's still angry at him," Nanette would later tell me.

But he's dead. Why be angry at a dead person? Talk about a waste of ruthless venom!

People get so weird about death, especially suicide.

What you should do is keep it real. Go through the drudgery. Express your pain loudly. Don't hold back. Call death "death," not "Going home to the Maker" or any other bullshit.

Thou shalt suffer, suffer, and keep suffering, I say. And when you're done, suffer once more. But don't go outside without your shoes and socks on. You'll catch a cold. It'll turn into fatal pneumonia. You'll die. And your suffering will be for naught. We can't have that.

Wait, what am I doing to myself?

Okay, there's keeping it real. And there's masochism. I'd attempt to stay on the healthy side of that line.

This was not until after Colleen said, "Robyn, don't let your traumas define you."

This was also not until after I sat by the Chico free clinic's rose garden, waiting on Douglas.

"Are you all right?" a sweet soul asked. "I'm a Reiki instructor, and I sense a lot of tormented energy here."

"It's that obvious?"

"Yes, honey."

I heard myself sigh. "Well, actually, my ex-husband died. It was a suicide. I'm not all right."

"You're carrying his energy. Let it go, sweetheart."

I needed that.

I'd let it go. It's not that simple, yet it is that simple. Let it go. I'm not Justin. He wasn't me. Sure, he was my soul mate, I believed. I did everything I could to keep him going. I lost myself to him, in him, with him, until I had to save myself.

I'd allowed Justin's chaos to take over anyway. That's what I deserved and needed to do, I believed. It hadn't happened consciously. But it happened forcefully.

As I looked towards a bed of white roses, petals laced in subtle pink streaks, I clarified to myself that I do choose life.

I'd claim my unique, life embracing identity separate from my late ex-husband's.

I'd choose me.

And I began to let go.

Chapter 3: She's Lost Her Mind

"The statistics on sanity are that one out of every four people is suffering from a mental illness. Look at your three best friends. If they're ok, then it's you."—Rita Mae Brown

Upon my return home from the Bay Area, Stephen asked, "How was your time in San Francisco? I know it wasn't a leisure trip, but I hope it was good for you."

"Yeah, thanks for asking." I huffed out a breath. "It's hard, but I actually got to walk through our old apartment in Oakland, where we lived when we were married, and I met Justin's sister. A bunch of us honored him in the Embarcadero, right by the water. So that was healing."

"That's good. Sounds like you got some closure."

"I did, yeah, it's a nice buffer to be living here now too. You know, separated from it."

"I'm sure. I just found out, by the way, that one of my friends from high school's boyfriend did that. I tell you, she's such a mess right now. It's terrible. It's a selfish thing to do."

"Yeah, it's selfish, and"—my volume dropped—"complicated."

I wasn't going to debate Stephen. I appreciated his thoughtfulness. As for the "suicide is selfish" philosophy, it's likely said with good intention—a way of acknowledging the indescribable pain left for surviving loved ones.

But labeling the deceased as "selfish" is off base. We're all selfish; that's not a bad thing. We need to be selfish in order to survive. In the mentally ill mind of a suicidal person, however, thoughts are the opposite. When people feel suicidal, they're certain that they're a burden. It's generous to relieve others of hardship.

Also, in their diseased brains, there's one and only one escape from insurmountable pain.

"By the way Robyn, not to change the subject, but I decided to clear out the office and rent it out as another bedroom."

"Oh, okay. We're not using it, so yeah, you might as well."

"It's just my old computer and some junk in there. It'll be a decent bedroom when I move that stuff into the garage. Only thing is, you'll need to share the bathroom. But on the plus side, I'll drop your rent by fifty bucks."

"That's fine. I mean, I'm not thrilled about sharing a bathroom. But I like the rent reduction."

A considerate homeowner, Stephen invited me to interview prospective housemates.

Lizzy seemed sweet—a drifter, couch-surfing hipster. She'd started a full-time job and should be reliable financially. Lizzy sniffled upon mentioning a slight cat allergy. We otherwise liked her low-maintenance, go-with-the-flow disposition. She'd fit in nicely.

Within minutes after the interview, though, Lizzy texted Stephen to say that she'd broken out in a rash and must be more allergic to cats than she thought. That was that. Any housemate would need to fully respect and love "our" (Stephen's) Mojo.

For a series of months thereafter, Stephen had no other inquiries. Many students were scrambling for housing at the time, but that didn't impact the south end of town. His home was too far from campus.

Eventually, one hopeful inquiry came through. An older (as in, my age, far beyond college years) professional woman.

Carrie arrived for her housing interview wearing a formal black business suit, nylons, and heels. She appeared a medium-sized woman, with shoulder length white-gray hair and thick red-framed glasses. After formalities, Carrie pulled a clipboard from her briefcase and began to interview us.

"I'm very much invested in water conservation," she reported. "Hot water is especially precious, as we know, living in California."

Carrie awakes at four in the morning "to attend to hygienic needs and use the facilities." Was I okay with that? What are my bathroom habits, and how much time do I need for them?

Seriously? I don't poop or pee on schedule. Four in the morning? That's when I hit my deepest sleep. Don't wake me, bitch.

"Well, I can be flexible, and I definitely don't get up before seven. I also prefer to bathe in the evenings. We can work these things out, I'm sure."

"You actually use hot water to fill the tub every evening?"

Oy vey. Yes, there was a serious water drought, and guilt plagued me. But an evening bath had been a staple since my youth, and one that provided solace. "Most evenings I do, yeah. But I'll keep it short when you're around, and I stay conscious of water conservation too." I feigned cheerfulness.

"Okay, my next question," Carrie continued, "What is the dress code here?"

Are you kidding me? Dress code? Let's see, Mondays through Thursdays are clothing optional. Kneecaps and nipples are fine on casual Fridays. Nudie Saturdays are the bomb! But then we have white-garb-only Sundays.

"We're respectful and comfortable. Right, Stephen?"

We underscored our flexibility and easy-going nature. We get along fine and respect each other's space. Stephen discussed how we conserve energy, leaving the windows open at night to attract cool air, taking turns cleaning, and the like.

Carrie needs the place to be germ-free and she likes to clean. Obsessive-compulsive nutter. This could work. She'll do all the cleaning.

After she left, I told Stephen that Carrie and I have opposite schedules, so that was good. "She does seem a bit uptight, though."

The decision was his, of course.

Carrie brought her air mattress and suitcase the next day. Initially, we were cordial.

"How was your day?" I'd ask, as she stood at the kitchen sink to rinse leaves of kale.

"Fine," Carrie would respond, before spilling a tedious monologue. "Well actually, my boss was extra grouchy because he experiences stress-related migraines at least four times per week, and his wife is undergoing chemotherapy for cancer treatments. She has uterine cancer and although her doctor says her health is on the upswing and she's almost completed chemotherapy, my boss has been struggling. You know, I understand it's hard. However, that doesn't justify all the changes in our procedural regimen."

I slowly, indiscreetly, inched backed into the hallway further from her. She didn't look at me and didn't notice. Carrie was fully focused on thoroughly cleaning her kale.

"I'd rather keep things the way they are," she continued. "I don't like change. And my ex-husband might be stalking me again because he wants me to pay for what amounts to his alcoholism and morphine abuse. My son inherited his father's addictive personality. I told them both, I said, 'You choose the life you choose. After all, I took care of you all these years. You're on your own now.' It's going to work out because God is good! We need to help the ones we love, but I can only stretch so far for so long." She shut-off the water.

"Sorry about all that. I've gotta say, that's a little scary, if your ex-husband knows where we live."

She turned to face me. "What?" Carrie's eyebrows shot up and down. "Oh, if he's going to come after anyone, it's going to be me. In fact, I saw what I think was his old white Nissan, driving past the house last night. Don't worry. Yes, he most likely only wants me dead. He doesn't even know you. Why would you worry? Do you have an ex-husband?"

"Yeah, and I know what it's like, Carrie. I'm divorced. And he wasn't nice to me. I worried a lot about him coming after me. But now he's dead."

"That's good," she nodded.

Good? Weirdo!

"Are you dating anyone (that I should also worry about)?"

"Oh no, no. Praise God, no. Are you?"

"Yeah, I am dating, casually." I sound cool, I mused. Yep, the no-strings-attached thing worked so well for me, I gave it another go. "He's a nice man, but he's going away soon for work."

"Well," she turned back to face the kitchen counter, "I need to make and freeze my green smoothies now."

Since Carrie wasn't interested, dear reader, I'll fill you in.

I'd gotten back on antidepressants, so my mood had stabilized when my friend Donna and I met as planned at the Elks Lodge for a Latin dance fundraiser. I followed her and her boyfriend du jour, Enrique, to get drinks. The Lodge, I'd learn that night, includes a spacious reception hall and a small bar in an adjacent room.

Donna led Enrique to the far end of the bar, smiled flirtatiously, then stepped slightly behind him. (This prima donna gesture means, "What are you waiting for? Take your wallet out and pay for both of us.")

Ugh. I hate third-wheeling and needed a jolt.

I nudged my way to the middle of the bar and placed my order. "Rum and Diet Coke, please."

"That makes sense," I heard, in a deep male voice. A man inches to my right turned to face me, approving my drink request.

"Right." I replied. "Why waste calories on soda when you can get gobs of them in rum?" As if I'm a knowledgeable drinker, much less a frequent one.

"Exactly." He imparted a charming smile. The man's handsome, I noted, in a classic film noir way, like Gene Kelly. But bigger, somewhat husky. Not the kind of guy I usually go for. No, this one's rather attractive.

"My name's Robyn," I extended my hand.

"I'm Troy," he responded with a firm handshake.

Troy sipped his drink then asked, "What do you do in Chico?"

I told Troy about the dance event, third-wheeling, and that I'm a writer and social worker. He listened thoughtfully. The dreaded question followed: "What kind of writing do you do?"

Crap! "Well, I dabble in lots of things except fiction. I published a small poetry book and I'm working on a novel these days." I stopped there. My brain continued . . . it's about my spectacularly unromantic romantic life and my remarkably sexless sex life. I've had a string of failed romances, through no fault of my own, of course, except that I'm drawn to the deficient. You're an alcoholic, aren't you? You're awfully cute.

"Nice. I like poetry," Troy said.

Damn. A gay alcoholic. Well, I could do worse. I *have* done worse. I smiled at him.

"So what do you do around here, Troy?"

"It's kind of complicated," he said modestly. "I work on a spy ship."

"A spy ship!" My eyes widened, like an elementary school kid. "That's so cool!" A voice inside my head yelped loudly: Date him, girlfriend. He'll give good story!

Donna and Enrique suddenly appeared behind Troy, waiting on me. Damn.

"Sorry, Troy. It was nice meeting you, but my friends are ready to dance."

"Nice meeting you too."

Troy reached into his pocket and handed me his card. "Give me a call if you'd like to do something fun before I leave."

"Great. I will."

And so I would.

Troy and I were the only customers at House of Bamboo, a quaint Thai eatery in downtown Chico, site of our first date.

"So tell me about your work on a spy ship," I said, "or would you have to kill me?"

Troy appeared amused, however suave.

We perused the menus, took sips of ice water, and chatted.

"It's all confidential. I'll be leaving in a month or so, but I don't know for sure, and I don't know where I'm going or what I'll be doing. On one project, we drilled at the bottom of the ocean. I'm sure we were looking for oil, but they didn't tell us what we were drilling for."

I contorted my face, perplexed. "How can you look for something if you don't know what you're looking for?" Then again, that defines my dating life.

"Oh, I *knew*."

The waiter approached, pen in hand.

"I'll take the chicken curry soup with red curry," he said. "Really, really spicy if you will."

After I ordered Thai chicken with veggies, Troy emphasized, "Don't go easy on the spice please. I like it really hot."

Troy glanced at me, spooning his soup. "Go ahead. I'm listening."

"Okay, well,"—I began chewing my chicken—"long story longer, I came to Chico for a writing job that fell through. Then I went back to social services. It's great, even though"—I sat taller—"I got abused. Like called nasty names, hit, had things thrown at me. There's one client who's really big, and she said she's having God's baby. Her doctor did an ultrasound, to prove she isn't pregnant. Of course, thankfully, she's not. But hey, immaculate conception is a wondrous thing, right?"

"Wow!" Troy squinted, his face tightened.

"It's not that bad, really." I feigned modesty. "I'm pretty tough and quick to respond in crisis and—"

"Here, try this." Troy fed me a spoonful of soup, after which I quickly finished the rest of my water.

"Yeah, that's hot! Woo, very spicy," I confirmed, while disappointed that his "wow" wasn't in response to my bravado.

"I like it this way," he said nonchalantly, pearls of sweat forming on his brow.

Troy continued to eat, sweat, and dab his forehead with a white cloth napkin. This cycle repeated itself. Meanwhile, I rambled as if I didn't notice his self-induced torture.

"Woo. Oh wow!"

The waiter rushed over. "Are you okay, sir?"

I couldn't help but laugh. "He's trying to be tough. The man's gonna finish that soup, if it's the last thing he does."

With a chuckle, the waiter left to bring a pitcher of water.

"I'm fine," Troy assured me. "I like it really hot." You are, I thought, and so do I.

As he ran the back of his hand across his forehead, I said, "Anyway, I spend all my spare time, if there is such a thing as spare time, what a concept, huh? I spend all of it on writing projects like . . . ."

I finished my meal a few minutes before Troy proudly displayed his shiny, empty soup bowl.

We walked through downtown and learned more about each other. Troy goes away for four-month stints, eight months of the year. This is really good and maybe not so good, but mostly really good, I decided.

Like me, Troy doesn't want to get married again. I'm overdone with marriage. I don't say "never," so I'll say: "I won't ever get married again."

Troy's last girlfriend cried after sex and confessed to being a sex addict. I assured him, I'm not addicted; addicts get a lot of something. I'm more prone to boisterous fist-pumping versus hysterical tears after a roll in the hay.

Troy reached for the door handle and opened my car door. He then leaned in and imparted a nice kiss flavored by really hot and spicy Thai red curry soup.

"Give me a call," I said, as I scooted into the driver's seat.

"No, you call me. I asked you out, so you make the next call."

Interesting rule, Ken Cool. "Okay, I will."

And actually, he would.

Troy's cozy cabin in the heart of Magalia—a small, forest-y town 20 miles northeast of Chico—hosted date number two. He'd grown up in that cabin. Hours earlier, he asked me to visit him with a bottle of wine at sundown; he'd show me his *property*. Yeah, I was excited to see the guy's *property*.

We sat on bar stools, drinking wine at the kitchen counter, flirting, talking about family and life.

"It's nice that you're close with your family. I've had a bunch of losses, but I'm close with my family in Southern California."

"What about siblings?"

"Yeah, one brother and one sister, and"—I took another sip of wine, then switched to a quieter tone, "well, I had a second brother. He had mental illness." It took him to the top of a very tall building. Shit. Let's not talk about it. It's been . . . maybe, almost 25 years. Breathe.

"Sorry to hear that." Troy patted my arm. Nice—no need to get into the whole story. "I used to give no credit to mental illness. I didn't think it existed. You know, the macho thing. But one night on the ship, it changed me forever. I was alone in my room. There were all these voices in my head, and then I saw people. Real people shouting at me in low pitched robot voices. I thought I was going insane."

"Were you drinking or on drugs?"

"Yeah, I'd been drinking, but I always drink. No drugs." No kidding about the alcohol. Notice I'm conveniently ignoring your alcoholism and boozing it up myself? I wanted to feel cool and sexy, so I drank with him. Not smart on my part, I suppose.

Now, as I type this, I don't drink at all. It's not worth it, and I have enough self-respect to inform others that I'll take water or juice or best yet, a mint chocolate chip milkshake, instead.

"It was different, though," Troy continued, "like my mind went into this other world of reality. I heard and saw things that weren't there. Men with no faces telling me that I should take my life, laughing at me, calling me a 'useless thug.' And they were vicious. I was scared as hell. It was really real, seemed like it lasted for hours. Since then, I have a lot of sympathy for the mentally ill."

I sat thoughtfully. Substance-induced psychosis is a thing. I and experts believe it really happens. That might explain his experience, even though he says it doesn't. But it was only a one-time incident. Strange. Still, it happens.

I believed Troy to be fairly stable—a high functioning alcoholic, perhaps. Maybe his stint with demonic nuisance was an atypical moment of extreme mental illness. Perhaps alcohol contributed. We can never know for sure.

Troy poured me more wine. He also served olives, Wheat Thins, and brie.

Discourse lightened, when he turned the focus to my writing. I was happy to talk about that—my blog, some pieces I'd been working on, publishing goals.

Alas, following extended build-up, Troy hooked his feet around my legs to pull me close.

Kissing ensued. "Mmm."

"Mmm." Quick heavy breaths.

"Can we move to the couch?" I asked.

He scooped me into his arms, merged us over, and adjusted the maroon couch pillows.

We lie horizontally facing and groping each other. "I don't want to smother you. Let's get you on top."

I complied. The room heated, bodily movements accelerated, and we tossed clothing aside.

Will there be sex?

"Mmm." Maybe. Heavy breaths. "Mmm." It's soon, but it'd been a long time. And it's pretty long and big, but not moving. Wait, did it budge? He subtly shifted me up and down along his warm, manly body. Will there be—"Sorry, this feels kind of weird for me. My mother's couch and all."

Shit.

Our heart rates eased. Breathing slowed, and I collected my clothes.

He escorted me to my car, then watched me drive away under a blanket of stars. I got lost several times on the way home. Wild dogs barked viciously when I mistakenly turned down dirt paths towards them. Still, a wishful, devilish grin brightened my face.

Troy had expressed interest in my poetry. So, with poetry book and an overnight bag in hand—because, um, you never know when you might get stranded overnight a few minutes from home and need poetic verse to keep you safe—I got lost trying to find Troy's condo. I know, he had a condo and a cabin. Sexy.

Impatiently waiting, he contacted me. "For a smart lady, you're directionally challenged." I argued that I was in the correct spot; they wrongly numbered the building. Not my fault.

My date greeted me with a hug and quick kiss.

Next, we visited Sipho's for delicious Jamaican food. He paid for our meals and impressed with his usual charm.

Back at the two bedroom condo, which Troy shared with roommate Matt, and which Matt conveniently vacated to attend a concert, Troy offered me a drink.

"I'll take a fruity, girlie one."

He handed me a pinkish drink and mixed a gin and tonic for himself.

We sat on a cozy loveseat to peruse my book.

"Very nice," he approved, grabbing a pen from the side table. "I want you to sign it. You'll be famous someday."

I wrote: "Thank you for being interested in my poetry (and me). =) xo."

Troy placed the book on his coffee table and started kissing me.

Our breathing deepened, our arms wrapped around each other, and we moved to his bedroom.

As we stood by Troy's regal king-sized bed and kissed, he shifted to adjust his plush silver pillows.

"Would you look at this!" he exclaimed, reaching under a pillow. Troy pulled out a pair of very, very wide white cotton granny panties. Oprah's? Rosie O'Donnell's? Honey Boo Boo's Mama's? Confident (because I'm not nearly that wide, or wide at all), I casually asked, "Whose are those?"

He shook his head in disapproval. "Matt did it. We pull pranks on each other."

Two grown men acting like silly jokesters. "That's pretty good,"

I chuckled.

Troy left the bedroom, granny panties in hand, and positioned Matt's bedroom doorknob through one of the big granny panty holes.

We began heating things up again, when he uncovered another pair of granny panties, this one under the comforter. Then another under the pillows. Oy, joke's old.

Kissing, touching, entangled bodies. Will it happen? I prayed, but not really. I deserve it, I knew. I'm a nice lady. I do good. I could use a dose. Hell, I need sex. And then—Yes! It's in! Hallelu—Wait! Where'd it go? Was that it?

Oh well, it happened. Right? I'm pretty sure. Yippee! I think.

A phone call rattled us out of sleep. Troy took the call, and I heard raucous male laughter. "Matt. You prick!" Laughter again. "She asked whose they were. So whose are they? No way! Your mom's? That's disturbing . . . . Alright. Goodnight, bastard."

The roommate's mommy's granny panties? Yeah, that's not Freudian. Impressive prank, though. We fell back asleep, both smiling.

"Thank you for the best two minutes of my life!" he joshed later that morning.

"When do you leave?"

"I won't know until right before, but it could be real soon. A buddy got his assignment yesterday." Troy looked serious, "I'm thinking maybe even Friday."

Shit. Stay calm. "I'd like to see you before you leave."

Troy pulled his pocket calendar off the kitchen counter, flipped some pages, and we confirmed a rendezvous for Wednesday—three days away.

I arrived home to find the bathroom ceiling vent fan still on. Carrie had gone, likely to church. She must've forgotten.

But when I got home from work on Monday, it was on again.

Thirty minutes later, the front door slammed shut. I didn't hear Carrie enter her bedroom. I figured she was making dinner in the kitchen.

I finished the paragraph I'd been editing and stepped out to talk. When I approached the kitchen, Carrie stood with her head dunked down under a running faucet.

"Carrie?"

She snapped her water-drenched-hairy-white-gray mess of a head up. "What?"

"Are you okay? What's going on?"

"I'm fine! You didn't tell me your bathroom schedule, so I'm washing my hair in the sink." She grabbed a towel from the counter and began to frenetically dab her hair.

"Okay, well, you can use the—"

Carrie breezed past me and headed to her bedroom. I followed.

"You don't have to wash your hair in the sink. You're welcome to use the shower. And you left the bathroom ceiling fan on."

Facing her closed bedroom door, Carrie paused, shifting to look at me. Not just look at me, mind you. She glared at me with murderous eyes. "Yes I did!" Carrie then slammed her bedroom door shut.

KNOCK, KNOCK, KNOCK!

The door swung open. "What is your problem with the fan being on?"

"I'm just trying to talk to you. Why do you purposely leave it on when nobody's home? I'd like to understand this."

"I need to diffuse the smell after I use the facilities. Is that enough information for you, Miss Robyn?"

"But you could open the bathroom window. I thought we all agreed to conserve energy."

"Apparently, I could say the same thing about the air conditioning unit. I don't know why you have this problem. You left the air conditioning on for the past two days."

"Okay, but it's extra hot these days, and we talked about using the A.C. when it's really necessary. It's been in the late nineties, so I thought we could use the cool air. I'll keep it off, though. I'm not home much anyway."

"Well, mind you, I can't open the bathroom window because it slips off the track and it won't close properly when I attempt to close it. I cannot manipulate it at the exact leverage necessary. Therefore, my only recourse is to use the ceiling fan. This is my place now as much as it is yours! You need to work with and not against me, Miss Robyn. I didn't like you from the start, but I'm willing to give this a chance. It appears, however,"—Carrie raised her right index finger and pointed at me—"you are not!"

"How about this? I'll crack the bathroom window before I leave in the mornings, and we'll keep the fan off. If I can't work the window, I'll ask Stephen for help."

"All right!" Her bedroom door slammed inches from my nose once again.

A text from Troy: "Aunts and cousins coming Weds to see me before I leave. Mom told me becuz she knows I'm seeing you. So, tonight? Only prob is Matt's having party at condo. Can come to you tonight."

"Sure, but we'll have to keep quiet—roommates."

"Well then you can't be your loud and naughty self. I can't stay the night tho. Too much to do in the morn."

Disappointments piled on, I shook things off for the sake of a few more minutes.

We sat facing each other on a pair of bar stools at a small upscale place, for a dive bar, close to Stephen's house. As usual, Troy needed alcohol.

"Since this might be my last chance, tell me that story again about when you jumped ship and survived. I have to write about it."

"That's so lame," he scoffed. "All right, but if you're going to write about it, you have to get it right." Troy proceeded to expel details. I madly scribbled notes on the backs of business cards I'd stashed in my purse.

"For $100, totally hammered, Troy jumped ship. Alarm sounded 'Man overboard!' Strong winds pushed him 2 anchor chain. Lucky bastard! Climbed chain ladder, 2 lower levels, 2 room waist high in grease, ran thru ship tracking grease, took rm key outta pocket & tossed clothes in trash, ran naked in circles so they wouldn't trail him. Found rm. Showered, dressed in tux 4 job as waiter on ship, Captain's men knocked on door. 'Are you Troy Alvarado?' He said 'yes.' 'Did you just jump overbrd?' 'No, I don't know what you're talking abt. I was showering 4 work sir.' They believed him & left. Capt called 4 him days later. Asked how he did it. Capt said, 'For the pure audacity, u can keep job. Don't let it happen again.'"

"I just can't believe it. You're amazing. I got all the details."

Troy grinned. "Well, I was a lot younger and in good shape then, dear. It was an asinine thing to do. I'm lucky to be here."

"Dang, I know. I can't believe it. You're like James Bond, and I think you're in pretty good shape now, Mister."

He rubbed my thigh. "Then you ready to leave and test my stamina?"

"Sure."

Troy and I were enjoying each other in my bed, when Carrie shut her bedroom door.

"Shh!" I whispered, "Crazy roommate's home."

"Well then control yourself, woman! Don't take out the whips and chains," he joked in a near whisper.

Giggles. "Don't make me laugh. You'll get me in trouble."

"For having a bed guest? Is she that crazy?"

"I think so. The woman washes her hair in the kitchen sink, and—"

He distracted me with kisses.

I rested my head on Troy's chest, as he stroked my back.

"I'd say that was a good four minutes."

"I was thinking the same. Yeah, twice as good as last time." I lifted my head and imparted a half-smile.

"I'll double the staying power every time."

"Promises, promises," I paused, nervous to say: "I'll miss you."

"I'll miss you too, sweets."

"GOD Morning Robyn," Carrie's Christian email welcomed me to a new day. Lovely. She further expelled the "results of a cost analysis on bathroom ceiling-fan costs in comparison to air conditioning unit costs per hour. Please note that the bathroom ceiling fan costs five cents per hour compared to nearly one dollar per hour for an air conditioning unit. I have been making extenuating efforts toward being an amiable roommate. Your hostile behaviors make me feel minimized and dismissed. You're monopolizing the bathroom and not allowing me to utilize the bathroom fan. This is not the team I believed I had joined. Please do better. Have wonderful day.

Carrie."

I emailed back with a cc to Stephen: "Dear Carrie, As I've said before, please talk to me directly anytime. If my door is closed, feel free to knock.

Thank you.

Robyn"

Perhaps she'd finally stop the madness, knowing that Stephen now knows about it.

Nah, didn't work. In fact, the shared bathroom became a free-for-all for Carrie's trichotillomania[1] and other means of cathartic expression. Long white-gray strands of hair had been spewed in bunches all over the tile floor, the walls, and my side of the bathroom counter.

My soap, which I'd kept in my soap dish, now on the top shelf of my side of the floor cabinets.

My black hairbrush, formerly in my makeup bag, now on the toilet tank cover.

Her fingerprints decorated my side of the mirror.

When I heard her come home that evening, and as she washed kale for smoothie preparation, I approached. "Carrie?"

"Huh?" She didn't remove her gaze from the kale.

"I'd like you to please clean your hair off the bathroom walls, floor, and counter."

"I don't know what you're talking about. My hair falls out sometimes. I can't control that. You don't seem to mind a messy bathtub." She shrugged her shoulders and filled the blender with her precious kale.

"I don't know what *you're* talking about. I keep the bathroom clean."

Now, turning to me, Carrie asked, "Well, why do I find your hair in the bathtub then?"

"When I see it,"—my tone intensified—"I clean it up. Be a grown-up and quit playing games!"

---

[1]An anxious condition that involves pulling out one's hair.

"Well, you're certainly very angry. Let's talk with Stephen when he returns from work."

"Fine!" I started walking through the hallway, then turned around. "Actually, no, Carrie, I don't have time. I say 'hi' to you and you talk for 20 minutes about your boss' migraines and how you're a wonderful team player but I'm not, and all sorts of crap that I don't care to pretend to care about. All I need to know is that you'll respect my things."

"Well, I don't know."

"You don't know? Okay then, maybe you don't know what you think about my calling Stephen at work right now to see what he says about all this."

"Well, that's not very considerate of you, Robyn. He's been nothing but cordial."

"Yeah, well, Stephen doesn't know that he's living with a demon!"

"Name calling isn't necessary."

I stomped to my room and slammed the door.

Her door blasted shut a few seconds later.

Troy's text message calmed me: "What if I should desire a little more?"

"You know where to find me, babe. xo"

"I like a cute, witty, sexy woman. What to do? xoxo"

"Ah, thank you, hot stuff. Wink. xo"

"At winery. Thinking about you a bit. It's all good!! xoxo"

"Let me know if you can squeeze me in, or squeeze into me, before you leave. xoxo"

"Of course, just held hostage by job. Waiting for itinerary. Frustrating!"

"It'll come, hon. No worries. xxoo"

"I like the way you are."

Really dude? Afraid to say the three little words: *I like you*? "I like you too," I wrote.

I'd finally figured him out. Troy played it cool, but cowardice took control. He hadn't gotten his assignment yet, so we could've had more hours or even an extra week or two together. And why'd he go to a winery without me? He showed tinges of interest but was quick to shift focus.

In fact, Troy wasn't a communicator. Not a good one. He refused to deal with human emotion, killed it with booze.

I kept stupidly giving Troy a free pass too. For what? Six minutes total!? Damnit.

While tears rolled down my face, I changed into my Hello Kitty nightie then entered the bathroom to collect tissue.

Fuckin bitch! Carrie's blow-dryer was now on my side of the bathroom counter, plugged into the outlet.

KNOCK! KNOCK! KNOCK!

"What?"

"Carrie, remove your blow-dryer from my side of the bathroom counter, please!"

No response.

I marched to the bathroom, yanked out the plug and grabbed her blow-dryer, then charged back to her door shouting: "I took it hostage until you agree to respect my space and belongings. Looks like a nice blow-dryer. I could use a new one. Will you agree to be respectful?"

"Well I don't know."

I was conflicted. I can't steal. Here I am, lowering myself to her level, treating her like a kid, acting like one too.

I re-entered the bathroom and placed the blow-dryer on her side of the counter.

In the meantime, Carrie had left her bedroom. She stood in the hallway, on the phone.

I approached. "I put your blow-dryer back. Consider yourself warned!"

"My roommate isn't stable . . . yeah. I don't know. I don't know what she's going to do . . . I think she's having some sort of psychotic episode. I feel threatened."

Can't believe it. "Yeah, I'm the psychotic one!" I shut my bedroom door and signed into Facepalm, wherein I updated Dawn on the situation. "What do you think her diagnosis is?"

"Well that's easy," Dawn wrote. "She's batshit crazy!"

"Yeah, she's on the phone now. Maybe it's her psycho stalker druggie ex-husband. I can't imagine she has any friends. I'm too upset to write anything more. Talk later. Thanx."

Next, I made a phone call. "Hi, Stephen, sorry to bother you at work but the situation with Carrie is unbearable. She's constantly doing things to provoke me and then acting as if she's the innocent victim. She's leaving hair all over the bathroom, purposely touching and moving my things, and doing whatever she can to get at me."

He sighed. "Look, Robyn, I don't know because I'm not there, so I'm not going to take sides. You'll need to work it out together."

Are you kidding me? "That's insulting, Stephen. I've been a good, reliable roommate for over two years, and you don't trust my integrity? She's a lunatic!"

"Look, we're all grown-ups here. I can't be like the father of two kids. I can't be bothered at work either. If you won't cooperate, then I'm afraid, I hate to say this, but I'm afraid you'll both have to leave."

I can't believe this! "Fine, Stephen. You'll lose your best roommate."

"Robyn, if she's that crazy, it will come out."

"Sure, but it'll be too late."

"Okay, look, let's just talk all together when I get home."

As the call ended, I heard loud, abrupt knocking at the front door.

"Chico Police!" Shit. Seriously? She did call the police. Can't believe this bullshit.

Two broad shouldered, fully armed male Chico officers walked towards my room, tentatively, as I slowly emerged – in my Hello Kitty pajama shirt covering my white granny panties, bra-less and barefoot.

When their eyes met mine, their subtle smirks were bemused: "That tiny woman is the source of a domestic altercation?" (Note: I'm four foot eight, 105 pounds.)

"Oh, hi." I said casually, showing my free hands. "I'm Robyn. There's two of you, huh?"

"We travel in pairs," the officer nearest me said. "Why don't you come out to the front and we'll all talk."

"Sure." I followed the officers to the front entranceway where Carrie stood, arms crossed.

"We're officers Johnny and Mack. What's the problem here?"

I looked at Carrie to respond.

She uncrossed her arms and held them rigidly by her sides. "I didn't like Robyn when I first met her, but I thought I'd give her a chance because I'm a fair person that way, and I needed a new residence. My old landlord decided to sell and paint the building, and that's a very long story. Anyway, I've only been here for one month or so now, and she's been here for over two years. She's had her own bathroom, but now we need to share."

Carrie glared momentarily at me, then looked back at the officers and continued. "Now I can understand that she doesn't want to share, but that was part of the entire arrangement. When I interviewed, and I made sure to cover all of my questions so I wouldn't get into an untenable situation like this, I asked about bathroom schedules, dress code, and important details. She withheld information,"—Carrie glared briefly at me again—"so I've needed to wash my hair in the kitchen sink. Now I'm feeling minimized and she knocked on my door really loud several times, which I found to be very inconsiderate! She refuses to pay her share of the electric bill too—"

What the hell? I refuse to pay my part? "What are you—"

"Ssh!" The officers hushed me. Both of them. Alrighty then. I'll shut up. You keep indulging her verbal vomit and see who's cray cray. You are too, by the way, for the indulgence.

Why are the most irrational people given the most space and time for their irrationality? I never understand this.

"I told her, I said, when you run the A.C. unit it's far less cost effective in comparison to the bathroom ceiling fan. She said 'well, then you can pay P.G. and E., because we talked about conserving energy.' Now, we did address conservation of water, energy, and whatnot when I interviewed. However . . . ."

"Uh hmm," Officer Mack uttered.

Both cops stared at Carrie, empty-eyed. They asked for it. "She's small in stature, as you can see,"—she once again abruptly glared at me—"but she's very threatening. Robyn has a temper, and frankly I don't think she's at all stable."

Exhausted, the officers eventually advised us both to lower our expectations. "Just be civil. You don't have to be best friends. Just make it livable and start anew. You'll both need to make compromises. It's not going to be ideal for either of you but do the best you can. Okay?"

"Okay," I said, "Carrie, I'm sorry for upsetting you and I'll be respectful of your space and things."

"Great," Officer Mack said. We all looked at Carrie. "What about you?" he asked.

"Well, I've been cordial and cooperative all along. I just was trying to understand their structure for doing things, their dress code, rules about expenditures and bathroom use, so we don't waste water because there's a grave water shortage that's getting worse every day, you know. I was just trying to cooperate and be an asset and team player, but Robyn isn't at all accommodating."

They gave up, imparting a courteous "Goodbye and good luck."

Carrie went straight to the bathroom, closed the door, and came out within seconds. When I noticed strands of white-gray hair all over the floor, I slammed my bedroom door so viciously, I'm surprised it didn't fall off the hinges. Carrie blasted her radio, turned the bathroom fan on, stomped through the house, and finished by slamming her bedroom door.

I raced to gather all my bathroom items, then brought them into my room for safe keeping.

How? How can I deal with her any longer? And there's going to be a fuckin meeting tonight. Need strategy to stay distracted while she talks. There's no way of listening to her for any length of time without losing it.

I thought about what makes me laugh. I remembered one outrageously fun night. Kathryn, Susan, and I went out to celebrate my 23rd birthday. We rolled down the windows and shouted the lyrics to Barry Manilow's *Copa Cabana*. That's it. I'd write Barry Manilow's song lyrics while Carrie talked about how unstable and antagonistic I am. It'd keep me focused and in a silly mood.

Stephen, Carrie, and I assumed the same positions we'd taken during Carrie's interview—each woman on a separate cushioned chair in the living room, and Stephen on the couch between us.

"Okay," he started, "this cannot continue. Either you live together cooperatively or, I hate to give an ultimatum, but you'll both have to leave. Second of all, the police department contacted me. He said it could be worked out. Now, I'm very serious about not wasting city resources on a nonemergency." He looked at Carrie. "Call me first. I'm the homeowner. I'll take it from there."

"Oh, it was an emergency, Stephen," Carrie defended. "I felt very threatened. Robyn's diminutive, but she's intimidating and—"

I started scrawling: *Lola at the Cope-ah Cabana the hottest spot north of Havah-nana-nah banana my cabana boy and passion were always in fashion blah blah. Psycho bitch lady won't shut the fuck up at the Coca-Cola place. They fell in love, ignored the Pepsi and again. Repeat, yada hot spot, the hottest spot north of all hot spots. Then Rico had a diamond. Cubic Zirconia, I bet. She had yellow feathers in her hair and a dress cut down to there. Where's "there?" Pretty high up, I assume. They sit there all refined and shit and drink themselves half blind and shit.*

Damnit, does she ever shut the fuck up? They lost their something (not their virginity. They lost that way earlier.) And they lost their mind. Wait, they only had one mind between them? She lost her mind, hell yeah she has.

Doing great, keep going, she's not shutting up.

"Stephen, I just want to know the structure and rules to be a team player, but when she stole my blow-dryer . . . ."

I've been alive forever and I wrote the very first song. Barry, you're awfully arrogant. But you're so good, honey. I wanted to marry you when I saw you in concert forever ago and even now. You put the words and thoughts of me holding you when we spent time in New England will this strong yearning melody together. You're music, and you write the songs so you ooh can mooove."

"And Robyn's defensive posturing in response to everything I say, Stephen, isn't conducive to a harmonious housing situation."

She sits there so I remember all my life, raining just as cold even now the world has come so far when I can't live without you even now is wrong without you can't smile Mandy Sandy you're mighty randy, my love I'm doing great, but that was forty years ago. Now it's the disco. How much longer?

Thank goodness; I eyed the clock and stood up. "I'm interrupting because this has been going on for 45 minutes and I haven't said a word. I'm going to grab my jacket and leave. I have to be somewhere." That is, I had to be anywhere else.

"See, Stephen," Carrie argued, "See how defensive she's being. I'm trying to cooperate and work things out. You had your processes in place. I'm just trying to understand how I can accommodate."

When I put on my brown denim jacket, Stephen came to my bedroom doorway. "Hey, Robyn," he said quietly. "I just want you to know that I don't want you to leave. I'm going to suggest that maybe this isn't the right place for her. I'll let you know."

Phew. "Okay, thanks for telling me that." I won the war! Woo-hoo.

As I drove along Mangrove, I was drawn to Cozy Diner—the word "cozy" and all. Lucky me, it was karaoke night. Perhaps I'd be entertained.

The friendly emcee introduced himself when he saw me sit at a nearby booth. "Are you performing tonight?" he asked.

"Oh no. I can't sing," I chuckled. "I'm just here to listen and get a bite to eat."

"Come on! You should sing. First-time singers get a free dessert!"

Crap. I laughed. "You really shouldn't have told me that."

I signed up and wrote down the name of the song I'd sing.

The waitress had just taken my order, when a text came through.

Troy wrote: "Leaving for airport 5 a.m. tomorrow. Thank you for your company and poetry. Take care, sweets."

"I'll miss you. Be safe, handsome spy."

"I'll miss you too. xoxo."

"Robyn," the emcee called me up cheerily. "You're on!"

I took the microphone, nervous at first, somewhat quiet and shy for the beginning lines. But I relaxed into my performance, tossing in some dance moves. In fact, I was soon giving it my all for approximately five sweet families. I imagine I looked like Elaine Benes and sounded like Cosmo Kramer on acid:

"At the Copa, Copa Cabana, the hottest spot . . . she lost her youth and she lost her Tony, now she's lost her mind!"

It was a quiet night when I returned home, the calm after the storm.

I awoke late the next morning. On the kitchen table, a note from Carrie:

"GOD morning, Stephen and Robyn, I have decided, because of family complications, and because Robyn won't accommodate my presence here, I will be living with my son across town effective immediately. I appreciate everything you did, Stephen, in an attempt to make me feel at home here. It wasn't going to be possible, however, because of Robyn's attitude, instability, and erratic temper. I will contact you regarding rental payments. I'd like to be refunded for the remainder of the month, which I paid in full. God's blessings, Carrie."

Is this too good to be true? I knocked on her bedroom door. No response. I cracked, then pushed it open—nothing, nobody, empty, vacant! Woo-hoo!

Alone at home, at peace, victorious. Mojo scampered by and playfully rubbed against my calves, as if he knew that he too was free now. (The poor kitty had spent most of his days in hiding under Stephen's bed.)

"Her name was Lola!" I broke into spontaneous dance and song, boogieing throughout the house, like Martha Stewart at the thought of fingering Chuck Norris' most protected pistol.

Now she's lost her mind!

Chapter 4: Shrinking

"Just because I'm having a bad day doesn't mean I didn't take my medicine."—Sarah Howerton Kakkuri

<u>Note to self:</u> Don't be so naive.

<u>Note in response to note to self:</u> How? I mean, whenever I'm sure I've reached some potbellied guru level of enlightenment, I abruptly fall butt first onto broiling hot asphalt wondering why the hell I was so slow on the uptake.

I guess I'm too trusting. They say you should be trusting, though. Having faith in others, trusting humankind's a good thing. You just need to balance that with smarts.

I didn't exactly detect that Carrie's batshit crazy from the start—like when she asked about my poop and pee schedule. I gave her a chance. We know how crappy that worked out. Shit.

Potty time? Potty time!

Takes me back to my preschool teaching days. A bunch of rambunctious little boys dashed by me through the school halls, shouting what I heard as "Party time!" I began to sternly reprimand them. Silly me. They were just excited about going potty. Yippee! Potty time!

Ricky Goes Potty. Stupid book. Stupid company that chose to publish a whole damn stupid series on Ricky's toileting triumphs instead of my book.

"Ricky sits on potty. Ricky pees in potty. Ricky flushes potty." Really? You want acclaim for your treasure trove of empowered women's stories, so you monitor Ricky's bowel and bladder action?

"We like your book. We'll get back to you. We'll get back to you." Next thing I know, they've published a series on Ricky's potty successes. Pretty crappy if you ask me. They didn't ask me.

Maybe I should just let it go. All of my resentments. Denial. Blissful ignorance. Keep moving and grooving. Shake it off, off, off, off, off. Nah, carrying grudges is fun—delightfully empowering and judgmental.

Hey, kindly quit judging me. You like gossip and vindication too, right? I knew it. Wink.

Earth to me. It appears I'm in Facepalm now, staring at the right side of the screen: "Boost Post," "3 event invites," "Trending." What was I going to do? I forgot.

Oh, I'm naive. That was the point.

Perhaps it's not as much about my naivete as it is about reducing an intricately complex problem to a simplified label (e.g., "naive," "batshit crazy," "mental health").

<u>Note in response to response to note to self:</u> This note is too long. Long isn't always good.

<u>Note in response to response to response to note to self:</u> True. Over.

I received a message in the Facepalm chat thing, so I tap the touch pad. A friendly check-in from Ernie.

Our email chatter had been relatively spectacular. By this, I mean that the man proved capable of two-way written correspondence. Also, he claimed to look like Ernest Borgnine.

This took me to Google. Therein, I found the goofy *McHale's Navy* guy plus a highly impressive acting career, numerous Oscars, five marriages—including a one-month union to Ethel Merman— and his trademark gaping space between the two front teeth.

"I see it," I said, studying my suitor's photos. That's a good thing," I wrote. "Borgnine has character. Or he *had* character. No offense to the dead, but one's character flattens once they flatline."

Ernie didn't respond. Does he lack a humor gene?

It seems I'd find out soon enough. We scheduled brunch for Saturday at Beatniks.

I signed off, closed my laptop, and attempted productivity. Yeah, that didn't happen. A blissful nap had taken precedence.

"I'm going to take an online psychology class," Ernie said, as a barista placed our meals on the table. "And I'm gonna learn Spanish once I get my truck fixed so I can drive to Butte College 'cuz I'd rather use it than my little Kia. Funny, I had to get the neighbor to give it a jump-start yesterday morning when I ran out of dog food and the truck needed an oil change so I didn't want to drive it until I took care of that. That thing is really old. It's like an '82, and I got over 240,000 miles on it. I got it when I . . . ."

I grinned with polite insincerity, as I poured syrup on my French toast and watched his lips move up and down, up and down. Borgnine died at age 95 in 2012. The similarity hit me over the head; they're equally interesting in the aftermath of Borgnine's death.

I chewed the last piece of French toast upon realizing that boring is better than crazy. Maybe. At least it's predictable. Predictably dull to a seemingly never-ending extent.

In attempts to dodge crazies, I manage to find apparently sane ones, at least. Problem is, in the words of author R.A. Salvatore, "Sane is boring."

As Boring Borgnine reached for his coffee, I chimed in. "I studied psychology as an undergrad. It was all Freud, Freud, Freud. Things like the Oedipus complex and anal stage and weirdly perverse stuff that every psychology professor seemed unnaturally fixated on. Now I have my license in clinical social work. I've done therapy here and there. It's rewarding, but I tell my clients 'You're the expert, not me.'"

"Well, after I learn psychology, we'll shrink each other."

I countered cheerily, "No thanks. I'm short enough."

"No I mean—" he explained what he meant. Seriously?

Nope. No sense of humor.

"I know. I was just kidding."

Boring then shifted the conversation to talk about . . . I don't know. I wasn't listening.

He paid for my meal, held the door open for me, and was gentlemanly. But this didn't negate my strong urge to interrupt his ramblings and flamboyantly extend my arms to both sides, sweep our plates off the table, launch atop it, and belt out "Everything's coming up roses!"

The date ended badly: Boring wanted to see me again. I froze and replied with a "sure, yeah, me too." I called a few days later to tell him, with apologies, that I wasn't interested. He felt bad. I did too, but not nearly as bad as I felt listening to a droner with the personality of an expired Borgnine, compelled to explain a conversational, life-sustaining tactic known as humor.

He was a nice man, however, and Boring showed me that people still use the term "shrink" in reference to the helping profession. An interesting term, figuratively accurate. We shrink people to a single word or phrase, then watch them attempt to function in a "socially acceptable" manner despite ingesting an unwieldy amount of potent, brain-altering drugs. If they can do this, we take all the credit for "fixing" them. If they can't, it's solely their fault. They're "bipolar with borderline tendencies," after all.

Our bible in the mental health realm, the DSM (Diagnostic and Statistical Manual of Mental Disorders), is so fraught with controversy, it's been given a full upheaval eight times in the past 65 years. And when the current version, the DSM V, was published, I recall being told, as a licensed clinical social worker, basically: "Wait. Don't use it! There's no consensus that it's relevant." By the way, $25 million was spent on its publication.

I waited for an answer—do I use it or not? What did the pros decide? All these years later, no word from the experts. One wonders how many extravagant vacations they've been enjoying in the duration, though.

Yep, a $25 million investment, as useless as the Democratic National Committee. My Bernie. I love him so. He's a as good as they get. The DSM, not so much.

Substantial sections of the Manual remain troublesome. Homosexuality was cited as a mental disorder until as recently as 1974.

And as a kid, I'd have fallen neatly into one diagnosis in the second edition: "Withdrawing reaction of childhood or adolescence." Symptoms include detachment, sensitivity, shyness, and inability to form close relationships. Actually, that still describes me. Heck, it sounds fairly normal to me.

In the current edition, you're not allowed to experience grief when someone dies. Well, you can, but you'll risk being diagnosed with Major Depressive Disorder and subjected to trials of powerful antidepressant medications that cause stomach aches, headaches, lack of interest in sex, a feverish appetite and, if you're lucky, an uplifted mood. Caution: Might cause death by suicide. (We warned you. Your family can't sue us if you kill yourself. Happiness always. Love, Big Pharma.)

Oh, and gentlemen, Premature Ejaculation is a full-fledged mental illness too! Show some restraint, would ya? Be punctual and never early.

Parents, beware that your tantrum-raging children will be labeled "mentally ill." One of the most ignorant statements about clients that I've seen documented countless times over the years: "Little Jimmy behaves badly when he doesn't get his needs met."

Apparently, children are not supposed to have needs. If children have needs, they will express said needs. If children express said needs, they're pathological. When said needs are not met, children behave "badly." "Bad" children are consequently subjected to lifelong target practice by a slew of "professionals" who want to make "bad" kids "good" (i.e., happy).

<u>Per www.Dictionary.com:</u>
Happy adjective, happier, happiest. 1. delighted, pleased, or glad, as over a particular thing: to be happy to see a person. 2. characterized by or indicative of pleasure, contentment, or joy: a happy mood; a happy frame of mind. 3. favored by fortune; fortunate or lucky: a happy, fruitful land.

I was never a happy kid. I don't consider myself a "happy" adult either.

In fact, I was feeling anything but cheery at this time. Rather, depression had achieved a tight, suffocating hold on me. I wouldn't let it win.

There I sat, in a confining, bare walled room at the county crisis center. I'd given my information and was told to wait. I waited. And I waited and waited, feeling incrementally worthless and alone with each passing second.

"Ma'am, are you all right?"

The woman who asked sat comfortably across the room from me. She'd been through the routine before, likely many times. Her relaxed posture, and the police officer by her side, told me so.

"Yeah, I'm just tired of waiting." I looked towards her, my vision blurred by weighty tears. "Thank you for asking."

In a fully genuine, thoughtful tone, the officer who'd escorted her said to me, "It will get better, it will."

Eventually, I met with a counselor who informed me, after all that waiting, that I was in the wrong place. You know what? I was okay with that. The sole reason for my okay-ness is that she was kind. She was invested enough in my well-being to call me several hours later to see how I was doing. The woman who asked if I was okay was kind. The officer who assured me, also kind.

I'd met with another caring professional, Dr. Vangel. "Promise me you won't do anything stupid," he said, after providing compassion, a prescription for the one antidepressant that I needed to restart, and a referral to a local clinic.

"I promise." I added, confidently, "Too many people care about me."

It was the standard check-in window you find at any crisis center or Wendy's drive-thru.

"Dr. Vangel referred me," I told the young woman with short, shiny black hair and a frazzled expression. "I'm here to meet with the psychiatrist."

She took my information then handed me a cup—a flimsy transparent drinking cup.

"What's this for?"

"We need a pee test." She raised her arm and pointed towards the restroom behind me.

"No, I'm not here for a drug screen. I'm here to see the doctor."

"Standard procedure, we screen everyone for drugs." She turned her back on me and walked away.

What the hell? I've never done drugs, and I rarely drink. I don't even eat poppyseed muffins!

Feeling utterly humiliated, I sat on a cold toilet seat, catching my pee in a flimsy cup.

I walked out, cup of my urine in hand.

Robyn goes potty! Robyn pees in cup! Robyn hands cup of her pee to nearest person wearing badge and white jacket! Yay, Robyn! Yay!

Within the week, Robyn receives a $392.48* bill to cover laboratory analysis of her urine. (*Number wasn't falsified.)

Next, Robyn writes scathing Yelp review about this clinic and does not pay bill. *Bad Robyn refuses to pay nearly $400 to pee in cup! Noncompliant, oppositional defiant bad girl!*

The remainder of my experience at the clinic further eroded my mental state.

The doctor sat across the room, official clipboard in hand. He watched me cry a few tears, informed me that I needed intensive treatment (i.e., expensive treatment that's not covered by insurance). He rushed me out of his office within 10 minutes—so as to bill for a $350 "hour" of service delivery.

Incidentally, as a Licensed Clinical Social Worker—I'm a therapist, but not a doctor—I can bill for $3.47 per person for one hour of treatment when I lead group therapy. Yeah, $3.47 per hour: the state reimbursement rate as I type this. It seems California doesn't apply minimum wage laws to therapists. Meanwhile, doctors get all the loopholes they can find, create, or lie about.

Desperate, I agreed to the intensive (expensive) treatment that the psychiatrist had suggested. It included a group of peers. I needed that.

Dad forwarded me a chunk of money for it. I was touched. Without a thought, without a care (i.e., with care), Dad was consistently there for me when I asked for help which, as he knew, was fairly rare.

Mom was the same way. I missed her so much, it stung.

I showed up on the day the group was to start. "There's no group," they informed me. I spouted off some angry words to the woman behind the I'm-protected-by-you-because-you're- crazy-crisis-center-slash-Wendy's-drive-thru window and left, more wrecked than before.

"Your brother has schizophrenia, paranoid type."
That's it. That's all that was said to me, and said in that manner. No support, no explanation, no caring, just the medical terminology.

I'm a professional. I diagnosed it. It's true. End of story. Have a nice day or not. I don't care. I get big bucks. Go Big Pharma. I'm the expert. End of story.

It's an exasperating search to find "helping" professionals that are more helpful than harmful.

Mind you, I have met some kindhearted psychiatrists.

One in particular, a lovely, sharp, young woman, sat by my side to deliver my diagnosis.

"Do you know about Dysthymic Disorder?" she asked.

I nodded.

It's a benign label to claim. Basically, I'm high-functioning and managing depression that comes and goes in full force but chronically simmers under the surface. Come to think of it, much of humanity likely experiences dysthymia.

Her diagnosis gave me something concrete, in addition to relief. It doesn't carry the same ugly stigma attached to other clinical labels. We're simultaneously high-functioning and equated with a multisyllable medical term. How cool is that? Lucky us.

Dysthymic Disorder for the win, Alex!

Research, scientific research, clear evidence. Expert testimony. Research, research. The DSM's based on it, so it's valid, right? Negative.

This "research" is incredibly subjective—a slew of opinions, observations, "best estimates" that are put to a vote by a small committee of doctors. Specifically, they're psychiatrists representing the American Psychiatric Association (APA).

Yep, certainly we learn all we need to know about the truly objective distinction between normalcy and mental illness from a small elite circle of mercenary, drug-pushing "healers."

One book cover says it all. Dr. Allen Frances, Chair of the DSM IV Task Force, wrote *Saving Normal: An Insider's Revolt Against Out-Of-Control Psychiatric Diagnosis, DSM-5, Big Pharma, and the Medicalization of Ordinary Life.*

Some of us do need meds, but just one. Okay, maybe two. Not some five-item combination package deal to rob you of human emotion. They'll eagerly start you on this regimen when you're six years old.

Justin relied heavily on one sole antianxiety pill. "Forgot to take my Lorazepam, need my Lorazepam, running low on my Lorazepam," he'd whine. After our nuptials, Justin generally behaved a piss ass. I can't imagine him without this medication.

Glenn was put on Thorazine. Or was it Haldol? Or both. I don't remember, but I do remember watching him walk around like a zombie—slow-motion movements, wide-eyed, cold, pale, stoic. I hated the sight, can't imagine how he felt, if he felt anything at all. That was too much to think about. I couldn't and didn't.

"I think Justin is bipolar," Nanette wrote in an email message, when she'd learned about our marital demise years prior.

"You're probably right," I answered. "He has too much pride to ever admit having any mental health problems. That's why we're at this place."

Too much pride, far too much.

Nanette called me a few days later, furious. "Justin ended our friendship of 25 years because you told him that we agree he has bipolar disorder!"

"What? I never told him that! I've been too scared to talk to him. Wait, shit. He must've broken into my emails."

"Change your passwords, Robyn."

After his death, Nanette started an on-line memorial page. Through it, I connected with people who'd been in Justin's life decades earlier—a former girlfriend, a long-term guy pal who'd lost touch with Justin in the past decade or so, relatives I'd never heard about.

NOBODY, not one person in the handful, asked how Justin died. They all knew. "It was a suicide, right?" they either said or didn't say. Justin had been openly suicidal all his life, it seemed. Everyone knew. His relatives, his friends, his ex-girlfriend.

Everybody except me.

Nanette told Dawn—during our wedding reception—that Nanette had contacted the police several times to check on Justin. She and Betty basically had Justin on a suicide watch sporadically over the years.

Nanette's point was that meeting me had forever changed Justin's life. She thought Dawn would be thrilled to learn this. What a stress-free place Denial is.

I had no idea Justin was suicidal. Or did I?

I acted as though I knew. I did everything to prevent that type of guilt I felt after my brother's suicide. I did everything to keep my husband afloat. I gave up sex, gave up dancing, gave up time to myself, pushed us into counseling, packed him lunches, bought him cards and gifts, everything to keep him alive. For what? Sure, I don't feel guilty that he took his life. I was the best wife a woman could be. In that sense, my self-sacrificial stance worked beautifully.

How weird—to be so self-preserving and masochistic at the same time. How strange that I tried unconsciously to relieve myself of guilt over my brother's suicide by marrying and catering to Justin's emotional needs.

That's kind of deranged, but it also makes sense. When mentioning the divorce these days, I simply state, "He was seriously mentally ill."

NOBODY asks questions about that. Everyone understands.

They do ask about me, though, "Didn't you see the signs?" As if I'm to blame.

Per www.Dictionary.com:
Naive 1. having or showing unaffected simplicity of nature or absence of artificiality; unsophisticated; ingenuous. 2. having or showing a lack of experience, judgment, or information; credulous: She's so naive she believes everything she reads. He has a very naive attitude toward politics. 3. having or marked by a simple, unaffectedly direct style reflecting little or no formal training or technique: valuable naive 19th-century American portrait paintings. 4. not having previously been the subject of a scientific experiment, as an animal.

Are you as perplexed by number four as I am, dear reader? If any person or animal can explain that one to me, kindly contact me. Thank you.

Naivete isn't all bad. I wouldn't have landed in Chico if I weren't naïve.

In fact, great things are birthed of naïve seedlings. So why do we judge it harshly?

In order to dodge clinical depression in extremely depressing circumstances, naïveté is required.

You're not supposed to be depressed. Naïveté in the form of denial is (wrongly) seen as strength and cheer.

Oy. Societal norms are such that you can't win. Don't be naïve.
Don't be cynical. Don't be clinically depressed. Worst of all,
depression is so stigmatized that it feeds itself. There's no
alleviating it, when we refuse to be open about it.

I got so fed up with general blame towards the depressed and
suicidal ("wimps," "selfish cowards," etc.), I needed to do
something. I thus wrote an article to explain the strong grip of
depression; people clearly don't understand its power. You can't
will it out of existence.

When I approached the local paper with a cursory draft, they
agreed to work with me on it.

It took a while.

With every revision, it was as though I'd unwrapped another
layer of duct tape from my soul—layers of societal rules, false
pretenses, stigma; what you're not supposed to say, feel, or admit
to, protective barriers from what's too ugly for public viewing.

I edited until I felt I'd given accurate voice to my grave wound,
an injury infected by the suicidal sentiment: "I don't want this
life." I'd known this feeling in childhood too. I'd also known that
one can—like me—have this mentality and never act in a
purposefully self-destructive manner.

<u>1/23/1983 (age 17)</u>: Do you know what's scary, Diary? On
Saturday, I cried and cried—I cried about everything—how
nothing ever goes the way I want it to. God, this is supposed to be
the <u>best</u> time of my life. Things are going to be 100000 times
worse for me when I get older. How will I handle things? Oh Di,
I'm afraid. I used to think of people who commit suicide as crazy
and insecure, but now I know different because it's just an escape.
I would never (now I can say) kill me, but I know the feeling
though. I'm scared.

When I linked to the article on Facepalm, responses poured in.
Over 100 "likes" and comments expressing compassion, tears,
admiration, empathy. Several long-term friends disclosed privately
that they'd also been struggling with chronic depression.

Strangers stated, "She gets it. She understands."

Nobody said anything to the effect of: "Oh, now I know more about depression."

Everyone already knew.

Everyone already knows.

I didn't educate the masses as I'd intended. Instead, I was gifted with a massive "thank you," added to loving connections that healed me in a way no pill ever could.

Chapter 5: Saving Face

"Human tragedies: We all want to be extraordinary, and we all just want to fit in. Unfortunately, extraordinary people rarely fit in."
—Sebastyne Young

I don't think I'm insane. I don't want to be. Am I merely in denial of my insanity? As we know, denial is its own form of insanity. So, I'm insane for believing that I'm sane and not insane. Right? If you're confirming my insanity and you're insane too, can we be normal together? Because if you're sane but I'm insane, I don't want your company. And if you're insane but I'm sane, feel free to drop by whenever I'm bored. You entertain me. Don't stick around too long, though. You exhaust me.

Thing is, I possess all of this insane brain cell activity, and—at times—behave like a crazy person. For example, I'd apologized to Justin during our final fight. I'd heard a beastly screeching hysteria come out of me.

That's so "not me," I thought, feeling horrible. Yet it's understandable. At that moment, he was raging at me for . . . trying to make him happy. I'd been attempting that for three years. Nothing worked. My ultimate explosion was inevitable.

Great! Now I'm questioning if there's something wrong with me for always feeling a need to make amends. There's no harm in an apology. Right? The whole pride thing's at stake, I suppose, especially for men. They're supposed to be fully "manly" all the time.

Dad demonstrated this. He didn't cry. An armor of sarcasm walled off his genuine emotions.

He neglected and mistreated me in ways that I both can and can't remember. What I remember mostly are daily "attacks" that took the form of blatant ignoring—walking by me in a huff, not saying anything when I sat on the living room couch to await his arrival from work; not acknowledging my birthday but taking Dawn out to dinner on hers; playing baseball with my brothers and never inviting me to play.

To his credit, Dad was a good man. Annoying at times, yet a more than decent person. He wasn't a terrible father, and there was a soft heart underneath. I was an extremely sensitive kid. And honest. Brutally honest. Still am. The combination of the two of us, and our respective tenacity, made for a chronically tense relationship.

Compared to what my clients experienced, though, I'm extremely lucky for all that was good in my childhood, including a father who made ends meet in a high-level professional job. He also never physically abandoned us. Furthermore, he had a playful, warm-loving side and introduced us to Kenny Rogers' *The Gambler*. "Every hand's a winner, and every hand's a loser."

I tried to turn Justin onto Kenny Rogers, but he wouldn't have it. He hated country music. Justin's favorite: Italian opera. I can't stomach that excellent stuff. Play music I can understand and relate to, or don't play anything.

I've been devoting less thought to Justin these days. He rarely if ever inhabits my dreams, the ones I can recall. Those are full of family tensions, and family—well, hope.

Since I've been writing this chapter, which seems like a solid decade now, Glenn has been entering my dreams, alive, sick and zombie-like from the meds, but very sweet. A new opportunity to nurture him.

In last night's, I was planning to take my brother to a doctor for a thorough exam, as the start to helping him get his life back on track. He was amenable to this. Then I woke up.

Contrastingly, I don't feel the need to make amends regarding Justin. It was all said and done. Things shifted when I'd read his final words. Anger can make letting go easier and more complicated.

See, Justin left a suicide letter, only to Ruthie. His words served to console her in his absence. He wrote how wonderful she'd been, how special she was, to not feel guilty. It'd ruin the friendship had he moved to Paradise to live with her and her husband.

Justin didn't want to die, he stated, although he didn't want to live anymore—an ambivalence very common to those grappling with suicidal feelings.

Within five neatly typed, double spaced pages, the man who'd been the love of my life, whose existence ruled my world for a time, whose suicide devastated me to the core, this man hadn't mentioned me once. One reference to "two divorces" being too much to bear—that was it! Seemed I was hardly a sidenote in his life and his decision to end it.

His focus, instead, was on a woman (Ruthie) who he'd had a short romance with years earlier, then no contact until his final chapter. She went out of her way for him in the end. The letter was only for her. I'd quote it here, but frankly, it's boring. Repetitive compliments to this woman. No genuine emotion.

As relieved as I was insulted, I realized then that, at a certain point, guilt-driven grief is a choice. We (caring people) invest intensely in grief, with every ounce of our being, especially when a loved one dies by suicide. All the "what ifs," all the gut-wrenching feelings about the bond we shared, their final decision, their indescribable pain that consumes us in their absence. We wrestle with whether or not we deserve to live. (Suicidal feelings are not uncommon to those who've lost close loved ones to suicide. It's a tremendous loss, attached to a tremendously overwhelming guilt-infused pain.)

I pondered all that I'd done to keep Justin going, our "everlasting" love. My feelings that we were one and the same. Ha. Hardly. I chose and still choose life. He chose death. Nothing I or anyone else could've done would have changed his decision.

Time to call bullshit on myself. No more "poor me, poor Justin" energy.

No guilt.

Glenn didn't leave a suicide note. We didn't need an explanation. He didn't need to give one.

I struggle with the nurture versus nature conundrum. Was he "troubled" because he (like I) was labeled the less deserving, more contentious, middle, problem child? Or was he unbalanced all along? Something's not right in my brain; thus, chronic depression and medication that I need to endure for a lifetime. In him, it appeared as a different, indescribable "something."

Written on the final back side page of my diary because I felt so bad about it. <u>10/10/1973 (age 7)</u>: In my mind I think bad things about Glenn David and I know there true. But things are worser then I think. He is greedy, selfish and all the other things.

Sometimes hes a cry baby like now. He asked mommy what should he have to besize a hamberger and mommy said that he should'nt fuss or something then he starts yelling, you make me mad. You make me very mad. Probably just to get attention.

It's perfectly normal for a young child to yell at their parents when they don't get what they want. That's what kids do. And he was an adoring, live wire most of the time. A star athlete, an honors student, a charismatic boy whose skills and charm drew the neighborhood kids together for football, baseball, basketball, backgammon, frisbee—you name it, Glenn took the lead, with Jonathan by his side.

Was I onto something being "off" about the older of my two brothers (1.5 years younger than me), though? I took care to write that on the final page of my diary, despite the fact that there were gobs of empty pages available to me. I remember a sharp sentiment of shame. There's something to "in my mind" and "worser then I think." Possibly. I was a deep thinking girl. Was I trying to say "I can't pinpoint it" because he was in the very early stages of mental illness?

Then again, I was probably merely projecting my issues onto the other neglected middle child. Maybe.

I like to say that a family's level of dysfunction is directly proportional to the number of therapists it produces.

Two of the four Engel siblings, my sister Dawn and I, are licensed therapists. One of the four of us died due to mental illness and suicide. Jonathan, fortunately, turned things around. Not only did he become a teacher, he married Angela. They're raising Josiah—our tribe's heart.

Still, 50 percent is impressive. Right?

As I suspect you might have noticed, dear reader, the "helping" field is overflowing with troubled "helpers." To locate a seemingly sane therapist can pose challenges.

Years earlier, so exhausted from changing counselors in a search for one with compassion, or simply one whose office I'd leave feeling better and not worse about myself, I figured I'd give my then therapist the exact wording I'd been pining to hear. I thus told

Julie this: "I want you to tell me that I'm not messed up." How hard could that be, right?

"But you are messed up, Robyn," she countered. Gee thanks. That information for $60 of your professional counsel? Methinks somebody forgot the motto: "Do no harm." Perhaps you didn't take your medications today?

Another, Shelley, was relatively supportive. I'd told her giddily about some fun I had with a man in my car, after dancing together at Kimball's in Emeryville. Shelley was appalled: "You're acting like a woman who gets raped." Yeah, those were the words of a therapist I liked because she was much nicer than the others.

My theory on the apparent overabundance of messed up psychotherapists? In chaotic families, we're hardwired from infancy to ignore our emotions in order to focus on others' needs and demands. And these others can never be adequately satisfied, though we tried relentlessly. In a real way, at the time, our lives depended upon it.

Consequently, we grow into astutely skilled beings—extremely resourceful, perseverant, and self-reliant, albeit deeply disturbed. Everyone else comes first. They always have. We're a natural fit for the helping field. We find ourselves in the profession as if it happened unconsciously. In a way, it did.

As grown-ups, should we choose the path of insight and self-awareness, we're able to move our lives onto a healthier track. The labor involved in this isn't enticing. That's no excuse, but many of us simply don't choose this route. Or we're so layered with denial, we don't feel the need. Or we take a few steps, then retreat. And repeat. Or not. Or we dodge the whole self-work journey because we're "all that." After all, we're therapists who have the power to diagnose and slice others to bits. Why bother looking inward?

Client quote: "Justin Bieber was 17 when he dated Selena Gomez and she was 18. They were setting a bad example for teenage dating."

Sometimes it's plain difficult to decipher client from professional. (Hint: Clients tend to be nicer, more genuine, and less malicious.)

Throughout my social work career, I was hard pressed to find a healthy employer, too, who wasn't driven by insatiable ego and control needs. Many or most were outright mean and unethical.

Raquel was, and likely still is. That bulging, ugly boss limped around the office with a cane, moaning about her pained ligaments due to her fall from the "damned step ladder." She was 40 then, nearly as wide as she was tall, and utterly unrefined. Plus, most irksome of all, Raquel bore a rather obvious dark brown moustache. But I was extremely lucky to have her as my boss. They all told me so.

"She has exceptional skills with the toughest of clients, Robyn," they said. "You'll learn so much from her!" "You're very lucky, Robyn!" they emphasized.

I said something different: "She's fat, ugly, and needs to shave her moustache."

It was my 34th birthday (June of 2000) when I got the offer. The salary was twice what I'd earned at my last job.

"Is the amount okay with you?" the director asked.

"Oh, hmm, yes, it's fine." I suppressed my enthusiasm about a higher salary than I'd ever imagined.

"Welcome! Welcome! We're so glad to have you here." They were warm and hospitable when I arrived. Alas, I was a professional in a professional setting earning professional pay at one of the world's biggest health and medical professional establishments. (Hint: It rhymes with "miser.")

I quickly befriended colleagues who joined me on weekend dance excursions. Management consultants adjusted my computer space to assure ergonomic correctness. I participated in free tai chi classes during Tuesday lunch breaks. Chocolate eclairs graced the conference room tables, sweetening the toll of lengthy staff meetings.

What more could I ask for?

Slam! She'd invade my office, week after week, abruptly shutting the door behind her. Raquel sat across the room from me, eyes piercing, both hands clenching the handle of her cane. She opened her mouth and the words cut through me. It was disturbing enough to view her—this blubbering mess of a moustached woman, hailed as the department goddess—but I was subject to regular doses of her ruthless critique in the name of invaluable mentorship.

"What you said during staff meeting wasn't appropriate. You need to watch your words. Don't speak up until you clear it with me first. You need to learn people skills. This isn't the right work environment for you. You don't know the first thing about being a clinician . . . .

After each weekly bashing, I returned to my job with a friendly smile.

At the 10 week mark, Mrs. Williams called me in for what she termed "an evaluation."

"So how are things going with Raquel?"

"Well, we've had some differences but we're working through it. Things are getting better."

Mrs. Williams' eyes punctured me in a Raquel-like fashion. She snatched a post-it from her desk, scrawled some words of nonsense down, then invited me to leave her office.

The stage was set. I was laid off the following day.

Ever resourceful, I transitioned to a new employer rather quickly. Shantel hired me, and she'd become my long-term supervisor.

Months later at a party, I met Dean. He worked with Raquel at the place that rhymes with "miser."

"Kindly pass on a message for me," I told him. "Tell Raquel that she's fat and ugly and needs to shave her moustache."

Supervisor (in front of large training group): "Robyn, are you a midget or a dwarf?"
Me: "Can I have a third option?"
Director to whom I reported the above disciplined me for not getting along with this supervisor. Prior to the write-up, I'd reported that this supervisor regularly napped at her desk too.

Bad Robyn! Bad, noncompliant midget or dwarf Robyn tells the truth.

Gina and Helen were fun colleagues. We kept each other laughing. The clients, a spirited clan. We'll call them Caroline, who dominates the upcoming scene, Rosie, innocent and loved by all, and Tanya, who knows how-to-do-as-little-as-possible-for-the-biggest-reward-possible. This capable client pulled in approximately the same earnings as we did. (Note: We worked full-time. She didn't work. Actually, she aptly worked the system.)

Caroline and I had been spending a lot of time together. I even took her to a book reading, and she did great—she sat patiently, asked relevant questions, enjoyed the event. I felt successful; no other staff had formed that type of meaningful connection with her.

A big woman, tall and chunky, she used her stature to intimidate. But we got along great. I hate to admit it, but I think she began developing a crush on me. I could tell by the quick, sporadic glances I'd receive unexpectedly. Ugh.

One afternoon, Caroline went ballistic. She'd convinced herself that she played a very special role in the world. Caroline was pregnant, she insisted. The father could've been any one of a number of male adolescents. But Caroline was selective and went straight to the top. As in, the father was The Father. God had impregnated her.

So, yeah, who wouldn't go ballistic, when carrying God's baby? Can you imagine the Virgin Mary's pre- and post-partum angst? And do you negotiate a prenuptial? Whoosh! Such pressure.

To squelch her delusions, Shantel had taken Caroline for an ultrasound. No sign of an unborn child. That's because only she and God knew about it, Caroline argued. Baby's due in five months and twelve days.

Per www.Dictionary.com:
Sane 1. proceeding from a sound mind: rational 2. mentally sound; *especially*: able to anticipate and appraise the effect of one's actions 3 healthy in body.

I picked up the clients' medications at the start of my shift. When I arrived at work, Gina and Helen told me that Caroline was in her room. She'd been shouting at everybody about her unborn baby.

"Robyn, don't go in there," Rosie said, pointing at Caroline's bedroom door. "She, she like"—Rosie pressed out her belly and patted it—"'I'm gonna have my baby and we're gonna live here together.'" Rosie giggled, then joined Tanya in the recreations room.

Gina recapped: "I just told her that I'm not God or a doctor, and she knows her body best."

"And that pissed her off?" I chuckled, bewildered.

"You gotta understand, Robyn," Helen chimed in. "She's pregnant. It's hormones. Holy hormones!"

"Of course, how insensitive of me. Do you want me to talk to her?" She's cool with me.

"If you want to." Gina shrugged her shoulders.

Helen added, "Be my guest."

Relaxed and unafraid, I walked to Caroline's door. Knock, knock.

"WHAT!"

"It's Robyn. I'd like to talk to you. Can I open the door?"

"Go away! I fuckin hate everyone!"

Eye roll. KNOCK, KNOCK.

I heard the thuds of heavy feet, a noise that grew louder. The door swung violently open. Then, faster than my brain could pull together a—Caroline's fist was at my nose! Whoa. She just punched me in the nose!

<u>Note to self</u>: You got punched in the nose. It wasn't too hard. It happened so fast. There was a pinching pain for a fraction of a second. You're fine. I'm fine. Yippee!

<u>Note in response to note to self</u>: You're lucky she had a crush on you; you might've been flattened otherwise.

<u>Note in response to response to note to self</u>: True. Lucky me.

"I hate you! I'm going to kill you all! I'm getting the fuck out of here!" Caroline stormed out of her room, unraveling at the speed of lightning on methamphetamines.

"I'll help you pack," I said casually, as I slipped into the bathroom to examine my face. No blood. I fingered my nose from top to nostrils, no broken bones, nothing. I stepped out of the bathroom.

"You okay, Robyn?" Gina asked.

"Yeah, I just got punched in the nose, but I'm fine. Should we call the police?"

Gina and Helen said that, yes, we should. "Okay, I guess I'll do it, since I was the one hit."

Meanwhile, Caroline ran out of the house screaming. Rosie and Tanya joined us in the office—scared, staying close.

We scrambled to lock the doors and windows.

I gave the police a full report.

"Why did you call the police?" Shantel interrogated, when I updated her. "I can't believe you did that! You're acting crazy Robyn! Do you even hear yourself?"

"I can't believe you're saying this, I can't—" Too upset to talk to Shantel, I walked with the phone and handed it to Gina.

The police arrived within minutes. I stepped out to speak with an officer who pulled her car in front of the lawn. At the same time, Shantel jumped out of her car across the street and ran towards us. She abruptly nudged me with her elbow.

"I got this, Robyn, go home! You can't be working with a client you're afraid of." She looked at the officer, "She's scared. She needs to go home!"

As I walked away, I heard Shantel tell the officer to "Please find Caroline and bring her home. I'm really worried about her." The police car sped off to retrieve the client who'd threatened to murder us.

<u>Client quote</u>: "I'm a pet peeve."

I sat alone on a wooden picnic bench in the backyard, to settle my nerves.

Shantel barged inside the house, walked by everyone, stood under the back doorframe and shouted at me, "I told you to go home, Robyn!"

"I'll go as soon as I'm ready!"

"Is Robyn getting fired?" Rosie asked. Shit. They know I got punched in the face and that yeah, I'll be punished.

Thing is, friends, many clients are smarter and saner than the systems established to serve them.

<u>Client quote</u>: "You're short, but I don't mean to make assumptions."

At home that night, I checked the bathroom mirror. Strange. No marks, no blood. My nose, completely intact.

Sigh. I wanted to talk to Stephen. He'd always been supportive. But he was in the living room, on a webcam call. I saw from the side of my eyes a woman with long shiny brown hair. Stephen said to her, "You're different." Sounded as though my roommate met someone special.

Mojo ran to welcome me, then followed me to my room and hopped onto my bed alongside me. Sneaky boy.

I stroked his back and thought about the words: "You're different." Being different, a good thing. "It's good to be different, sweetie." We all want that, and we want to be with someone who's different.

I'm different. "I got punched in the nose today." There's a price for being different, or is it just me? Am I different in that when I'm different I'm punished for being different? You're supposed to conform to the status quo. Don't help. Don't get punched in the nose. Don't go all Marcia Brady: *My nose! My nose! My nose!* "Don't do it, Mojo." I kissed the top of his head.

Bad Robyn. Don't do your job. People who sleep on the job don't get punched in the nose and lose their jobs. Be good! Go potty. Pee in cup. Sleep at work. Good girl!

<u>Client to my coworker</u>: "You need to pull up your pants. Your butt crack is showing."

The next day I learned that Caroline had been located. She was admitted to some faraway psychiatric facility, and sent back to us the following afternoon. We were given no treatment suggestions, no new diagnosis, no change in medications, not a word.

So it goes.

I expressed my concerns about safety to Shantel's supervisor, Eileen, and Eileen strongly urged me to document my concerns. I complied. That Friday, I handed Eileen an articulate, three page letter about Shantel's efforts that repeatedly undermined workplace safety.

Next followed the meetings I was required to attend "Just to talk to you, Robyn." I sat quietly, taking nonsensical notes. I know the drill.

Her name was Lola Mandy can't you see that God I wish you knew when I never hear your name even now I wake up crying at the cabana Pepsi boy. Bring me a tall margarita and give me a massage dude. Real deep. Deep, deep tissue. I wrote the very first song. She was a showgirl. Rico wore a diamond thirty years ago. Don't fall in love. She lost her mind.

"Clearly, by the way you're behaving during this meeting, Robyn, you're NOT going to cooperate." Those words spoken by the executive director <u>because</u> I sat quietly and said nothing.

"You don't seem happy," Eileen whined. "I want you to be at a job that makes you happy."

I contacted a lawyer friend to discuss the situation and learned that I had a legitimate lawsuit. I didn't want one. I didn't even make a doctor's visit to have my nose checked. They had no reason to worry that I'd so much as file a worker's compensation claim. Were they smart, they'd have been nice to me. It could've been that simple. Be respectful. Leave things as they are, you know. But they intensified the mistreatment. Idiots.

It wouldn't happen for a lengthy stint of time, that is, if it happened at all. We'll say it didn't. Or maybe it did, hypothetically speaking. Wink. I thought it'd provide a good chapter ending to inform you, dear readers, that perseverance pays. Good conquers evil. Little beats big. Rhetorically speaking. A woman like me might have been punched in the nose by a client like Caroline. Next, management might've attempted to push her out, taking— we'll say—most of her hours and all of her benefits. Arrogant lawyers and mean-spirited administrators possibly provoked and threatened her at every turn. She held her ground, let's imagine, throughout the ugly, elongated process. In the end, she won a settlement. It was piddly, for example. But it was worth it. She saved face in insane circumstances. Wink.

Chapter 6: Oneness

"The reason I talk to myself is because I'm the only one whose answers I accept."—George Carlin

When I happened to see an ad that week, I was elated. "Out of the Darkness, 2012." Dramatic, honest. It alludes to "coming out" as a survivor of suicide loss. At the bottom of the ad, a phone-number.

Mike's a rare soul—purely good through and through. He has no hidden agenda, no rough edges; just heartfelt, solid, genuine kindness. When I told him about my brother and my late ex-husband, Mike said the only right thing worth saying: "I'm really sorry."

I'd soon learn about his family's tragedy. A star student, daughter Suzanne (aka "Suzy") went to college across the country on a full four year scholarship. She was 19, a passionate young lady with an infectious smile. So free-spirited, Suzy would pull her car over to the side of the road at night, hop out, and catch fireflies—to gawk at them, then set them free.

She kept a dark secret, though. A growing depression plagued Suzy's spirits. She sought help online, where Suzy landed in pro-suicide internet sites.

Who knew these sites existed? How outrageously twisted and horrid.

Suzy was preyed upon by a man who'd befriended her, gained her trust, and encouraged her to end her life. There was no hope, it'd only get worse, he promised. This man went so far as to spell out a specific formula for poisoning herself, and he provided Suzy with a suicide letter to post on "delay" after her passing.

What kind of sick person would do this? Well, he's a seemingly "normal" one. A married father of a then 18 year old daughter himself.

This man would continue to prey upon depressed and vulnerable youth, causing more deaths by suicide.

He's reaped no consequences whatsoever. See, no laws forbid a person from instructing and encouraging suicide this way. It's not illegal.

Mike embarked upon a focused nationwide advocacy campaign. He did this, knowing their daughter's predator's name and address. He did this to save others' lives. Imagine that level of kindness, integrity, and resolve, in the face of such a profoundly shocking, sick and twisted loss.

Suzy's Law criminalizes the act of endorsing, promoting, and instructing suicide through the Internet. You'd think this would have been readily approved. No.

The bill's been resting since 2003 amid swarms of paper that collect dust on Capitol Hill. Every two years, Mike needs to start anew and re-author it, in hopes that at least 50 Congress members will cosign. Then, it might bounce between committees and subcommittees and it definitely collects more dust, while more young lives vanish.

At the end of our phone discourse, Mike had invited me to an upcoming planning meeting. They're getting ready for Chico's fourth annual event, he informed me.

I sat on a plush, brown cushioned recliner in a beautiful, upscale home in the heart of Chico. The host served homemade vegetarian pizzas on artisan flatbread, fresh out of the oven. A large cooler housed ice and sodas, a plethora of drinks.

Agenda topics included whether or not to have tablecloths on the resource tables at the event. A great amount of fervor, and a ping-pong back and forth, depicted this heated tablecloth debate. I believe that Dollar Store plastic tablecloths won out, and all were appeased.

"Do you mind helping with registration?" Mike asked me.
"Sure, that's fine."
How hard could that be?

Scores of people lined up to check in, looking at me impatiently.
A handful of packets containing lengthy rosters floated amongst us—lists of folks who'd registered online; horizontal lists organized by teams, other lists in alphabetical order. A few precious pens. I got this.

Smile. "Welcome! Your name? Sorry, can't find it. "Are you sure you're preregistered? Under a team? Team's name? You don't know? Didn't already register?" Smile. Find registration form. Find pen. Ask about donation. Done. I assume. Not sure. They want to donate, great. "Thank you!" Find envelope. Line grows longer. Take envelope with donation. Keep line moving. Smile.

By 9:10 a.m., heat hit. Speed it up. "Good morning. Name? Already registered?" Give them pen. Where's pen? Someone walked off with pen. "Good morning. Your name?" Checkmark their name. Find it first. I can't. Keep line moving.

Young man doesn't want to be photographed. Shares personal, tearful story. Line grows longer. Be caring. Be patient. Smile. Oops, don't smile. Sad story. Remember his face, the one who just walked away. Point him out to photographer, in crowd of hundreds. When? How?

As if he and photographer will be right next to each other when I'm in their vicinity and able to tell photographer which person in crowd of hundreds to NOT capture in any of her photos. Not once. What about everyone else taking pictures? Wait, what'd he look like? Wait, am I sure it was a "he"? Smile. Shit. We're gonna get sued. It's my fault. I'll cost them hundreds of thousands of dollars. Help, Mi—iii—ke!

A tense quiet pervaded the scene. Mike stood in front of the crowd to give an introduction.

No more line.

Hundreds hovered around the stage to my right.

To my left, one young man, in a tattered white t-shirt and faded blue shorts. I assumed, by his appearance and sad eyes, that life had pushed and shoved him quite a bit.

This man took slow, shy steps towards me and asked, "What's going on here?"

"Hi. Thanks for asking. It's called Out of the Darkness. We're raising awareness about mental illness and suicide, to fight the stigma and prevent suicide loss. It's a fundraiser. Mostly, though, we're here to support each other and come together as a community."

He nodded acceptingly.

"You're welcome to stay. There's food and water." I pointed behind him, where volunteers distributed refreshments and bottled water.

"Thank you."

I hesitated but asked anyway. "You don't have to. But would you like to make a donation?"

The young man dug into his right side pocket. He pulled out a crumpled dollar bill.

"It's all I have," he said, extending his arm to give me the dollar bill.

"Oh, are you sure?"

"Yes, I want it to be used for this."

He joined the crowd.

I slipped away to my car, parked across the street.

I'd kept a few things in a grocery bag by the passenger's seat that morning. One of those items, a slim, stapled book that Dad had given us after Glenn's suicide. The cover shows my brother in his most current photo. Under this picture: "PLEASE SHOW ME YOU CARE, Glenn David Engel (November 28, 1967 - September 21, 1988)."

Glenn's writing filled the pages, mostly poetry from the last few years of his life. I'd brought it to, in a way, have my brother with me that day. I clenched the book, to take it back with me to the plaza.

Next, I quietly made a monetary donation.

If one person can give his all—literally one hundred percent of what he had—I could certainly make a monetary contribution.

One man.
One dollar.
Invaluable.

Client quote: *In small Chico gift shop.* Client pointed at a pair of earrings and asked cashier, "How much are these?"
Sales clerk: "Those are half off."
Client: "Half off? Dang! That's expensive!"

The walk itself was short. I joined a small group at the finish line to cheer enthusiastically and give high fives to all returnees.

A few speeches followed. One person talked about God; God saved her after she lost her son to suicide; God was her strength; she wouldn't have survived without Him. Blah blah blah.

Jesus Christ, how do non-Christians deal with suicide loss, in this beautifully diverse world?

We have to find internal strength. All of us. Regardless of religious or a-religious beliefs.

Exhausted, I planted myself on a quiet patch of grass to sift through pages of Glenn's poetry and pontifications.

<u>By Glenn David, 1988:</u> "Labeling people crazy is not an admirable job, but I am. A crazy consciousness can be linked to unclear judgment and a failure or inability to recognize right from wrong. God has given a spirit to such people for that reason. A crazy consciousness may be the result, in my opinion, of genetics, or perhaps some people are rightfully, purposefully, atheists."

"Rightfully, purposefully atheists." I like that. I loathe religious dogma. It's patronizing, damaging, destructive to one's sense of self.

<u>By Glenn David circa 1987, age 20, around the time of his diagnosis</u>: "I don't believe we should pass the buck when we have a chance to help someone. I think we can be better people if we live for others as opposed to only living for ourselves. When someone is happy at the expense of another, then there is not enough caring going on."

We thought alike.

We fought a lot too—purposely doing things to antagonize each other. I remember having a fit when he cut my Barbie's hair off. All of it. Made Barbie bald. Barbie appeared to be a chemotherapy patient. I was enraged. It was wrong.

Actually, that was a good move on Glenn's part. Barbie needed humility. The bitch still does.

Other times I'd provoke my brother by turning the channel to watch what I wanted on our monstrous Zenith. This was long before the days of the television remote. He'd proceed to chase me through the house. I think the worst I'd get from him, though, was a soft (perhaps deserved) punch in the side or belly. He held back.

Once I ran into my bedroom and locked the door. He scurried outside and attempted to climb into my bedroom through the window. The moment his fingers were on the windowsill, I slammed the window shut.

"Ouch!" I can still hear him scream.

And I still feel like shit about that.

He was okay, though.

He let go in time, didn't lose any fingers or need medical attention. Thank goodness. I'd otherwise struggle even more with the memory.

In the aftermath of someone's suicide, every interaction is up for scrutiny by the always critical judge and jury living in one's head. It's not fair. None of it.

I didn't become consciously aware of our respective roles as the contentious middle children until one night, when my family sat in our red and white striped Rebel station wagon at Culver City's drive-in movie theatre.

I consistently took to the far back seat, alone—as distanced from the family as possible. Dawn sat in the front seat between my parents, Glenn and Jonathan were in the middle.

We stared at the big, blank screen, waiting for *Blazing Saddles* to start.

"I think the lights blinked. It's about to start." I said.

"Yeah, she's right. I saw it too." Glenn added.

"Well, they agree on something, they must be right!" Dad chuckled. Mom giggled.

That exchange stuck with me in a weird way. I didn't think that I routinely argued with Glenn, but I guess I did. Or was it a matter of being the less favored of the four, the roles we were supposed to play, even though we usually got along okay? No, probably not. There was a lot of conflict between us. I'm just unsure of its source. I mean, did our parents unknowingly put the conflict there, or was it typical sibling rivalry? Or both? Likely both.

We were sensitive, deep thinkers, highly fragile and insecure. Like me, Glenn would sit alone for long periods of time to write. I noticed this more often after he got sick—several years following Mom's death. (He was diagnosed in 1988, but sick for months preceding that, and we lost Mom in 1985.)

I looked down at the book and slowly turned a page.
The four of us loved to watch *Bonanza*. I'm guessing that inspired this one.

<u>"The West" by Glenn David Engel, circa 1985</u>: "Tell me about the days of cobblestone and chuck wagons, of jerky and rodeos, of the winning and the combat, of the deserted and the deserters, of the saloons and of the goons, of the fables and of the foibles. Tell me about the smell of the leather and the tap of the boots. I long to know how the west was won."
That one's my favorite.
He had a curious and curiously playful side. Glenn would challenge Jonathan to marble races, for example. This involved both of them climbing up the backyard slide ladder simultaneously. I can't picture it now—that ladder was small and flimsy, yet they were both quite limber. Atop the slide, each with a marble in hand, each ready to fling said marble with their thumb on the count of three, they did. They'd spend an hour at a time competing this way.

"You all right, Robyn?" Mike wiped sweat from his brow.
"Oh yeah, just sitting for a bit." I closed the book and centered it on my lap. "It seemed to be a big success, right?"
"Yeah, it was great, over 300 people. We raised a lot more than last year. I'll have the exact numbers soon. Thanks for all your help."
"It was an honor. Thank you for getting me involved." I stood up.
Mike and I hugged.

Chapter 7: Disappearing Act

"You sometimes think you want to disappear, but all you really want is to be found."—Unknown

Upon his return from Phoenix to visit his new girlfriend, Stephen reported having had a great time. Lauren even introduced him to her family, and they toured local hot spots. He really liked the city. It seemed he'd met "the one."

"The one." Is there a "one?" For me, "the one" is more like the one…the one-thousand, twenty second dating disaster. I was sure Justin was "the one." I suppose he was for a short time. How long does "the one" need to stick around in order to be "the one"? Plenty of couples do stay together for years—happily some of the time, working on their relationship all of the time.

Monogamy is a given factor, you'd think, in the concept of "the one." Reality (i.e., the rate of infidelity) dictates otherwise.

Heck, I can't even find one single man who wants monogamy. They tend to want to be "the one" for more than "their one" woman. Like Paul E.

I met him at this time. It was fall of 2012, and I brought a poem to an open mic at Has Beans Café, Creekside.

"When darkness falls, I'm at your door," I began, taking my turn onstage, reciting my silly "Halloween Erotica." "To raid your stash, then beg for more." Some people laughed shyly. A few appeared appalled. Chico is mostly a churchgoing crowd, but one that's usually readily loosened up.

"Don't fall asleep, there's no reprieve. I'll nibble 'til next Hallow's Eve."

A loud applause made me smile. They loved it.

Paul E. approached me afterwards. "Robyn, would you like to go for coffee some time?" My *Halloween Erotica* attracted a man. Sweet.

"Sure," I responded, and we exchanged numbers.

The hostess walked us to a table by the back windows at Italian Cottage, when I noticed black hairs protruding from his nostrils. Yikes. Paul E. was gentlemanly enough to pay, though, and he's a nice man. The guy's probably ten years older than me, I realized, yet he looked every bit twenty years my senior.

After that, we walked around Bidwell Park, talked about family, travels, work, the standard realm of miscellaneous categories covered when getting to know someone.

Client quote: "I have a belt, so no one can see my tiny whineys."

He dropped me off and imparted a nice long hug. Paul then asked if I'd like to go out again. I agreed.

I ordered a scoop of mint chocolate chip, and Paul got rocky road. We sat on a faded wooden bench outside of the ice-cream shop.

"Mmm, this is so good!" I glowed. "So how've you been?"
He proceeded to tell me about problems with a long-term friend. They had a chaotic history, his friend owed him money, etc.
I listened, somewhat intently, very supportively.
"Mm, mm, yeah, that's tough."

Have you ever noticed that when eating ice cream with someone, they don't annoy you? You don't see hair protruding from their nostrils. In fact, they're the most beautiful person in the world.
I didn't even notice that Paul E. asked me nothing about myself. I played the supportive, caring woman. All was good.

"Where'd it go?" I joked, looking into my empty cup.
My date laughed, stretched his arm around my shoulders, and moved in for a quick kiss.
"You have such a fun, playful spirit."
"Thank you."

Paul E. drove me home. He exited the car when I did.
"I'll walk you to your door." He approached, putting his arm around my back.
At my door I told him, "You're welcome to visit for a bit."
He didn't decline.

As we sat on my couch, Paul E. initiated kissing. It felt nice, a good chemistry.

"You kiss like you mean it," he declared.

"I do (mean it)." But wait. That's a weird, corny line. How many women have you used it on? It doesn't even make sense. "Like you mean" what? Like I mean, "I like you and I don't even mind that you're over a decade older than me and have long black hairs protruding from your nostrils"? If that's what I mean when kissing you, yeah, I do mean it. I think.

We started kissing again, and he got a bit handsy.

"We'll wait 'til we know each other better," he curtailed activities.

I walked him to my door.

"Thinking of you. Hope all's well," I texted two days later.

"Thinking of you too. Swamped with work stuff. Maybe a walk on Saturday?"

"Sure."

Paul took my hand as we stomped browning leaves in Bidwell Park near an area called One Mile.

"I'm wondering"—I treaded nervously—"Can I ask some pointed questions?"

"Sure, I have nothing to hide."

"So, what are you looking for, in terms of a relationship?"

"Well, I don't really know."

A few seconds passed. He started to ramble. "I'm not into casual sex, online hookups or anything like that. That's not me. I'm too old for that." He chuckled. "And I'm done with marriage, that's for sure."

"Yeah, me too."

"I just want to get to know you better." He looked at me and smiled, satisfied that he'd thoroughly and accurately responded to my inquiry. Hoping he passed.

"Thanks," I paused. "What I'd really like to know is, are you wanting monogamy?"

"That just, no, I"—Paul E. stuttered—"my last girlfriend wanted that, and I couldn't give it to her. She's a great woman, don't get me wrong. She has every right to want monogamy. I respect that. Thing is, there are at least three women in town who would sleep with me,"—pride dominated his tone—"and it means nothing to them."

I let go of his hand.

"Okay," he continued, "to tell you the truth, Robyn, I have a dinner date tomorrow night. We'll probably end up having sex. That's how it goes when we get together. She's just a friend, though."

I was fairly shocked.

Now, my friends, perhaps you understand the reason I dubbed him Paul E. Say it quickly.   "PaulE, Polly, poly." Not a Mormon, not a parrot, just a grown man who can't get enough. Apparently, there are plenty of women in town who accommodate that and long black nostril hairs too.

I reclined on a park bench, and Paul sat next to me.

"This is so frustrating." Tears started. The hope, once again, of having possibly met "the one" or at least a good one. The almost immediate letdown. Feeling foolish. He's not worth the tears. I knew this, but that didn't stop them.

"Relationships take investment. I'm worth it," I argued. "I'd like to date you if you cancel your date for tomorrow night."

He looked out towards a grassy field. "Maybe we need to stop. I hardly know you."

"Okay. Well, I hope you have a good fuck tomorrow night, because you're losing out."

"A really good fuck!" I wished him this again, at least in my mind, before I hopped out of his car when he dropped me off at my place. Actually my final words, stupidly, were "You know where to find me if you ever decide to be monogamous."

"Thank you for leaving the window open."

A good fuck to you, fucker! A really good fuck!

<u>Client quote</u>: "If you get ammonia, you're like really sick."

As the holidays approached, Stephen announced his decision to move to Phoenix. I wasn't surprised. I also wasn't happy. I'd have to move. He'd do some repairs and remodeling, then enter into some sort of co-ownership arrangement with a local agency. I could stay and possibly get kicked out, or I could find a new home and relocate.

Sigh. Moving again. He gave me plenty of notice, though; I had until year's end.

I'd miss Stephen and Mojo. Yet the thought of living alone again, nice. Very nice.

The first time I moved far from home, I planted roots in a little studio apartment by Oakland's Lake Merritt. This was in 1992, and Glenn visited me. I don't mean to confuse or freak you out, and you'll likely decide now that I am in fact insane.

My brother was dead. He quietly entered and left in a peaceful, comforting way, though. And nothing like that has happened to me before or since, except in my dreams.

It was a normal evening, as normal as life could be given I'd lost Mom seven years prior, Glenn four years earlier, and I was living alone for the first time in my life—hundreds of miles from home. I was soon to undertake the daunting task of graduate school at U.C. Berkeley.

The days and nights were long, lonely, and infected with trepidation.

As I faded into sleep, or tried to, there was a gentle, distinctive tap, tap, tapping. I turned towards my coffee table, and I saw a faint image of Glenn. He was making the tapping sound by using a little wooden spoon to hit a little wooden cup—both of which Dad had gifted me, along with Russian dolls painted in similar colors (blacks, reds, greens, and yellows), upon his return from the former Soviet Union.

We have ancestry from Russia; I've never been. These seemingly trivial objects were a family heirloom of sorts. Dad made the visit between Mom's and Glenn's passing.

When my brother noticed that I saw him that night, he disappeared as quietly as he'd arrived.

His message seemed clear, "I'm here. You're not alone. You'll be okay."

Whatever it was—a hallucination, a wish, a dream, or a real visit from Glenn's spirit, it was an unexpected gift. I still treasure it.

Back in Chico, while 2013 got dressed behind the scenes, a spry young woman showed me an apartment in the center of town. It's spacious, with stained carpets, oddly placed outlets—a funky design. There's a nook in the hallway near the bathroom. The nook isn't quite big enough to be a room of any sort, perhaps a closet. But there's a closet directly across from it, a few feet away. I liked this oddly placed nook.

The deal breaker, though, was the flimsy, light (fake) wood paneled walls in the dining room. Reminiscent of the patio room Dad built before Mom died. He took great pride in that room, set in the back of our house in Westchester.

We were all excited. The walls were comprised of Styrofoam encased by flimsy (fake) wood. An air hockey table, ping-pong table, and my brothers' free weights would take residence. Throughout, piles of dirty laundry and miscellaneous items.

The Engel home was filthy, disgusting really. Neighborhood friends would joke with us (truthfully) about seeing giant insects (roaches and others we couldn't identify) they'd never before seen in the pantry or elsewhere. The bathrooms were filled with grime (to put it nicely), toilets rarely flushed properly, doors didn't lock. Ugh. I could go on.

It's perplexing. Perhaps our parents expected that we'd do all the cleaning. If so, that was never made clear. And the mess didn't seem to bother them. Did they even notice? Maybe they grew up in similar conditions.

I wiped and cleaned counters, the base of the toilets, tossed a lot of garbage, swept and mopped, etc., only for things to abruptly revert to sloppy dirtiness. I wanted a simple "Thank you" too, but my efforts weren't seen or acknowledged.

It was home, so I convinced myself it was fine. Home sheltered a mostly fun-loving family for years until Mom's death broke us.

This now nostalgic feeling evoked by a Chico-based flimsy (fake) wood paneled room drew me into the rental space that I'd take over.

I relocated, stayed in town, and had an uneventful holiday season. Until New Year's Eve.

Brandi didn't want to go out. I get that. She's older than me. I'm older than I like to pretend I am, and I wanted some New Year's excitement.

Donna agreed to join me. She's the same lady I was with when I met Troy at the Elks Lodge. The type of friend a woman both loathes and loves to be with: a sweet, outgoing, gorgeous blonde who can fit into a size zero with room to breathe.

We disappeared in the swarms of people, as we readied ourselves to welcome a new year.

The band stopped playing to announce the countdown. Anticipation cut through the walls of the boisterous nightclub. Champagne made its rounds. Beer was chugged, wine imbibed, and the time, eyed. I stayed back, on the fringes of the commotion.

"Ten!"

An intoxicating energy surrounded me—to my right, and in front, and . . .

"Nine!"

I glanced left. Whoa. Cute guy. Standing close.

"Eight!"

Mm. Dark hair. Young. Handsome. Glancing at me and . . .

"Seven!"

. . . moves slowly closer and closer to me and . . .

"Six!"

I think he's going to kiss me. Nah. He probably just . . .

"Five!"

. . . wants to look at my watch to check the time or something but
. . .

"Four!"

. . . his lips look nice and closer and full and closer and . . .

"Three!"

. . . juicy and closer and I can almost . . .

"Two!"

. . . taste them as they come even closer and . . .

"One!" YES! His aim and timing, perfect. His lips—moist,
gentle, assertive, not aggressive or slobbery. They press against
mine for one glorious moment, lingering sweetly as I pucker in
response.
Then they're gone.
I freeze, wide-eyed. Happy New Year to me!
Donna stammered through the crowd, arms extended. "There you
are, Robyn. Happy New Year!"
"Happy New Year, Donna!"

Funny that I didn't think to watch him leave. I wouldn't even
recognize my kisser if I saw him again. I mean, he was cute and
approximately half my age and maybe five feet, eight or so, give or
take. I was in heels, so I don't know. Regardless, he made my
night.

CL; chico personals missed connections
<u>New Year's Eve Kisser</u> – w4m (chico CA) <u>map</u>
Dear Kisser,

It's all a bit fuzzy, but you kissed me on the lips on New Year's Eve at midnight in a club in Chico (the dark one with a lot of people). I'd like to thank you repeatedly. You made this 46 year old woman feel like I still got it or, at least, can still get it if I want to. And I do. I'm fairly certain you look like a perfect combination of Tom Cruise pre-Scientology-sofa-aerobics and Brad Pitt pre-wolverine-Jolie-won't- notice-if-I-give-Aniston-a-few-of-our-kids-right? You're five foot eight give or take, and you're at least 18. You're athletic and toned, with a physique not unlike Michelangelo's David. You're perfect, sweetie. Plus you appreciate the premise behind the movie, *Harold and Maude* (i.e., much older women turn you on).

Please respond with a close-up selfie of your lips, so I know you're not an imposter. Thank you. Looking forward to our next encounter.

I was tempted to actually post this ad but decided against it. Trying to recreate experiences like that, to get more out of them than they already offered, that only disappoints.

Treasures reside in oneness, and oneness can't be replicated.

Chapter 8: Speech Impediments

"I know exactly what words I am wanting to say, but somehow or other they is always getting squiff-squiddled around."
—Roald Dahl

Truth be told, Kissing Bandit wasn't the only one.

By 1 a.m., another young man lunged towards me. "Hey! How're you?"

"I'm great." Do I know you? You're cute, like Woody Harrelson back in the day. "Happy New Year!"

"Oh"—Woody stepped back, befuddled—"sorry, I thought you were a friend of mine. But Happy New Year anyways. Wanna dance?"

"Sure, no worries."

After a more formal introduction, Woody excused himself to place his beer on a nearby table.

I figured he was in his early thirties. Despite this, he kept up with me just fine on the dance floor. I'm kidding, though I was ego-energized by the double dose of youthful male attention.

As his hands grazed the sides of my body, Woody said he's been in Chico for seventeen years. He's currently working on his master's in psychology. Pretty good, I think, admiring the man's soft blue eyes, dirty blond hair, and marginally innocent smile.

"You're fun," I spouted.

"So are you. You're great, Robyn."

"Thanks."

"So what do you do?"

"Social services. I'm a—" I stopped myself from saying that I'm a writer. And that I write humorous snippets about my mostly nonromantic romantic life and sexless sex life. He'll likely be the subject of my next blog post, especially if he proves himself a jerk or dweeb—"Social Worker. I do social work." Phew.

We continued dancing.

Time escaped.

Woody pulled out his phone and asked for my number.

"Sure." I enunciated each digit.

"Can I take you to dinner sometime?"

"Yeah, that'd be nice."

He stepped closer and wrapped his arms around me. Woody stroked the sides of my face, then kissed my lips with fervor and a teaser of tongue.

Am I dreaming? I don't think so because my feet hurt like hell. Damn heels. Kisses from, not one, but two men? This only happens to real women like Carrie Bradshaw.

"You made my New Year's, Robyn."

"You made mine too." Well, Kissing Bandit did first. He was cuter and younger than you. But your kiss was just as good. Almost. I mean, he won by courage and remarkable timing. Otherwise, it was distinctly close. Keep practicing.

I clumsily approached my door at 2 a.m. when my ringer went off. Woody.

We spoke briefly, sharing that we were glad to have met, and confirming a dinner date for Friday night.

January 1, 2013, text messages:

Woody: Good morning. I'm feeling a little hong over. How about you?

Hong over? Is that like finding oneself, penis exposed, on a stranger's balcony in Hong Kong after a night of drunken debauchery?

Robyn: I'm still waking up, tired and feet are sore. Only had a lil champagne so I'm ok.

No response.

Robyn: I hope you're feeling better. Good night.

No response.

January 3, 2013:

Woody: Hey.

Robyn: Hi.

Woody: What are you doing?

Robyn: Not much. About to make dinner. You?

Woody: Empty frige. Need to go to the store.

Robyn: I know how that is. *At least my fridge has a "d" in it.* Are we still on for dinner Friday night?
Woody: I hate to disappoint u but I have my kids to marrow.
I didn't know he has kids. I like kids. But he has "to marrow" them? Sounds intensely painful. I wonder if it's anything like a spinal tap. Well, I understand why dinner wouldn't fit into the equation. Still, the hurt. Disappointment. Irritation. What do I say?
Robyn: K.
Woody: Need to reschedule. Maybe we can talk on the phone.
Whoa! Talk on the phone? Slow down, tiger! What kind of girl do you think I am?

I called Woody.
"I've tried dating single dads before, and it hasn't worked out. They say they want to date, but they don't have the time. If that's your situation, I'm not going there."
"Yeah, that's my situation. I just want friends. It's like anything can come up with kids. I just messed up on the custody thing, so I have them this weekend."
We're silent. I don't know what to say.
Thing is, I'm thinking that I don't tend to stick any portion of my tongue into my "friends'" mouths. Thus, I don't want to be "friends." I'm also aware that I liked him much better when he liked me much better when he was drunk.
He broke the tension. "I guess we'll leave it at that."
"Okay. No hard feelings." "I had a great New Year's" (because of my Kissing Bandit).
"I did too, Robyn. It was fun with you."
"Thanks," my voice faded, "goodbye."
"Bye."

A lump dominated my throat. Damn.
Why must I fall, again, so quickly from a high? Why must I hurt like this and feel so damn foolish, yet again, and again, and again?
Be forgiving, I told myself. Self-loving, even. There's nothing stupid about opening your heart to love and romance. Just because it didn't work out doesn't make me stupid.
Sure, it's not smart to go for the stupid ones. Yet how could I tell? Everyone seems stupid, in a fun way, on New Year's. The

smart-stupid ones hide their stupidity throughout the year. It's only the stupid-stupid ones that can't, and they're easily detected. Usually. Ugh.

It seems I continue to pick the wrong men, not intentionally.

Deep down, maybe, I still feel unworthy of quality relationships. Why should I get to? My brother didn't.

<u>"No More" by Glenn David Engel, 1988:</u>
The last of my wishing
To want of the kissing
To smell of the flowers
The touch in the showers
The stroll on the shore
Please no more!!

I recall a piercing confusion tangled up with seeing him on campus. While I knew I should at least say "Hi," I couldn't—it seemed. As if a concrete wall engulfed me. On that vast expanse of UCLA, we even had a class together. Unplanned.

Neither of us acknowledged the other. He was already sick, already in an abysmal place. It was up to me, his sister eighteen months older, the healthy one between us, to talk to him. I didn't.

I treated my brother like he was invisible, like he didn't exist.

How could I have done that? I'm compassionate and loving and I knew how it felt to be treated that way. But I acted like a stranger who wanted nothing to do with him.

I still struggle to make sense of this.

Maybe I wasn't healthy. Maybe I was equally mentally ill.

I didn't know how to talk to anyone in my family. My place was alone on my bed, or in the back of the station wagon that I occupied solo.

A distance both expected of, and chosen by, me.

Words carry power.

Unspoken words, even more powerful.

The squiff-squiffled around ones, the ones perhaps chillaxing in the frige when your date's hong over, verbiage that suggests a need to marrow the kids, linguistics choked by exponentially confused

injustice packed tightly into acute but tender self-demoralizing
hatred for loved ones—those words? Did they ever even exist?

Chapter 9: Explosive Blows

"To be uncertain is to be uncomfortable, but to be certain is to be ridiculous."—Chinese Proverb

I don't have answers. I do have theories, suggestions, thoughts, concepts. We'll start there.

By "there," I mean "here." It's the summer of 2013. I'm loving my new, old and funky Chico apartment; it feels like a palace—so much space.

Being alone affords me sanity, too. I'm at peace.

Yeah, moseying freely throughout my abode, wearing only bright pink fuzzy slippers and big cotton granny panties; squishing my rapidly inflating belly bulge with both hands to form various shapes (hearts, a frog's mouth, a baby's butt); engaging myself in daily discourse about how weird and silly I am—all sorts of oddities like these help me to feel normal.

Somehow.

Actually, I'm considering the idea that we're all "normal," except the truly extremely irrational ones who are often or sometimes entirely disconnected from reality—through no fault of their own. They can't function productively, and they experience delusions or hallucinations with fair regularity. Professionals call them "psychotic."

Per www.Dictionary.com:

Psychosis 1. a mental disorder characterized by symptoms, such as delusions or hallucinations, that indicate impaired contact with reality. 2. any severe form of mental disorder, as schizophrenia or paranoia.

The rest of us maintain your standard neuroses—moments of irrational fear, panic, frenzied catastrophe mode; deeply pained, hopelessly depressive bouts of morbidly marginal existence; mania worth enjoying the heck out of because it disappears the moment after we've decided to give in to it; obsessive fixations on trivial things that we know are trivial but that we obsess over anyway, etc.

<u>Per www.Dictionary.com</u>:

Neurosis 1. Also called psychoneurosis. a functional disorder in which feelings of anxiety, obsessional thoughts, compulsive acts, and physical complaints without objective evidence of disease, in various degrees and patterns, dominate the personality. 2. a relatively mild personality disorder typified by excessive anxiety or indecision and a degree of social or interpersonal maladjustment.

Why can't I find a man who's only a little bit neurotic at worst?

As usual, when I ask these questions, another man presents himself. This one, Hank, seemed pleasant enough. We'd met on a dating site called HereIGoAgainBeingStupid dot come on.

Yeah, lining up another internet date. What do they say about insanity? It's defined by repeating the same behaviors, while expecting different results. Nah, I disagree.

Einstein never said it either, though his name's linked to it. Albert knew that science is about repeating the same actions, repeatedly, and then again. That's how we derive new knowledge. It's good to persevere and perseverate. "If at first you don't succeed," and all.

Okay, for me to keep dating strange men who are in fact strange, especially the ones I meet online, year after year, and to hope for a winner in the mix? Yeah, that's not sound. Every one of them seemed at least a bit, and sometimes very, unwell.

Yet let's not confuse naive hope with delusional antics. They aren't equal. I don't think.

And let's not forget the desperate behaviors that loneliness incites. Depression and loneliness are so common, they're normal.

So is "crazy" just a normal state?

"We used to think that only people with psychosis heard voices or had delusions, but now we know that otherwise healthy, high-functioning people also report these experiences." -Dr. John McGrath, www.cbsnews.com Rachael Rettner May 28, 2015.

I remember when Justin and I strolled through Costco on what unbeknownst to me would be our final excursion. He took control of the shopping cart with firm grip of both hands.

Our relationship, extremely tenuous.

I kept mostly quiet, doing my best to maintain a guise of harmony between us.

We navigated aisles of household items, when Justin said matter-of-factly, "I'm going to need towels for houseguests."
Houseguests? He had no friends who'd visit. Plus, Justin forbid me from having house-guests.

Was he already planning to kick me out? It made no sense. I had no words. I simply denied that he said it. He did too; he let it go the minute it slipped out.

A few paces further, Justin stopped abruptly. He raised his hands from the shopping cart handle, clenched his fists, and stood frozen in deep, disconcerting thought (or madness).

In a mumbling back-and-forth argument with himself, Justin punched out the words
"No. No. This isn't happening." His rigid arms returned to the cart handle.

Two slow steps further, Justin said "No, I'm not hearing this."
It was too much to process.

We continued to shop, bought some food for the upcoming week, and pretended nothing had happened. No, Justin showed no signs of psychosis. He refused to acknowledge any mental health problems whatsoever, much less hallucinations.

By now this type of psychosis had become frighteningly familiar.

Glenn David, age 13: I am and always was a short, shy, unaggressive, intelligent and likable person.

"Glenn," the psychiatric emergency team addressed my brother.

My siblings and I sat on the sofa, tense. Minutes earlier, he'd punched me. Dawn called 911. A muscular male duo arrived within minutes.

"Glenn, are you seeing things, things that other people might not see?"

"There's a little man dressed in green there walking across a tightrope." He pointed towards the ceiling.

That was enough for my brother, a frail 20 year old, just over 150 pounds, to merit being confined to a straitjacket and hospitalized in UC Irvine's in-patient psychiatric unit.

As they wheeled him on a gurney into the front entrance doors, Glenn looked at me. "She hates me," he said, as they wheeled him through the emergency doors.

I couldn't type those words, I can't reread it or look at those words, without crying.

My brother took my silence as hatred.

They warned me, lectured me in fact, to not be that way.

"Robyn, you can't ignore your brother when he's sick," Uncle Leo reprimanded in the thick of Glenn's illness, "You have to talk to him."

"Talk to your brother," Aunt Viv ordered. "Don't pretend he's not here."

But Uncle Leo didn't speak to him, nor did Aunt Viv. I was supposed to. They knew best.

The onlookers are the experts, apparently.

I was the one who needed to be different.

I wanted to. I did.

I wanted to tell an emergency room attendant out of complete and utter desperation "Fuck me now. Um, please." I hadn't even had sex yet. I didn't know what that meant, but I heard it felt exceptionally good.

I wanted to feel anything but what I felt. I wanted to be anywhere else, in any other situation. And he looked hot in medical garb. He was caring and compassionate, a good healer. Clearly, the perfect gentleman.

Fortunately, or unfortunately, I refrained from making the request.

I mean, yeah, it's fortunate.

Because I'd proceed to do all this dating, and ultimately have mostly boring sex that wouldn't merit publication. I'd publish anyway. And I suppose I feel as though my life should unfold as it has and will. I like the person that I am today, after all.

That said, back to the Tilt-A-Whirl of my dating life. I agreed to meet the next dude, Hank, at Buffalo Wild Wings.

Upon my arrival, I watched a man stroll out of the eatery's front entrance. He appeared a much older, much more balding version of the man whose online photos I'd admired. So it goes.

"Hi, Hank, good to meet you," my smile, forced.

He conferred a side hug.

"Good to meet you," Hank grinned. "Say, I just went in, and that place is really loud and crowded. I'm wondering if you want to go somewhere else?"

"Sure. What else is around here? I'm easy."

"Why don't we go to BJ's?" On a first date? Maybe I shouldn't have said "I'm easy." But it can't mean that. Right?

"Okay, yeah, BJ's."

As we sat in the semi-crowded, semi-loud restaurant waiting for our food, painful conversation occurred. I was the only one skilled in basic discourse. Hank focused on his phone, showed me photos of himself and his brother, and was generally odd and boring.

"So, what does B.J. really stand for?" I couldn't let it go.

With pride and confidence, he blurted out "blow job!"

"Blow job!" Hank devolved into a laughing frenzy.

I sat awkwardly, alarmed and unamused.

"Blow job! Blow job! Blow job! Hahaheehee wuhmee hmeeheehee!"

It was like watching Beevis and Butt-head play an incessant game of "Pull my finger".

A sweet young waitress approached our table.

Hank ceased his giggling to ask, "What does B.J. stand for? She wants to know."

"Um, I think it's someone's name, but I'm not sure."

"Oh,'cuz I told her"—his voice got louder and prouder by the millisecond—"It means blow job!"

The waitress glanced at me sympathetically. "Well that's awkward."

"Yes. I don't know what menu he's looking at, but he won't be getting any of that."

Hank launched into more laughter after we placed our orders. Really, dude? You're like old and graying and a grandpa and you think you're the next Amy Schumer?

<u>Note to self:</u> Stop looking for a man, you strong, empowered woman. Did I teach you nothing? You have a rich life, a lot to appreciate. You're loved by me and many. You're all you need. Write. Write. Write.

<u>Note in response to note to self:</u> Right. Write, write. Right?

Hank walked me to my car and kissed my lips. "Can I see you again?"

"Yeah, maybe." Maybe? Yeah? Why'd I say either of those words? Even worse, I added, "Give me a call."

Hank never called. He did correspond, though.

"Hey, Im at Thunder Valley. Lots of food. LOL!" Hank messaged a week later.

"Enjoy yourself," I responded.

"Lightnin storms tonite. Crazy".

"Stay safe," my thoughtful retort.

"All good. Wanna go 2—Blow Job agen? LOL!"

Really? What could I say? Nothing.

"No reply? U have No cents of humor. Blojobblowjobbbb!! Blow job! LOLzzzz."

I mean, seriously? That's not the intended name of a fairly classy restaurant, and the lol-er is the only one still laughing. Why are not people who act this way labelled "insane" or even "neurotic"?

Those guilty of much less abnormal behaviors are given stigmatizing mental health diagnoses for a lifetime. It's not fair.

I mean, if you have nothing reasonable or courteous to say when you're trying to impress the other party, say nothing. It's the most sane choice.

Even if you're not trying to impress, be respectful. It's the reasonable choice.

Somehow, though, I'm the problem. I have no "cents" of humor.

I never heard from Hank again.

Phew.

Silence.
Ineptitude.
Flaccidity.
Impotence.

Glenn had been home from the psychiatric ward for several days.

I didn't know how to talk to my brother. I could barely survive that nightmarish episode, never mind find words for it or for him.

Somehow, I did it. We do what we have to, when we have to the most.

He lay belly-up, stone-faced, on his bed.

I stood under his bedroom doorframe, "Glenn David?"

"Hm, what?"

"I just want to say . . . I love you. I'm sorry for everything you're going through."

"Well, you have a lot less to worry about than I do."

He was right.

A sane response, it was unexpected. There was no connection or acknowledgement of my loving expression. But it wasn't about me. It was about him. Glenn's response made me feel perhaps even worse.

What could I say? "I know."

I turned my back on my brother and walked away.

Psychosis versus me.
Psychosis versus me and my brother.
Psychosis versus my brother and himself.

"Words" for Glenn David Engel by this Author:
If words were verbs, this verse would serve
To spin plight into light like you deserved.
To trade the pains and strife you bear
With regained faith in life that's fair
Erase all portions of your toll
Embrace and restore your gracious soul.
If words could expel your gravest fears
They'd repel what plagued you
And those you held dear.
Inject youthful zest and the same flashing spark

That helped move you through
Past patches of dark.
They'd kill the ills and cease disease.
Lift you in seamless steam, thrill, and ease.
If words could convey your out-of-sight worth
They'd bathe you in every last diamond on earth.
Words: they can blast, pop, and pound
And yet not make a sound.
They can crowd real loud
When there's no one around.
Yet in times of travail
When hours require fight
Words flail, fail, and
duck out of sight.
They can't serve as elixirs
Or tenderize the gruff
But they'll render
"I love you."
I wish that was enough.

Chapter 10: The Edge of Mad Rage

"He was insane with anger. Or is all insanity anger?"—Anais Nin

Sometimes I talk too much. Or so Justin would tell me. Especially when he was mad. This was, it seemed, every moment of our brief but belabored 13-month marriage. Anything I said or did to appease him only made him angrier. I was supposed to leave Justin alone when he was upset. Stay away and wait patiently until he welcomed civilized discourse. Which he never did.

They ("experts") say that anger isn't a real emotion. I (perhaps an "expert") say they're stupid for saying this. Ah, how nice life would be if anger wasn't real! Come on, seriously, what's more real than male fury? If you've been on the receiving end, you know what I mean.

Please don't take me for a chauvinistic piglet. I'm not saying women aren't capable of effusive madness. We are. At least, I am.

Thing is, men are generally more prone to rage because of societal conditioning; they're supposed to be tough, and this involves withholding all emotions except anger. Plus, males can generally do a lot more damage when enraged.

Men model their behaviors after their angry, abusive dads too. It's a volatile self-perpetuating pattern.

And let's talk pro sports like boxing wherein men are worshipped, praised and applauded, paid millions to demonstrate ruthless, unhinged anger. How twisted does it get?

Weirder yet, I fall for it. The glamourized pro athlete.

I didn't think I would. Besides being a woman of depth (sometimes), I'm uncomfortable talking to big, tall men. And all men are big and tall to me. But when they give me attention, and when I learn of their athletic prowess, well, in one instance, I swoon(ed) like Martha Stewart at the mere thought of Ted Nugent's 38-inch long 1892 Alaskan Takedown Cartridge Rifle.

<u>Halloween, 2014:</u>

The place was packed with your standard small town, boisterous yet good natured, drunken but "I'm just getting started" energy—taken up a notch by bloody zombies, big-bosomed nurses, stoned hippies (that's redundant), and a costumeless but clothed me. I made it to the bar, ordered a Pepsi per my typical "wild" night out, then pressed through the crowd to stand by the dance floor. Dracula and his monstrous pals played upbeat, catchy tunes.

"Do you know how to swing dance?" My face met that of a huge burly man. Actually, my face met his silver-plated chest. I looked up to see a pair of friendly brown eyes beneath a two-horned Viking helmet.

"Um, well, not West Coast," I responded. "I can do some East Coast, but it's been a while." Viking's face constricted. Seemed I'd confused him by an overload of syllables. Yet he held out a huge palm.

Next, I was slipping and sliding on the wood paneled dance floor, laughing hysterically. Viking swung and flung me from side to side and all around. I hung tight, one goal in mind: do not fall on my butt. Then I fell on my butt. Shit!

Viking abruptly swooped me up and resumed slinging me around. I realized the meaning of his question. He meant "Are you fine with me swinging you around the dance floor?"

Thankfully, eventually, the outrageously fun and incredibly awkward dance ended. I stretched my core to climb onto a barstool, when Viking introduced himself. "I'm Ken, Ken Kansas," he said.

Frankenstein walked by, "Hey Ken." I'd learn that Viking Ken Kansas is 6 feet, 5 inches tall and weighs 300 pounds. The bartender, a Dolly Parton wannabe, glanced our way.

"What can I get ya, Ken?" He told Dolly that he'd take another Corona and asked what I'd like.

"Thank you, I'm good," I smiled. "You seem to know a lot of people here."

"Yeah, I'm kind of a big deal. I used to play for the NFL. And well"—he paused in a 'If I must tell you, I will' manner—"I actually have a Super Bowl Ring." Whoa!

Viking didn't wear the ring, he'd confess, because his fingers got too big (i.e., fat) for it. The man was clearly either a football player or a monstrous refrigerator. I didn't think a monstrous refrigerator would go to a hick bar on Halloween, so I believed him.

We sat face to chest as Ken Kansas rambled. He scored points with me: "You looked beautiful so I asked you to dance," "I'm 45" (good age for me, a tad younger), "divorced" (me too), and that he'd played for an NFL team decades earlier (unlike me. I didn't make the final cut. Rude!).

I'd need to sleep with him to see the ring, I figured. Yet I'd suffocate and die in the process. It'd thus be challenging to share the story. Then again, I could be on top, but I'm afraid of heights. Have you seen his belly? It's huge. What to do?

"Why'd you only play for a year?"

"I got kicked off," Viking said nonchalantly. "There was a bad call, the refs jumped in, I tore into the guy's face. But we're cool. We're buddies now," he chuckled, lifting his third beer for another swig.

When Viking Ken asked for a ride home because he lost his driver's license due to extreme alcohol habits, I agreed. I'm caring and helpful like that. Don't get the wrong idea. I was safe as could be.

"I warn you," I reported, "I carry pepper spray."

Oh yeah, that would've worked. Pretty pink covered, full proof ladies' pepper spray, tucked away in my bulging purse for moments when I need to say, "Excuse me, sir, would you kindly keep your hands and body parts to yourself, open your eyes real wide and freeze so I can find my pretty pink pepper spray, aim, and then shoot? Thank you."

We approached my car. I opened the passenger's door to shift the seat as far back as it would go. "I never had anyone so big in this seat."

"It's alright, I got it." He's still flexible, I thought, as Viking Ken settled in.

Here's when I pause to make a <u>Public Service Announcement</u>: No matter how caring and thoughtful she is, and no matter what kind of ring a man's hiding or claims to be hiding, or how many charges of DUI (Driving Under the Influence) he's collected, no female should ever get into a car with a male she doesn't know—especially not one built like a stainless steel large capacity Frigidaire with double doors and bins deeper than the Suez Canal.

A dearth of streetlights made for a long, dark drive to Viking Ken's home.

"My shared custody thing is kinda crazy," he sighed. "You'll have ta come over for dinner this week to meet my kid. Maybe Tuesday or Wednesday. I'll fry up some fish. Can't wait ta get my license back. Gonna have it soon. Then, I'm doing more hunting. I'll call ya tomorrow see how your week looks . . . . " Oy, how badly do I wanna see that ring? "That's my house behind these bushes right up here."

I pulled up and set the parking break.

"Wanna come in for a minute?"

"No thanks. I need to get home."

"Okay, but how about stepping out of the car so I can kiss you proper?"

Endeared, curious, and drunk on the thrill of an unexpectedly exciting night, I said "alright."

Viking Ken dropped to his knees when I approached. He cupped my chin in his humongous hands. Next, a rather unnatural moment of kissing occurred.

Imagine a minuscule meteor shard being swallowed up by a black hole, or Moby-Dick attempting to suck all the flavor out of an extra salty baby sardine, or Homer Simpson attacking a barely perceptible pink-sprinkled donut hole.

Ken Kansas didn't get handsy or slobbery or anything of the sort.

We wished each other "Good night," and I returned home safely.

The next morning, well, yikes. How do I reject him? He ripped a guy's face off for, well, playing a game with him, on the opposing team. It took decades to say this: I like my face.

I decided that honesty is best, that and not running directly at him (his ankles) on a football field.

Ken called at 10:30 a.m. "I'm sorry I got carried away and started making all sorts of plans for us."

"That's nice. I appreciate it. Yeah, to tell you the truth, I don't want to date you because of the size difference. I'd worry about my survivability."

A curt joyous chuckle spilled through my phone. Then, "Well, this was a good talk," he said cheerily. "I'll catch you later."

Kinda strange, however relieving.

Okay then. That was easy.

Therapist, when dumping me on the spot in the aftermath of my brother's suicide: "Even if I could see you twice a week, I couldn't solve your problems. I'm fast, but I'm not that fast."

I turned to my Facepalm addiction.

A friend's question topped the page: "What's your biggest fear?" My answer: "Angry men." They can hurt me, they're incredibly unpredictable; they've shattered my sense of self. Dad was sometimes playful and warm-loving, sometimes mean, explosive, neglectful; I never knew what to expect.

This chronic not-knowing increased my angst, thereby causing subtle yet chronic angst.

If only I could comfort my former self. All that energy invested into feeling scared and anxious. It wasn't worth it. But kids know only that their parents/caretakers rule their universe.

And fear isn't always realistic. Often, it's off base. In fact, under a microscope, it's entirely irrational. We're scared of those parts of ourselves that are most human, most vulnerable, primitive, hurt and scared. We're afraid of fear.

Thus, explosive rage involves a very real paradox. Its building block: a sense of being threatened to the core.

In this chapter's introductory quote, Nin asks if all insanity is anger. But is all anger insanity?

Client to other staffer, in my presence: "Tell Robyn I don't pre-she-ate her making me say 'please' to go get my soda. That's her job. Oh and she's a 'b', 'i', you know the rest. Fuck it!"

In time, through that horribly bleak episode, anxious tension inhabited my family's lives without reprieve. Nights were worst. He'd climb onto the roof, where he sat for hours. I don't know if he thought about suicide when up there. I assume so. I also don't know how he got up there without a ladder; he was extremely agile though.

When not on the roof, Glenn wandered the streets at night.

One remarkably sobering night, he was picked up by the police. That night, he'd worn his blue jacket. That night, someone robbed the Thrifty's at Sepulveda and Manchester. The criminal, a boy I'd gone to Kentwood Elementary school with, also wore a blue jacket.

My brother was thrown into jail for a night due to circumstantial evidence. Criminalized for being mentally ill. A historical pattern, even before Reaganomics hit its apex of destruction.

I couldn't imagine the depths of my brother's demoralization. I remember, I think, trying to say something comforting to him by phone at the time (him, in jail). I remember, clearly, having failed.

His behaviors culminated in literally playing with fire. Glenn set fire to our old school pictures—gave them crisp black edges and burned some of them completely.

What causes this type of mad rage? Having been robbed of one's humanness?

"Loneliness" by Glenn David, circa mid 1988:
Spelling your name 100 times in a row
Going to a movie to see the same show.
Running till you're stiff at night
Where home's a purr, a screech, a light.
Family away with friends to meet
I turn on the TV and lift my feet
Loneliness is felt when no souls are there
I think I'll go out and cut my hair
Or maybe I'll write and sing a song
Only one around, it feels so wrong.

The big football hero kept contacting me. He seemed lonely. Me too.

It's strange that he interpreted "I don't want to date you; I'd worry about my survivability" as "I want you." Some men translate anything a woman says that way, I suppose.

"I don't want to date you," I'd reiterate.

"We'll see about that," he'd chuckle.

I suppose once you've won the Super Bowl, at least in your mind, women don't turn you down. This isn't in the realm of possibilities.

Still, I'd see Ken here and there, unplanned. I'd never be alone with him again, and I wouldn't give him rides of any sort. When there was music, I let him swing me around the dance floor for ole times' sake.

Once in-between bouts of swinging at The Graduate, we sat with drinks to catch up.

"So how've you been Ken?"

"I'm great. Work's good, everything's good," he nodded. "What's going on with you?"

"Not much. Well, actually my Dad's pretty sick, and work's lousy. But I'll be fine."

Dad's health had taken a bad turn. He wasn't aging well and might soon need nursing assistance. Jonathan and Angela were wonderfully invested in all aspects of his care needs. They visited him with Josiah several times a week. It was a huge relief to me and Dawn, both of us much further away. (Though we honestly wouldn't have made anywhere near the efforts our younger brother and his family made. We'd both had too many tensions with Dad.)

"I'm sorry." Viking placed his hand on my thigh. "Do you want to go for a walk and talk about it?"

"No thanks. I'll be alright." I removed his big, fat hand, which he then extended for more dancing.

A second source of stress, as I'd mentioned to Ken, was my employer. I was then employed by an adoption agency, managed by a mother-son duo. The mom, a seemingly sweet 76 year old with a hunchback. Her son, an angry, entitled White man in his thirties.

When Hunchback asked me to help with a difficult couple, I did. They came with scores of issues, including psychiatric meds and serious mental health diagnoses, inadequate bedroom space for expanding their family, an active open case with child welfare, and more. But they insisted on being cleared for adoption. I was told to do this clearance, whatever it took.

This particular couple demanded answers and help at all hours of the days and night. I thus wrote them a clear and respectful email about not being available around the clock except in cases of emergency, but to contact 911 first, and blah blah blah.

Hunchback was most grateful. "That's a great email. You spelled it out clearly, thank you."

Thus, I never expected the fallout:

"You'll meet with us at 9 a.m. Monday morning," Angry Son informed via email.

At a small circular table in Hunchback's office, with Angry Son, another director, Hunchback, and me, Angry Son abruptly shut the door.

"Here!" he handed each of them a printed copy of the email I'd forwarded to the couple.

Hunchback pretended she hadn't seen, much less approved, my message.

"Robyn, I can't believe you wrote this," she said. "After the first sentence, it's fine. But you know we never tell clients we can't be there to help—"

"That's not what—"

"Stop it!" Angry Son snapped. "This is completely inexcusable!"

"Well I—"

Hunchback shook her head, disapprovingly. "This isn't like you, Robyn."

"Yes, I think it's not professional," the other director colluded.

"Well, as a licensed clinician—"

Angry Son interrupted, "Then you should've known better!"

Clearly, it was a lost cause.

If you work on behalf of child welfare, you need to feed adult egos and ignore the kids' needs. In fact, put the children in the care of extremely troubled people. The more troubled, the better. It doesn't matter. It's about money and power, folks.

Bad Robyn puts kids first. Bad Robyn sets limits with troubled adults who want to adopt vulnerable children.

"You have NO BUSINESS in customer service."

Customer service? What the hell? Angry Son thinks we're in retail? I work at Walmart? Shit, were that the case, I could afford fancy new socks.

Angry Son reminded me of Justin.

It's a rage that seems boundless.

Once, my late ex-husband had actually permitted me to record our conversation. I was desperate to improve our communication. I'm not sure why he was okay with this—likely because he was such an astute lawyer, certain that I was the one being unreasonable.

Having transcribed it—and I'm including a segment below—I'm not entirely convinced he was the crazy one.

Mean-spirited and ruthless, yes. Insane? Not here.

<u>Robyn:</u> Thank you. Is there anything else you want me to work on?
<u>Justin:</u> Yes.
<u>Robyn:</u> What?
<u>Justin:</u> Having boundaries and not insisting on being heard. Even if I want to, it's counterproductive, it's destructive, and it just keeps pissing me off. I can't give you what you want because it just makes me more angry when you keep pushing. It's like sticking a bear with a stick, you're gonna get bitten.
<u>Robyn:</u> Okay, I'm sorry for what, from my perspective, is my tenacity and desperation to not have these problems in our marriage. It's not my intention. It does go back to my fear of abandonment and being successful with everything else in my life. I can't stand the idea of not being successful in our marriage.
<u>Justin:</u> Yeah, but this is different. Sometimes it means backing away for a while. But just poking and poking and poking will get an explosion in an enclosed space. And that's what a marriage is. If you just back away for a better time, that provides judgment and time.

And I need to not get so angry, true, but I give a lot of warning signs that I'm not in a good place and you need to back off and you think I'm procrastinating and you keep poking and poking and poking and kaboom! You know, sometimes you need to leave me alone!

Robyn: I need to feel like I'm being treated lovingly, honey. I don't feel that way. I feel like I'm being treated like I'm a pain in your ass.

Justin: I do not mean to make you feel that way. Sometimes I do feel you are that way, yes. And it's just that you need to leave me alone for a different time. I'm actually not that hard to please. I'm really not.

Robyn: Sweetie, when you're upset, you're impossible to please. Anything I do upsets you more. I give you flowers or a card, and it's dismissed. I cooked you dinner and you ate something else. I'd like to know how I can please you more, baby. I know, back off. I wish you could see that I just love you and I just want to work on our relationship instead of seeing that as a bad thing.

I'll work on backing off and giving you space, and I would like you to work at always being loving towards me and holding onto my motives as good and positive and loving, and that I don't want to cause you strife. I'm desperate to work on it, and that's perceived as controlling. I'm sorry for that.

Justin: I don't remember all the garbage you talk about. There's a lot of stuff you talk about all the time.

My crying is audible. The recorder is turned off.

They say you can't fix crazy, but I tried. Or was I trying to fix anger? You can't do that either. My intentions, heartfelt. The goal, unachievable, and perhaps crazy in itself.

Viking Ken contacted me. "I have good news."

"Yeah, what's that?"

"I got married! Well, I was already married." Wha, what? "We never filed for divorce. She said she wanted to try again, so I said 'sure,' and it's going great so far."

Hm, normally, I'm enraged by a married man who pretends he's not. In this case, I was mostly relieved. Bewildered too, though mostly relieved.

"Congratulations." I guess.

"So I'll see ya around town."

"Sounds good. Good luck to you."

Drop-kicked off the field by a swinging Super Bowl champ who remembered that he's married only when his wife regained interest in touching down again.

Well, I'd entered "cleanup" mode, so this was fitting.

One more door needed to be shut.

I didn't mind traffic during my final trek to work.

"Here you go," I stepped into Hunchback's office, wherein she chatted with Angry Son.

"I quit," I said confidently. I handed her a letter that spelled out my immediate termination because, as I stated then and there, in writing and verbally, "Workplace harassment is against the law."

They looked a bit surprised, flustered.

"Wa, wait, we have to pay you," she bargained.

"Uh, no. I never get paid on the spot. I'll expect it in the mail."

I placed my office key on her desk as Angry Son glared.

Turning directly to Hunchback, I asserted, "Your son has serious anger issues. He needs help."

"Oh no, he doesn't," she said awkwardly and turned to him.

As I made a swift departure, I felt his heavy glare. I also felt a broad smile across my face. Yes! Robyn pulls ahead in a victory against insane rage.

Sometimes the best we can do is call it what it is, turn our backs on them, and make a speedy exit.

Chapter 11: Cruise Control

"If you think anyone is sane, you just don't know enough about them."—Christopher Moore

Seduced by a former Super Bowl champ (or one who claimed to be)—there's something exciting about that. And "exciting" equates with "sexy" or even "crazy." At least, that's what we're taught.

Think about songs with "crazy" in the title: "Still Crazy After All These Years" (Paul Simon), "She Drives Me Crazy" (Fine Young Cannibals), "Crazy in Love" (Beyoncé), "Let's Go Crazy" (Prince), to name a few.

A curt perusal of Amazon book titles elicits similar results: *The Right Kind of Crazy* (Steltzner & Patrick); *Crazy Sexy Diet* (Kris Carr); *Crazy Brave: A Memoir* (Joy Harjo), and *Crazy Is My Superpower* (A.J. Mendez).

All told, crazy is good, right? Perhaps there's a good-crazy versus a bad-crazy. I'm often good-crazy, but sometimes I'm bad-crazy. Maybe I'm both. I'd suggest you are too. Agree?

I find it perplexing that the same word ("crazy") used to describe mental illness also means playful, fun, sexy, and/or strange in a good way.

Accordingly, the only segment of "non-crazy" constitutes that which is tiresome, mundane, and well, normal. Boring too. Let's face it, that's what sanity amounts to.

"Sane is boring."—R.A. Salvatore

In fact, I do feel "normal" when there's no thrilling activity in my life. I'm more productive and calm during stretches of celibacy, for example. Boredom is essential; it's not necessarily bad. I'm talking about a status quo, trekking-in-cruise-control status.

It's wonderful, really. I get to experience it because I don't have kids, and I'm not often subjected to the hormonal craze induced by sex. Not often enough.

Yet I and we itch to break free from boredom, because it's so different from what we're used to. And because we're taught that life is sexier when we traverse the crazy lane. Many or most of us grew up in it.

Calmness is unfamiliar. It breeds anxiety. Plus, physiology. Point-blank, sex is addicting. I like it on occasion, that occasion being when I get some. You know?

Male suitor to me: "I have church in the morning, so I can't see you tonight."
Me: "I've never been rejected for Jesus, so I guess I'm flattered." Amen? Argh, men!

Settled into living alone, for better and for worse, I needed a go-to spot in order to break the monotony. I'd been hearing about the open mic at Has Beans Café. Maybe I'd go there and recite some of my writings. I'd check it out.

Nerves kept me lurking in the back rows for weeks on end. Locals' talents far surpassed any description I could formulate in words. Once I started chatting with performers, though, their genuine humility impressed me.

Even better, when I finally summoned the courage to recite my poetry, they loved it and wanted more.

Several months into my engagement with this downtown hub, George showed up and sparked discourse. He's a nonmusician who also appreciated the show.

We began to look for each other weekly.

I got to know George as a sweet, smart, reliable man. So I delightedly accepted his dinner invite. We had a nice time at a popular Thai eatery. But of course, there was a red flag. In this case: politics. He's Republican.
Note to self: Can I date a Republican if he's nice?
Note in response to note to self: Sure, it's just a label. Right?
Note in response to response to note to self: I'm left but right, right?

"It doesn't matter," George stated. "People make too much out of political differences."

We agreed we wouldn't argue politics. In fact, per my suggestion, we wouldn't argue. Period. Harmony with a man, at last.

I won't tell you George's profession, but he mentioned wearing latex for his job in healthcare.

"A lot of people are allergic to latex nowadays, so we have to avoid it," he informed me.

"What do they do about sex?"

"I guess they have to abstain or resort to masturbation," he suggested, factually.

At once, we both giggled.

"When I ask men who come into the office if they're allergic to latex," George added, "they very proudly and in a deep voice say, 'Oh no! Not at all. I'm NOT allergic to latex.'"

(Fortunately, George wasn't allergic either.)

As he grilled fish for our dinner one night, I lounged outside on a beach chair. George went inside for a spatula, came back out, then closed the screen door between his kitchen and patio.

"Can I do anything to help?" I asked, as he returned with spatula in hand.

"You can go ahead and get some plates for us."

"No problem. Where are they?"

"In the right side cabinet above the microwave."

"Okay." I stepped towards the kitchen when BAM! My face smashed against the screen, knocking the screen offtrack.

"Are you okay?" He rushed over to examine my forehead.

"Oh yeah, I'm fine." Ouch. No. I'm embarrassed, everything's cool. We agreed I'd be of most help if I stayed seated.

"You know those helmets that kids wear when they have special needs and do the headbanging thing? I need one."

"No, you just need to slow down," he said evenly, "and take your time with things."

I'd surely met a good one.

Life has its polarities.

On the flip side of my new beau's steady demeanor, my next potential employer took me through a rapid-fire interview. He didn't stop or pause at all when describing the position. I'm doubtful he understands the term "slow down."

"You'll be the consultant at structured weekly point-five hour clinical meetings for the entirety of the treatment team that's inclusive of first and second year interns from multiple school programs in the greater region," I learned, "wherein you'll respond to their case scenarios in a didactic manner for example by way of informing them to utilize Motivational Interviewing conduct a BDI assure that their MSE is current and accurately assess for suicidality possible risk to others and refer them to their primary care physician for a medical examination. Always certify that you've obtained the appropriate disclosures and releases. It's quite simple really."

Whoa. Slow down, dude.

"Because of your wonderful experience we'll have you facilitate outreach with the university engage in groups in various community forums conduct multifaceted training classes and represent the program in the community at large."

Having never done drugs, I can only surmise that he might have just inhaled or shot up something unkosher and extra stimulating.

He (we'll call him "Speed") wouldn't take "no" for an answer, despite my emphasis on the fact that I had no experience in addictions work.

Speed said I'd be fine, and I accepted the job.

For several months, I enjoyed the work. I consulted with interns individually and as a group. Yet the employer prevented me from networking, or any of the other glorious things I'd been promised.

Instead, I was instructed to provide more specific drug treatment interventions. Even though I didn't have expertise in this. Even though he described an entirely different job.

I did the best I could, nonetheless, to bone up on trainings and specific techniques. I thought things were going fairly well.

Yet Speed stopped talking to me altogether. Whispers of fiscal problems and "reorganization" took hold (i.e., layoffs). Not a good sign.

What could I do but keep going?

Speech patterns or lack thereof (whispers or silences) can be as telling as they are puzzling.

My interactions with Dad, too, grew troubling in terms of communication.

He continued to deteriorate. A nurse suggested it might be Parkinson's. Shit. I thought, he might be showing signs of Alzheimer's, but Parkinson's sounded much worse.

"He's falling a lot," Jonathan said. Dad was now in a nursing facility.

"How are the kids?" Dad asked, when I called during a lunch break.

The kids? "Dad, I don't have kids, but Josiah's great. You see him a lot, right? He's eight now."

"He's fun," Dad chuckled. "He's a good boy. How are the kids?"

"They're, they're fine, Dad. How are you feeling?"

After pausing, Dad tripped over sound bites through a tearful outpouring of grief, sadness, frustration and perhaps drama.

I cried too.

"Dad, I love you."

"I love you too."

I realized Dad used to ask Mom "How are the kids?" I don't remember this, but I'm assuming that's why he asked me. It must've been a routine question for nearly twenty years—when Dad worked at the pharmacy and Mom was home with us.

Long-term memories are the most hardwired, so this makes sense.

However, that type of questioning on his part could easily be, and has historically been, viewed as a sign of mental and medical illness.

Let's face it, we'll never understand the brain—its 86 billion neurons; 125 trillion synapses in the cerebral cortex alone. We're talking about at least 1,000 times the number of stars in our galaxy. How arrogant are we to assume that we can define and test for "mental wellness" versus "mental illness"! And that this state is fixed versus fluid.

I admired George's memory for specific details. This didn't always work in my favor, though.

Seemingly out of the blue, he argued about all the red tape involved in running your own business. This spun into ranting about governmental regulations regarding energy saving light bulbs. I don't remember the nuances of George's contentions, but he huffed hot air as a prelude to "the damn liberals who want governmental control over everything."

Oh no he didn't. Oh yes he did.

"That's not it, hon. Everyone wants the government out of our business," this damn liberal countered. "Less government sounds good to everyone." There. I could be in a relationship with a Republican.

I continued with confidence and pride. "Stupid incompetents rise to the top of every system, and California loves regulations. That's just a fact, having nothing to do with the political leanings of those who create all the red tape. Plus what's wrong with being environmentally friendly? It's to everyone's advantage."

I was on a roll.

Thing is, I don't debate well. But I really liked George. I needed to prove that we could work as a couple. So I babbled about hippie-dippie systems and big corporations, about how slews of redundant policies govern every big system.

As I heard myself talk, I thought: That's pretty damn good. You're making sound points.

But then I heard myself say: "And I love you."

Holy shit. I'd dropped a big matzo ball on George's lap, only three weeks into our courtship.

For one fraction of one second, George appeared terrorized. He then continued, composed, as if he hadn't been privy to an awkwardness that could be detected by rabbis lost in prayer at Jerusalem's Western Wall.

"Anyway, I prefer regular light bulbs to that L.E.D. stuff," he countered.

"Excuse me while I go potty" was all I could say.

I examined myself in his bathroom mirror, my face flushed with complete and utter embarrassment. Maybe he didn't hear me? I whispered to my reflection, "Big, big matzo ball you sent flying, girlfriend." Gulp.

For weeks, I buried my feelings during shared breakfast smoothies that preceded romantic sleepovers, barbecue dinners at George's place, and snuggle time in front of his big screen TV.

We even took a trip to Lake Tahoe. There, George and I played in the snow, ate at buffets, toured the town, ate at buffets, shared a cozy hotel room, and engaged in indoor recreational activities—to stay warm between visits to buffets.

Holding hands as we walked through Harrah's, I felt a comfortable joy.

Nevertheless, surging emotions struck me on the ride home, inciting a silent spillage of tears. I positioned myself to look out the window and managed to stop long enough, after stretches of time, to make small talk: "You doing okay with the drive?", "The snow looks beautiful."

<u>Note to self</u>: I love him, but he doesn't love me.

<u>Note in response to note to self</u>: Stop it, you're always too negative.

<u>Note in response to response to note to self</u>: Yeah, but he never expresses his feelings. You must be right. You love him, I love him. But he doesn't love you, he doesn't love me.

The thought pattern repeatedly repeated itself. Correspondingly, my angst soared.

Alas, the long drive home ended. I dropped my bag on George's hallway floor, when he noticed I'd been crying. "What's wrong?" His tone conveyed warmth and nervousness.

We sat on his sofa for a talk.

I faced the door, eyes down, ready to make a grand escape if he said the wrong things or—more likely—didn't say the right thing(s).

"I'm just worried, worried that I have more feelings for you than you do for me."

"Well," he paused, "when you said you love me, don't you think it's too soon?"

"Okay, I do use the word 'love' pretty freely, but"—my voice dropped—"I'm starting to fall in love with you. That's just how I feel, so it came out."

George pulled me close and held me somewhat warmly, somewhat tentatively.

I eyed the distance between us and his front door.

"I can't take any more hurt. I can't tell you how painful the whole thing was with my ex-husband. I'm getting really scared that I'm the only one invested. You never say anything."

He looked at me. I had no idea what he was thinking. Shit. He fuckin said . . . nothing.

I wriggled away and stood up.

"I'm going to just go now."

"Why?"

"Because you're not saying anything now either. I'm feeling really stupid!"

"Yeah, I probably could be more expressive." Progress.

I patiently, hopefully returned next to him on his sofa.

"I'm starting to feel that way," George confessed. "Just give it some time." He rubbed his hand up and down my back, leaned over to whisper in my ear, "Have faith."

I rested my head on his chest. "Okay."

One afternoon in the midst of the holidays, I got a call from Speed's boss.

"Ms. Engel, we're terminating your contract effective immediately. There were some complaints about you."

"I don't know about any complaints. In fact, I've only gotten positive feedback. I've done everything Speed's asked of me. This isn't right."

"We are in fact terminating your contract. There will be no more discussion on the matter."

"Okay, well, then let me make a few suggestions: Hire a director who has an ounce of people skills and who is at least as educated as the interns. Learn some social skills yourself. You all talk like robots. Find your humanity."

I called George. He dropped everything to come over and hold me.

"Well, at least I'll have more time for my writing and for us."

"You'll find something else," he assured me. "It'll work out."

"Yeah, I always land on my feet." Except when I land on my butt.

On New Year's Eve, I prepared an Italian dinner for us (cheese-spinach manicotti, green salad, garlic bread). We sipped a bit of wine. Then we slept together. Well, only I did. I fell asleep, that is. On my couch.

"It's midnight," George whispered. "2015."

I pushed myself up and out of a snuggle position. We stepped outside to watch all of the fireworks that we'd been hearing for hours. We saw none.

George and I stepped back inside and readily fell asleep.

When did it get so difficult and mean so little to stay up past midnight on New Year's Eve?

"The worst part of holding the memories is not the pain. It's the loneliness of it. Memories need to be shared."—Lois Lowry

George and I seemed to be doing well. Mostly.

We'd been together for five months and three days. (I was counting.)

"I'm thinking up lines for my 'Easter Erotica' poem for open mic," I giggled. We snuggled in front of his TV. "Things like, 'Let's commit an original sin,'" I giggled again.

"Don't do it."

What? "Come on, it's funny. Original sin!"

"Don't do it." He was serious. "It's a small Christian town. That could ruin your reputation. Don't risk it."

"Are you kidding me? It's no big deal. It's funny. Nobody's going to be offended by that."

George, insistent. Me, not one to be controlled.

In fact, when bossed around, I'm inclined to rebel. But I liked and even loved George, so I recited my Easter Erotica for the audience when George was out of town on a business trip.

"It doesn't feel right that you told me not to read my poetry. I want a boyfriend who supports my art," I argued by phone one night. "Plus, it was fine. They laughed. They liked it."

"They probably didn't understand the references," he defended. "Anyway, it doesn't change how I feel about you. I didn't want you to—"

"Wait! How you feel? How do you feel about me, George?"

"What do I think?" No, dude. How do you feel—you, know, the male "f" bomb, "feelings."

"I think I'm in love with you and I think that you're a good friend and that you're smart and pre—"

"Stop! You said you love me?!"

"Yeah, but that doesn't—"

"No need to argue anymore, sweetie. I'm good. My baby loves me. Woo-hoo!"

George chuckled.

As we know, love isn't all it takes.

Slowly but poignantly, our relationship eroded.

We sat at my dining room table one evening. While he ranted, I reminisced about the good ol' days when we first dated. Our respective political views would not be a source of contention. We wouldn't argue. We'd be a harmonious duo, and we mostly were.

Little did I know what spurred this word vomit or that he'd slice me in two by it.

"A lot of the mentally ill are violent."

Blood rushed through my system. When Justin had expressed a similarly hateful, insensitive comment about mental illness years earlier, I was certain he couldn't have said anything more hurtful. And he'd said a lot of painful things.

But this one hit too close to home, caused too much pain, was coldly dismissive of me and my family. It ultimately meant that I couldn't and wouldn't continue to be with him.

"It really hurts to hear you say that." I looked directly into George's eyes, maintaining calm. "I told you about my brother, and you know about my depression and my work on suicide prevention. Not all people with mental illness are violent."

"Well, some of them are!"

"And some people without mental illness are violent too!"

I couldn't talk.

Memories.

The saddest of memories.

<u>Late September, 1988:</u>

My bright pink beanbag, at the foot of my bed, buffers my fall to the darkest of places.

I'm jolted by the ringtone, hoping desperately to hear Glenn's voice, alive and okay.

God, please don't let my instincts be right.

The man's tone is stoic with a slice of compassion. "I'm sorry it took so long," he tells me, after introducing himself as the coroner. The impact of the fall was so profound, he explained, that my brother's fingerprints kept slipping. But he finally confirmed that the body is his.

Glenn's jump from 10560 Wilshire Boulevard was his final act. I'd been working in a nearby high-rise at the time, but I stopped going to work when he went missing. The same numbers, differently ordered, had entered my dreams the night before. Did he intend to be near me, to prove something? To get even, to cause me guilt, or to add to it?

"Thank you for the call," I tell the coroner.

Numbness suffocates erratic emotion. No time.

Call Dad first. Call Irene, his girlfriend.

"Please take care of my Dad," I urge. She promises that she will, for which I'm relieved and grateful.

I make the other calls.

Dawn swiftly darts into the living room and gives Jonathan a hug, adding "I love you." She then hugs Dad with an "I love you."

I'm ignored.

Not for a moment do I, or anyone in the family, consider my well-being. I'm invisible like my brother.

Over the years, I've learned that tragedy does not alter family roles. It punctuates them.

Perhaps I'm not worthy of anything but tragedy. I think about his love . . . and his sadness, his desperation and loneliness. I was a lousy sister. I'm not only thinking about his pain, I'm incorporating it. Deep within, I believe it's my toll. I carry it. I need to. It's my burden, my punishment.

Perhaps that same sentiment which launched him off the roof of a Wilshire Boulevard skyscraper is an extreme form of the energy that instinctively pushed, and still pushes, me away from myself.

George also, perchance.

Maybe you too carry molecules of this energy, dear reader?

Primed to cut ties, I became increasingly irritated that George hadn't arrived at Has Beans yet. We'd planned to meet there. It was after 8:30 p.m. He'd always been timely.

Lightning shattered clouded skies, and thunderous blasts sporadically vied for attention. I checked my phone. Maybe the weather slowed him down. A message from George. I stepped outside the café to listen to it.

He sounded frazzled. "I'm not sure where you are right now, but I'm afraid to go out there tonight. I might get struck by lightning. I'll talk to you later."

 Might get struck by lightning? Are you kidding me?

"I'm upset! I didn't feel like coming here in the rain either, but I wanted to see you. We agreed on it. You didn't want to see me? You're not willing to drive a few miles in the rain?" My voice got louder and louder. George did nothing wrong, he insisted.

 "You're not even apologizing!"

"Okay, I'm sorry. I'm sorry you attacked me. Can we just get past this?"

"You're sorry I attacked you!?" I closed my phone and drove home shaken by anger.

George called the next day. We fought again. And again. He didn't do the breaking up, so I did, in a very nice way, after saying a not-so-nice thing that I won't repeat here for the sake of my already iffy reputation. (Alright, you convinced me. I told him "You just wanted someone to suck your cock.")

Incidentally, I'd finally realized that our sex had not involved an equal give-and-take. George expected me to please him but never even hinted at pleasing me. I wasn't bothered by this until the final stage of our relationship; I'd simply been thrilled to have a sex life.

Yet I didn't want to end on a sucky (pardon the pun) note.

Eventually, depleted, I told George, "I loved you, and I'll miss you, and good luck to you."

I waited a moment for his response.

Silence.

I closed my phone.

I texted George the following afternoon: "I remembered that you have my spare apartment key. Please tell me how I can get that back. Thank you." He said he'd drop by after work the next day.

George arrived. Quietly, composed, he handed me my key back. Standing under my doorframe, he looked at me endearingly but said—his usual—nothing.

I broke the silence. "Can I give you a hug?"

"Of course."

We held each other, briefly and for the final time.

Chapter 12: Gambling with Pride

"Guilt: the gift that keeps on giving."—Erma Bombeck

I question George's refusal to apologize. Is he incapable of expressing genuine remorse? I'm skeptical. The guy was sensitive enough to provide comfort when I lost a job. He's a bright man with an extensive vocabulary. He can certainly enunciate: "I'm sorry." But he chose pride. Pride in what? Insensitivity?

Yeah, in the name of pride, some folks—straight men, for example—take the robotic route. Societal conditioning dictates this. "Don't dwell!" "Be tough!" "Provide for the family," etc.

That said, many a man has appeared "antisocial." This condition doesn't necessarily involve introverted loner existence, as the term literally connotes. (Language is an insane entity of its own.) Rather, the "antisocial" person has no sensitivity to others, no apparent conscience.

We all know these people. If we haven't had them in our lives, we've heard plenty about them. They're also called "sociopaths." Extreme examples include mass murderers, serial killers, child molesters. A look into their history often reveals severe child abuse under torturous conditions.

Is that an excuse? No. There's no acceptable excuse for an unacceptable act. But it does perhaps explain an inability to connect on a human level with other human beings.

Now let's consider the less deviant, mainstream population of the semi-narcissistic, sometimes callous rest of us. Our mental health challenges don't stifle our abilities to extend an olive branch. So why do we withhold the genuine apology? To salvage a rapidly shrinking ego? Well, that's insane.

Yeah, on that note, I kept dating.

My hopes rose. This one'll be different—as if "different" is good. As if all men are alike. In a bad way, too. I'm trying not to add: "They are." Oops, I didn't try hard enough. Apologies.

Fred did sound nice and kind, though. We'd connected through HereIgoagainbeingstupid dot come on. He worked as a high school math teacher.

The guy's profile page displayed bitch after bitch: golden retriever eats her food, golden retriever runs gleefully through grassy field, golden retriever takes leisurely nap on a set of fluffy pink floor pillows.

How sweet. The man loves his dog. Good sign; I like a nurturer.

We made plans for tea that upcoming Friday.

I don't know if I'll ever do this dating and relationship thing well, much less "right." That's okay. I'm my best self when I'm single. I'm good with that. Yet I keep trying, and failing, and downing myself for the miserable outcome—all the while collecting good stories.

It's not me, my friends. It's the men I choose. Well, that kinda makes it my wrongdoing from the start. Most conveniently, however, it's my failed relationship with Dad that's at the root. We never got that right. That's his fault. Yeah, mine too, being as a I became an adult down the road. Mostly. Sometimes. For better or worse.

Years ago, Dawn and I agreed that Dad was the textbook "narcissist." He displayed compassion here and there, but in a confused way.

10/1988: An amorphous, weighty agitation—guilt perhaps—suffocated my attempts to fall asleep that night. Dad was awake. I knew it. He sat alone nightly, exasperated, nearly paralyzed by the painful numbness of repeated tragedy. The message: I can do this. I have to. I will. I need to.

Fear.

Will.

Courage.

Will. I forced myself up and into the living room. Slowly, deliberately, I sat next to Dad on the fat beige sofa.

"Dad?"

He turned to me with a mix of care and apathy. "What, honey?"

Words and tears spilled out. "Dad, I'm sorry for your pain. I just" I pressed my left fist against my chin. "I felt like you never loved me, like you always hated me . . . . Why?"

Dad rubbed my back with his palm.

In a soft voice, he explained, "You didn't say 'hi' or ask how my day was when I got home from work. Your Mom and I did the best we could with you, but you kept us walking on eggshells with your temper."

"Dad, I was just a kid."

Dad extended his arms to hold me. "We'll have to start over, baby."

"Okay."

"We need to do the best we can to love and care for each other from now on." Dad loosened his arms. "Okay?"

"Okay," I said quietly, not fully satisfied but prepared to sleep soundly.

I did it, and I slept through the night.

Mom was incredibly paradoxical in terms of affection. She could walk into a stiff room of hundreds. Suddenly, a sublime lightness filled the air.

Mom loved me infinitely; that, I knew for certain. Yet she didn't hug me, not ever. Not once, to my recollection, did I get a hug from my Mom. Strange.

Quick kisses on the cheek came at night, after we recited the Shema[2] as we lay in bed. Both Mom and Dad made shema-kiss rounds at bedtime. It was a sweet tradition we'd come to rely on.

Despite the fact that we were darn cute kids, however, Mom was hands-off. Even for photos, there's no snuggling, squishing, squeezing, or even touching. I can't imagine being so distant, especially not with my own babes. If I don't nearly suffocate my nephew, Josiah, in tickly affection whenever I get the chance, something's gone terribly wrong.

Weird. It's all mixed up—Dad, Justin, Mom, Glenn David, endings, losses, funerals. George and the exes. Narcissism versus sensitivity. Ego preservation by acting like a mule's tuchas.

Per urbandictionary.com:
Tuchas- This Jewish slang word refers to the ever expanding rear end. It is known that many Jewish women have a large tuchas and

---

[2]Central Jewish prayer that affirms the existence of One God.

large chest. This is particularly true after the Jewish holidays due to great Jewish cooking. It can also be defined as the Jewish cushioning device.

Get your tuchas out of my face.

by CtrlAltaDel December 11, 2005

The first thing I noticed about Fred is that his face was strikingly flat. I assume it still is. Unless he's dead. In that case, well, it's even flatter. It was dark, so if I squinted, I could almost imagine his face in two dimensions. Cool. And if I shut my eyes, I could imagine him as handsome. Sorry. I'm not trying to be mean. My goal is honesty.

Fred told me about his job, and he listened as I talked about mine.

Our tea arrived.

"There's this client," I giggled. "She tries with all her might to be grumpy all the time. I have fun attempting to make her laugh. She's been through the typical hell they've all been through— sexual molestation, abandonment, all of it. And like all of them, she's been diagnosed with mental retardation, bipolar disorder, and I don't know what else. We give her eight different meds twice a day. It's crazy." I noticed his eyes on me, so I continued.

"Anyway, she and I compete at blackjack. She usually beats me, even when I'm the dealer.

I tease her about counting cards. She's really good, but not quite that savvy."

Fred nodded attentively.

"Whenever I beat her in a game, I push the cards aside, get up from the table, and stand where there's enough room for my victory dance. This routine involves jumping and doing as close to the splits as I can in the air, which is pretty pathetic and deformed to watch, especially since my goal is to land with two feet on the ground. I then do a silly, I dunno, Roger Robot Rabbit or elliptical contorted Mr. Ed move. You know, Mr. Ed? A horse is a horse. I can't even describe it, really."

I felt my face pinken.

My date grinned. Couldn't tell if he was more afraid or endeared.

"Last week, in the middle of my routine, she said something that keeps me in stitches. She fought back laughter and told me, 'You look like a REAL mentally retarded person.'"

Flat Face Fred chuckled.

I giggled.

<u>Insane factoid</u>: It costs $1,500 to file for bankruptcy.

The bill came.

"Would you like me to pay my part?" Please say "no." It's only tea. I made the drive. You're the man.

"If it makes you happy." Strange response.

"No," I said cheerily. "It wouldn't make me happy. I'll let you pick this up." You get all the happiness tonight, babe. Enjoy.

As we meandered towards my car, I learned that his dog, Heidi, was gracing her position in the passenger's seat. "We go everywhere together. It's what we do." Before I could register the oddity of Fred's enmeshed relationship with a female dog, he enveloped me in a warm embrace—the kind that got me worked up and wanting more.

"Would you like to get together for dinner next week?"

"Sure. I'd like that."

I checked my phone, preparing to drive home. Two calls from Jonathan concerned me.

At this time in my story, dear readers, mid-2015, Dad's health was declining more rapidly. We'd heard this before.

But what we'd been told was years, then months, to prepare for his demise, had now become mere days. Shit.

"Do you want me to come home," I asked Jonathan.

"Yeah, true. By the time I got there—"

"I know, okay. Thanks for telling me. I'll call tomorrow."

"Love you all."

What could I do? Life happens. Death happens. We keep breathing as long as we're able.

I drove to the taqueria, saying out loud and to myself: "I like Fred, and I'm pretty sure he likes me. He'll kiss me this time. It'll be good. Or it'll be bad. Either way, I'll know if this is going to work."

We decided to share a taco salad, and we sat side by side—a doubly good sign, I figured. Fred and I chatted about our respective work days, family, dream travel destinations, other significant and trivial matters. Everything seemed to be going smoothly.

When I mentioned Dad's serious illness, he said "I'm sorry." I thought that was a nice sign of compassion.

Fred followed with, "We're going to Europe this summer, me and my folks." Really, dude? Whoopdi-frikkin-doo-for-you, fucker.

Calm down, Robyn. Don't expect anyone else to stop their lives because Dad's dying. You're not even doing that. Besides, a make-out session's in the waiting. Maybe. Keep faith. Smile sweetly.

The salad was so humongous, we couldn't finish. I asked to take the leftovers in a to-go container. Fred carried the food and escorted me to my car.

The deciding moment arrived.

We stood by the passenger side of my car. Fred handed me the to-go box. I opened the car door, placed the leftovers on the passenger's seat, and then shut the car door. Kissy, kissy now? "I've gotta go let Heidi out!" Fred blurted, dashing to his car several yards away.

I briskly followed him like—I don't know—a puppy in heat. There they were, man and dog. Fred held onto the end of Heidi's leash, fully focused on her. "She needs fresh air," he reported. "Go ahead, sweetie," he told her, as Heidi explored a nearby patch of grass.

What to do? I pet Heidi. "She's pretty."

"Thank you." Why are you thanking me? You didn't make her pretty. That's a weird, gross thought.

With one hand firmly grasping Heidi's leash, Fred extended his other arm to impart a flimsy cold-to-lukewarm side hug. "I'd like to get to know you better." Bad sign. Good sign. Confused sign.

"Sure, be in touch," I responded.

Driving home, I said this: "I like, no, I like_d_ him. What the hell!? I won't compete with a bitch for a man's affections. Not a bitch with two legs! Not a bitch with four legs! God damnit!"

Flat Face Fred never called, not anytime shortly thereafter. It's just as well. I felt inclined to bark at him, and that might've turned him on.

Perhaps there WAS a kiss or more that night, and I was not the recipient.

I got the call at work. "He transitioned," Angela said. Jonathan had been by Dad's side day and night. He was holding Dad's hand when Dad relinquished the fight.

"Transitioned" is a strange, sugary term for "died." I'd never heard that one. When we're dead, we're dead. So I believe. Our spirits and energy do surpass our bodies, in a surreal but real way. But we're done. That's it. Kaput. Life's over. It's nice to think otherwise, I suppose. Then again, who wants to live forever?

That thought scares me more than the thought of death. I think. I want to have this big, little job done at some point. Otherwise, what's the point? An eternal heaven would be hell, I'm thinking. Who wants to keep going and going and going?

Life is about this moment. This one, right now, all that's wrapped up in and around it—the pain, the promise, the boredom, hope, agony, and more.

Why would anything matter if nothing ever ends? We'd have no moments to cherish. That'd be like flat lining. And that's death.

No parents left. Orphaned.

In the moment of losing Dad, I didn't focus on his limitations or lousy parenting. Instead, I grappled with regrets and guilt. He'd suffered tremendously—losing his wife of nearly 20 years, and then his oldest son to schizophrenia and suicide. What a lousy lot.

Dad did offer me love and signs of a soft, playful side. If it weren't for his physical warmth, I'd have never been hugged by a parent.

I wish I could tell you, dear readers, the most effective way to manage and eradicate guilt. What I can say is that by sharing, discussing it with trusted others, it lightens greatly. Shame doesn't survive outside of ourselves, try as it might. Thus we have to process and express it, to get it out and get it gone.

"I have some things to say," an elderly man stepped towards the podium during our gathering.

This long-lost relative unexpectedly appeared. He must've been in his eighties, yet his wit and spirits, intact. The man introduced himself as a great-uncle, Ben.

"We took him in when he first came to California at age 25. We spent our last dollar on a beat-up old Dodge for Jerry to drive around in. It was the best we could do. He drove it to Las Vegas to take the pharmaceutical exam, but it broke down in the desert when he was halfway there. We felt so bad. Jerry hitchhiked the rest of the way. Somehow he managed to make it on time for the test. He passed. He was a sharp young man. We were quite proud."

Ben continued, "I remember him telling us about a double date he went on. Jerry didn't care much for his date. He was smitten by the other guy's date, and he made the moves on her, he said." Ben smirked, then looked towards me and my sister. "That was your mother."

Dad was always somewhat of a risk-taking daredevil. Ben's stories made sense.

Jonathan welcomed me to the podium.

From my Eulogy for Dad, 12/27/15:

Many widows and widowers don't survive one year after losing their spouse. But Dad made it for 30 more and another 27 after putting Glenn to rest. Against all odds.

I saw him sadly, longingly staring at a photo of Mom at home, after the funeral. I saw him loving and holding Glenn for days or weeks, when our brother was plagued by demonic schizophrenia.

I received cards and letters from Dad signed "Mom and Dad" after Mom died.

Dad introduced us to new worlds: to Kenny Rodgers and "The Gambler." We'd subconsciously walk through the house singing, "You've got to know when to hold 'em, know when to fold 'em—" (The audience continued to sing the melody with me.)

But our relationship wasn't always easy. It was often difficult, awkward, and tense. I think we were both expecting to get basic needs met by the other, and that wasn't going to happen. Despite our rifts, though, we always came back to a gentle, sad, but certain, love.

We've both looked at the world realistically, if not cynically, which takes courage. We've both lived out loud, which takes chutzpah.[3]

On December 14th, we were told that Dad had only a few hours left. But he pressed on, with Jonathan by his side, for another 44 hours.

"The dealin's done."

You didn't just break even, Dad. You pulled way ahead. And in your final weeks, I found many aces I could keep.

Thank you. I love and am inspired by you always.

Rest in peace.

I folded my eulogy and stepped down from the podium.

"Did that help?" Dawn asked, as I returned to my seat by her side in the funeral chapel.

I sighed contemplatively, "Yeah."

Five or six months later, I received this text message:

"Hi Robyn. It's Fred. Sorry I disappeared a while back. I was wondering if you would like to reconnect?"

Really, dude? No explanation? You're simply "sorry"? Are you sorry because you're horny right now? Or because you realize it's not good for a gal's ego to be dumped for a four-legged bitch? Did Heidi find a new bone? Whatever the case, I'm guessing you're not losing sleep over remorse's hefty toll.

Some people (the men I've dated, at least) only say "sorry" when they don't mean it.

---

[3]Boldness and sass.

"Thank you for the message. I hope all's well. I'm going to pass on the reconnect. Good luck to you . . . "

<u>Note to self</u>: Should I go there?

<u>Note in response to note to self</u>: Yes. No. Yes. No, it's mean. Yes. Do it for your readers."

"and your dog. Robyn"

"Every hand's a winner, and every hand's a loser, and the best that you can hope for is to die in your sleep."—Kenny Rogers "The Gambler"

Chapter 13: God and Guilt

"All religions are the same: Religion is basically guilt with different holidays."—Cathy Ladman

Unfortunately, those of us who experience guilt aren't the ones so deserving. It's perpetrators of abhorrent acts, folks lacking a conscience, who should be tortured and plagued by guilt's suffocation. They're not. Life isn't fair that way. Or in any way.

So why do we make it harder on ourselves than it already is, especially in the throes of trauma?

We, those sensitive enough to broil in remorse, are expert masochists. It's learned. It's reflexive. It's religious.

It's convenient and easy, in the moment. It's destructive and fatal, ultimately.

Mom used to abruptly shut the door on folks who trekked from house to house to impart the word of the Lord. I felt sorry for them, thought Mom was being rude.

Heck no! She was perfectly restrained, a great role model. They're lucky they're not targeting my door now—that lanky white-collar shirted guy glued to his pasty puritan female counterpart, both grasping "You're in His Care" pamphlets. Yeah, that doesn't go well.

"No thanks, I'm Jewish," I grin. "Just like your Jewish God Jesus. Your all-loving, all-accepting Jewish God Jesus. We Jews (like me and your Jewish God Jesus) don't believe in trying to convert people. Your Jewish God Jesus never converted. I suppose said Jewish God isn't thrilled with your whole new religion that rejects your Jewish God Jesus' Jewish beliefs in order to worship—your Jewish God Jesus. Ya know?"

By this time, my visitors are examining their "You're in His Care" table of contents—in search of "What to say to the sassy little Jewish bitch who hits you with Bart Simpson style basics."

"Well," he says, their smiles intact, "we haven't heard this response before." Eyes locked nervously on each other's, they cautiously step away from my door. "Thank you."

"L'Chaim!"

Slam.

Unlike me, however, Mom handled them with poise and restraint. Those were the days, the days when our parents lectured: "If you marry a non-Jew, we'll disown you."

Some Orthodox Jews have gone so far as to mourn the deaths of their kin, when said kin are still alive but in interfaith marriages. This seems outrageously abusive and counterproductive. If continuity of the faith is the goal, and it is the stated goal, why pretend to kill off living Jewish loved ones?

Further, this promotes the sentiment that marital satisfaction doesn't matter. Better to have miserable Jewish marriages, versus happy and healthy interfaith or atheistic families.

Thing is, I married Jewish. Didn't work out.

Perhaps I should've taken the route to disownment. Think of the benefits. It's a lot easier to manage marriage without extended family strife, problems with in-laws, on and on.

Karla and I were playing with my Barbie dress set when she snapped, "Robyn, if you don't promise to accept Jesus, I won't be your friend."

"No, I'm Jewish. I'm not gonna promise it."

I waited for her to leave my home.

She didn't.

The guilt thing—it doesn't work for kids or adults. Religions across the world have yet to comprehend this and give it up already. That's a shame.

There's a lot of beauty in religion, sans guilt and close-mindedness: The intoxicating aura of candle flames. "Love thy neighbor." "Do unto others." Spiritual hymns that transport us to our beloved ancestry—beaten down to their last breath yet chanting with the fervor of thousands upon thousands of generations. Faith in that which defies words or logic. This, the act of letting go in order to hold on, has saved so many lives.

Justin and I relished all of it. We'd sit kissy-kissy, holding hands in synagogue. Neither of us very traditional. But we enjoyed all the ritual, and we believed in some form—whatever a fluid, indescribable concept—of "God." This was never a topic of conversation, and it certainly never caused problems for us. Instead, it was a bond.

This isn't to say, though, that I can't have relationships with non-Jews. When I take a mental scan of my romantic life, I realize that religious views played an insignificant role in my relationship struggles—if any role at all.

Often their religion wasn't Jesus. It might have been alcohol, or power and control, or even tenacious rejection of all organized religion.

<u>Client quote</u>: "My Mom went crazy and they put her in the menthol hospital."

The minute I spotted him in a crowded Chico bar, I was hooked. A handsome, clean-cut man grinned in appreciation of the music. He sat alone at a table, one small glass of alcohol in front of him. I kept dancing. And looking his way. And scheming.

Finally, I casually placed my glass on his table.

I then departed to dance once more.

Upon my return, I lifted my glass for a sip (of water, which I'd finished hours earlier). Lucky me, a nearby chair was free.

"Do you mind?" I asked.

"Sure, go ahead." He motioned.

Conversation spilled from there. The guy works in construction and moonlights as an artist. He's divorced with a grown daughter. His marriage ended due to infidelity on his wife's part . . . . Though he has a drug history, he said he'd cleaned up his act eight years ago and never looked back. Impressive. Church has helped him find his way. Reddish flag.

I shared about my work and writing, marital demise, what brought me to Chico. "I'm Jewish," I added, "just thought I should put that out there."

The guy shrugged. "That's fine. I have no problem with that."

"Yeah, I mean, it's a very Christian area. I do get annoyed by all the 'Jesus' talk."

"Oh no, I just go to church for the support. It's nobody's business what to believe."

"Agreed."

"Last call for alcohol!" the bartender shouted, as the music faded. "Five minutes 'til closing!"

"I'd like to talk more. Can I walk you to your car?"

"Sure. That'd be nice."

We traversed the darkened but semi-busy downtown area.

He asked when my birthday is and informed me: "We'd be a good match. Scorpios and Cancers go great together." Okay. I'll go with that.

Mr. Scorpio walked me to my car, then put my number in his phone. "Wanna go for a hike tomorrow?"

"Yeah, sure. Well—" I paused. "I have a few things to do, but that'd be great. I just need a few hours in the morning before we go." I was interested. I didn't want to move too quickly. Actually, I did. I knew I shouldn't, though.

They say: "Take it slow. It won't work if you rush it." Yeah, well, it doesn't work when I "take it slow" either. So which is it? Speed up the inevitable pain or revel in its buildup? A quick dose of poison is less lethal than a gradual one, no?

And what if the relationship sticks, or it sticks for a while? They NEVER say "You moved too fast" after ending a miserable fifteen-year marriage. . . not even when you're crying on their shoulder.

Let's face it, moving too fast means you had sex too soon. But who's to say what's "too soon"? That's awfully judgmental of them. Besides, we want sexual compatibility, right? Well, I do. Most of us do. For some, especially couples with kids, this means an unstated agreement to not have sex. Or perhaps it's stated.

While I respect those who wait until marriage, or until they know this is a "sure thing," I don't choose to be one of those people.

And while it's considered sinful for Christians to partake in premarital sex, not so for Jews. In fact, it's a blessing, especially on the Sabbath. Really. (You'd think this fact alone would have scores of people vying for conversion.)

I suspected Scorpio of being more Jewish than Christian in that way.

"I want to kiss you," he whispered, and then he did. A brief chemical, fireworks-y kiss. "Wow, that kiss—"
We said "goodnight."

My date drove us towards a prime destination for hikers in Chico's glorious Bidwell Park. We gabbed like two besties who hadn't seen each other in years, mixed with a layer of *I want you.*

Hand in hand, Scorpio and I worked our way down steep slopes of dirt and scattered shrubbery. Eventually, we settled into a soft sandy patch of earth. Scorpio opened his backpack and pulled out a box of crackers, small block of cheese, salami, and a pocket knife. We munched slowly, taking it all in. The sparkly, cool water—runoff from the Sacramento River—was livened by mini-waterfalls.

Interim kissing and gentle hugs landed amid his expressions of gratitude for having met me. I felt free and just plain ol' happy. At the same time, yeah, what's going to go wrong? Maybe nothing. Maybe he's a keeper. Right?

A good challenge for me too. See, I'm a close-minded snob about education and job status. Scorpio is neither a high level professional nor well educated. But he's bright and doesn't likely spell "college" as "collage." Plus, he was a meth addict and terribly addicted years ago. Having never even touched a bubble gum cigarette, I find that dangerously sexy.

I know—I didn't stop to contemplate the meth addiction thing. That's a biggie. Simply and naively, I admired him for having kicked it all.

He might be a keeper. Finally. I really like him. He really likes me.

Shit. He might drop dead tonight or next week or month.
That's always the fear. For crazy reasons.
For reasons not completely within my control.

<u>Rabbi M., who had known our family for 12 years, 9/1988:</u>

"All of us are born with different abilities. Some of us grow taller, some of us shorter. Some of us stronger, some of us weaker. Some will have very quick reflexes and some of us, slow.

The same thing is true spiritually. There are a few people whose souls are very sensitive, like Glenn. There are a few people whose feelings are much more intense than those of others. If he had been exposed to the normal trials and tribulations of a teenager, this attribute would not have been a defect but a vital asset. He might have become a sensitive poet, a playwright, a dramatist. He would have been a good and loving friend and wonderful father. Unfortunately, he suffered a greater stress than most people do. Though most people can bear that stress, because of the virtue and sensitivity, in a sense because of the greatness of his soul, he died."

At home in my living room, Scorpio's fingers sifted through my hair along the side of my face. We kissed, and then some more.

"I know we should take it slow," I said softly. "I mean, I was planning to."

"But it feels so right."

Feels so right. So right, I thought. It did. "D'you wanna go to my bedroom?"

"Yeah."

He carried me to my bed, clothes lost along the way somehow, or were already lost. I don't remember.

"Sorry, the mattress is weird and lumpy," I explained, as if he was listening. "I'm in-between beds, getting a new frame. I thought it'd help us take things slow—" Kissing, stroking, and deep breathing ensued.

"It's awkward I know—" He worked. I rambled. "Sorry… mm, mmm."

Scorpio made an attempt. Shit! It didn't work. Why must I attract all the men in the world with penile incompetence? I'm so damn frustra—wait, I spoke, err thought, too soon. He's in. Oh, oh, oh my, this is good. Really, really, who knew it could be so good?

"Oh my God, Oh God, Oh my God." God, yes, yes, God is good! Lord Jesus Christ Amen!

The neighbors likely thought I'd just been Born Again. And again. Suffice it to say, especially for a man in his fifties, Scorpio greatly impressed and pleased me that night. Maybe I just needed a man with loads of speed in his system!

God bless meth!

After several hours of ecstatic loving, he shifted onto his knees. Scorpio pressed his arms along his meaty thighs as if to soothe them. "The only thing about me is," he said, "I have Restless Leg Syndrome."

"I'm sorry." I sat by his side, gently stroking his arm. "What can I do?"

"Nah nothing, just don't touch me."

Oh. "Okay." I dropped my arm. "It's alright. I mean, that's lousy. I know a couple that sleeps separately because he has a bad case of it."

"Yeah, I need a hard surface."

I gave him a sheet and blanket to sleep away from me and in the living room. Then I fell asleep alone on our first night "together," my first night with someone else, alone, in what seemed like forever. Coupledom.

At last?

"Funny, I don't get restless legs during sex," Scorpio said during a bout of foreplay the next day. (With me.) Of course not. Why be restless during sex? And what—you'd kick me out of bed mid-intercourse? Imagine if the guy didn't like me: "Go to sleep sweetie," he'd whisper while pulling me close. "I'm fading fast," he'd say. I'd hit deep sleep when all of a sudden Wham! Shattered glass all over the place, as I'm catapulted headfirst through the bedroom window. "Oh, sorry honey!" he'd shout, lounging snuggly in my bed. "It's just my Restless Legs. Here"—he'd toss a sheet out the broken window, snickering— "use this, it's cold out there."

"Had a good day. Thinking about you honey," Scorpio texted. "I'll call at 6."

Six o'clock came and went. I'm a stickler about punctuality and reliability. If a man's not good for his word, I go into crazy-angry-fierce-How-dare-you? mode. I'm working on it, though. Thus, by the time 6:20 rolled around, I decided to distract myself through exercise.

"Sorry honey, I was watching the debates," he messaged at 6:40 p.m.

"I'm going to the gym. Will call you by 8 p.m."

As I jogged on the treadmill, my pace quickened to a run, beads of sweat dripped down my face, and then: damn him! He'd rather watch Trump and Hillary than be with me? We're doomed.

Back home, I washed up and purposely let 8 p.m. pass. In part, I was very consciously being passive-aggressive. To my credit, though, I wanted to calm down before talking to him.

A knock at the door.

There he was, handsome as always, concerned. "You didn't call me. What's wrong?" He stepped in and saw that I'd been crying, "Do you not want to see me?"

"No, I do. I'm just upset."

I explained why basic follow-through and punctuality matter, and matter greatly, to me.

"I get it. I'm just not used to answering to someone. I'm sorry. I just spaced out."

"Am I asking too much?" I'd been making efforts to not push men away because of my deepest fears.

"No."

<u>Rabbi S., who had known our family for 30 years, 9/1988:</u>

"Glenn committed the unforgivable sin"

"Unforgivable sin." "Unforgivable sin." Ugh! I can hardly type that fuckin phrase. Thirty years later, those are the only two words I remember from his sermon. Unforgiveable sin. How could he say that? Did he want to relieve us of feeling guilty, thereby labeling my dead brother a "sinner"? It doesn't, and didn't, help. It stung with a sting that lasts, one I still feel.

I mean, I know my brother is the sole person accountable for his fate. But his fuckin disease posed a fight he couldn't beat. And he's no "sinner" for deciding to end his unfathomable pain.

Finger-pointing after suicide creates a tangled, messy, harmful poison. Blame the victim, okay. This is, to some extent, healthy. Be mad. Work through it, gently and safely. Ultimately, though, the dead made their decision. They likely didn't give you a chance to save them. Or if they did, and it worked once, if they were determined, they tried again—this time making sure you wouldn't stop them.

If you're going to go so far as to call them "selfish," though, that's selfish of you. They didn't ask for their circumstances. They took control, perhaps for the first (and last) time. They'd lost control over their sensibilities, trapped in a very sick-brained dungeon.

Plus, they probably thought they were doing you a favor. Or they didn't think about that—drowned in unbelievably wretched pain. Pain from which they could not possibly see an escape.

Is it sinful to take action to end one's pain? No. We do it all the time. Ever heard of drugs, alcohol, sex, or chocolate?

Furthermore, if you're going the "that's selfish" route, why doesn't anyone say that about the (seemingly) millions of people who engage in extramarital affairs? Seriously. That's awfully selfish! And why don't we say "That serial killer is a selfish bastard"? Or think about this one: Why don't we say it about the person who is truly selfish and sociopathic, the one who does ultimately end their life by suicide?

Imagine if people were honest at a funeral. How cathartic that would be.

Thomas James Wendell Johnston II was an exceptionally decent example of your barnyard shotgun racist pedophile. Assault of the earth, you might say. The entire region was on guard. What a piece of shit he was! Glad he did himself in. It's high time we celebrate in raucous mayhem. Bring your own keg, and let the festivities begin. We'll play that funky music 'cuz he died! Yeehaw!

It's unfortunate that guilt's legacy inhibits this type of honest expression. If only we'd stop dancing around the big unspoken monstrous tower of guilt. It's ever-present. It's normal and understandable, however unreasonable.

And tragically, guilt kills. Close loved ones of suicide victims are exponentially more likely to die by suicide. The only way to lessen guilt's power is to talk honestly about it with others who understand and feel it too. To be kind to ourselves and each other.

I loaded several heavy boxes into my car the next morning for Out of the Darkness. It was my third year of involvement with the event.

Meanwhile, Scorpio sat leisurely on my sofa. "I'll be there, don't worry."

Hours later, I stood on the plaza stage and stepped forward to represent all who'd lost siblings to suicide. My message: "Be kind to yourself. It's not your fault. You aren't alone."

Scorpio had moved quietly to a bench behind the stage.

Likely, the program was too steeped in intense emotions for him. I hadn't asked him to attend. He'd said "I'll go. It's important to you."

Having been in drug circles, I figured he'd surely have known people who died by suicide, if "passively." I mean, they hadn't necessarily intended to die when doing drugs. But they lived as if not caring to continue living. Some even say as much, again and again, until drugs win the battle.

These types of "passive suicides" happen to such a great extent, we can't know the numbers. Official reason for death is often not "suicide" in these instances. It's (implied accidental) "overdose."

Scorpio said he'd never felt suicidal. I'm not convinced, with his history. And so utterly uncomfortable that day, he kept a clear distance from me into the evening.

I treated him to dinner afterwards. He didn't talk, except to make his order.

After unsuccessfully doing things to get attention like tossing off my clothes, I yelped, "We're not even snuggling!"

"You're, you're"—his head abruptly shifted up and down. He

gritted his teeth. "You're making me crazy!"

Furiously hurt, I suggested he "just leave!" Scorpio abruptly took himself, and his phone, to my dining room table.

Tears started to leak, so I moved to my bedroom.

Moments seemed like hours when he stood calmly under my bedroom doorframe. "I need a break, and so do you."

With that, Scorpio turned his back on me.

The front door blasted shut.

<u>From Dad's Eulogy for Glenn, 9/1988:</u>

"I must admit, Glenn, at times it's been extremely difficult being your father, especially the past year and a half. The degree of difficulty is nothing compared to what I'll have to endure the rest of my life.

When you landed, much of me and much of your family died with you.

I could dwell for hours on what we could have done or may have done wrong to prevent you from your act of ultimate desperation, but that would no longer serve any purpose. We must instead, dedicate ourselves in your memory, to loving and caring for people who are part of our lives, with a greater intensity and sense of devotion than we have ever shown. I must never again turn my back on cries for help whether they are shouted out or expressed in silent anguish. In your memory, I must strive to be a more compassionate leader to what is left of our shrinking family, in order for your death to have any meaning."

I loved him.

That was it!? Permanent breakage. I couldn't change his mind. I couldn't alter his brain functioning. I couldn't make decisions for him. I had my own stuff, and lots of it, to juggle too. I couldn't impact him more than the strongest of drugs--illicit or psychiatric.

It's over.

I was naive, even heartless, at times. I made mistakes.

But I'm a very loving, sensitive soul. I did my best under restrictive circumstances.

He made a unilateral decision. Had he given me the chance to make things right, I don't know. Maybe I'd have made a momentary positive impact, extended things a bit longer. The end result, though, would've probably been the same.

It's not my fault.

<u>Rabbi S., 9/1988:</u>

"The concluding words of the Kaddish[4] praise God for having established a harmonious universe, creating a heaven and earth, man and woman, creatures and natural phenomena. Light and dark, sorrow and joy. There is balance in our world. There is a possibility of developing harmony in all of our lives. In this moment of deepest distress, it is our prayer that the Lord will grant you causes for renewed joy, for new and happy experiences, for a life that is filled with causes for thanksgiving.

And we say together: Amen."

---

[4]Prayer recited at times of bereavement. It affirms God's existence and life's many blessings.

Chapter 14: Nurture Versus Itself

"It is sometimes an appropriate response to reality to go insane."
—Philip K. Dick

When you've outlived a parent, you understand the barrage of feelings upon facing that quantum leap: the birthday defining you as officially older than your parent's age at their passing.

And when you've lived to your 50th birthday, you understand a similar yet different eerie milestone.

Imagine my twofer ensemble bonus deal. Or just keep reading.

"I heard she slept with Charlie, Robyn."

"Wait, Charlie? The cute guy who frequents this place?"

Donna was privy to all the juicy gossip. She'd pointed out a 58 year old grandma stuck in a perennial free love hallucination. A wide gap between front teeth eclipsed her face.

"Eww. That's gross. Why'd he go for her? I mean, she's nice I guess. We're sort of friends, but she's a loon."

"I know. I think it's that circle of partyers. They've all had each other at some point."

"I mean, okay but that's gotta be strong stuff they're using. Meth destroys your mouth like that. Right?"

"Oh yeah, big time. I have a cousin who went through years and thousands of dollars of dental work because of it."

We sat in cushioned seats near the dance floor, awaiting live music. There was nothing much going on in Chico that night, so I'd decided that with a friend, I could handle the risk of running into Scorpio. It's where we met.

I scanned the crowd, twenty or so folks chatting in small clusters by the bar. "I don't want to see him. My getaway was so nice. I forgot he existed."

"Oh, how was your trip? I forgot to ask. You were there for your big birthday, right?"

"It was so heavenly, Donna. Tough too. I worked through some dark stuff. But great scenery along the ocean, great people, amazing food. I didn't want to leave. I'm in a much better place now." I think.

"Excuse me, hon," I crossed my legs playfully, "I'm gonna go pee."

"No worries. I'm grabbing a drink."

<u>Esalen in Big Sur, CA 6/2016:</u>

I can't get enough: fields of fresh grass line an endless sheath of cyan blue. Earth's star activates my pores with forceful yet tender intensity. Pools of natural hot springs slumber amidst jagged cliffs. All the while, far below, ocean waves thrash in harmonic discord against white-gray rock.

This place, this experience, this moment, the people, luscious foods, an impenetrable energy—it's keeping me alive and glad to be.

I inhale wisps of crisp air, remembering Mom.

"It's all so beautiful," she turned to Dad and said from a space not unlike the one I occupy now. Dad and Mom had crossed the ocean on a cruise, her last trip, a glorious opportunity for Mom to bid the world "goodbye." At 49.

I feel more connected to Mom, to Dad, to Glenn today.

I feel partly dead too. Dead with them and dead with Justin. We were one. I'm not whole anymore. Or am I? I want to be fully whole, fully alive.

I am. I'm at peace. Maybe. I don't know, I wrestle. I want to do so much more. I want to be so much more. My vulnerability scares me. My limitations, I can't tolerate. I, we, can and are everything. I, we, can and are nothing.

I got to live until this moment—this spectacular moment in this incredible place—beauty envelops me. I'm nurtured. I am safe. This place. This day.

I'm still here, and I'm still . . . here.

Thank you, Mom. God, I want to tell you this. I want you to hold me. I miss you. I'm crying. Tears of sadness, gratitude, loving tears dance down my cheeks.

Here and still. Today.

50.

Happy Birthday to me.

"Turning 50 doesn't kill you, nor does it make you stronger. But it does scare the shit out of you."—this Author

Earth to me. I'm at a bar, need to urinate.

As I brushed by the puffy jacket sleeve of some guy at the bar, "Hey, I was sl-looking for you!" he said.

A familiar face greeted mine. He appeared aged, dopey, and ragged.

Scorpio?! "Oh hi. Are you drunk?" (It just came out.)

"Maybe," he shrugged.

"What are you doing here?" As if it wasn't obvious. "You're looking for me?"

"Just wanna paul-jise. S,sorry for the way we endid-dit. Mish communicay-shun!"

"I didn't miscommunicate. I did nothing wrong! I wanted intimacy and you stormed out on a break, or breakup, or whatever. You hurt me."

"Well ya gotta all whiny and yell-ing an,and I canned hand-lit."

I did an internal eye roll and heard my voice relax, "Do you miss me?"

"Yeah."

I nodded, but didn't know what to do with that.

"Okay, well" I extended my arms, "thank you for apologizing. Good luck to you."

The hug, caring and brief.

<u>Thoughts at Esalen, 6/2016:</u>

The most unhealthy of people don't admit to having mental health problems. One key to "mental illness" is a fundamentally skewed sense of reality. So this makes sense.

We're all mixed with healthy and unhealthy facets, though. The most healthy of people know and acknowledge this.

It's a shame that we're conditioned to believe that mental wellness equates with happiness. That's wrong.

Granted, reality is harsh. To choose it seems an ill or masochistic act. It'd make for a more rational coping strategy to detach from real world experiences, at least some of the time.

Don't get me wrong, I loathe the ever-cheery. A Pollyanna persona is incredibly annoying, right? Far too disingenuous and just bizarre.

I keep spinning back to the question of mental "wellness" versus "illness"—where's the line, or is there one? It can't only be about saying "I have mental health issues" versus denying such. Or acknowledging that the world and life can be excruciatingly painful and unfair. There's more to it than brave, bold honesty and vulnerability versus stubborn denial and ignorance.

Glenn's voices were real. His visual hallucinations, painfully vivid.

Reality is an illusion.

Illusions are healthy, happy survival tools when we use them selectively.

This, life, is maddening.

To impose an accurate metric for sanity or insanity, maybe that's insane.

"What so-called normal people are doing when they define disease like manic depression or schizophrenia is reassuring themselves that they don't have a thought disorder or affective disorder, that their thoughts and feelings make perfect sense."—Mark Vonnegut

Midway between the bar and dance floor, Donna sipped a gin and tonic when I returned.

"I can't believe he's here."

"Where, Robyn?"

I turned back to point to Scorpio, but he wasn't alone. The 58 year old grandma ("Methie") was standing close to him, chatting and smiling emphatically. "What the hell? They know each other? Is something going on there?"

"Sure looks that way." She swished her drink around and took another gulp.

Minutes later, Methie approached with a smile.

"Hi Methie. You were talking to my ex?"

"I know, but he said you're not dating anymore. We're just talking, we both like hiking"—her speech rate increased—"we're only talking, Robyn, we're going hiking, we both like to hike, we've been hanging out for three weeks, we're only friends. I'm so sorry. Okay?" Methie's face contorted into an expression of: I'm getting some and you're not but I'm pretending to care about you.

"Well no, it's awkward. You don't date a friend's ex. Girl code. That's dis—"

Methie interrupted with a shout: "I didn't know you dated! We both like hiking. That's all. Okay, I won't hang out with him. That's how much I respect you."

Methie nodded before stomping off.

Next thing I noticed was Methie with her arm around drunken Scorpio. They'd maneuvered to a booth within direct eyeshot several yards away. There they sat snuggly, as if performing for me.

Blood pounded through my veins.

"Wait, Robyn, you were friends before, right?"

"Well, yeah, not good friends, but we were friendly."

"That's wrong of her. And Robyn," Donna extended her neck to take a hard look, "At least you have all your teeth!"

"One person's craziness is another person's reality."—Tim Burton

"Let's dance, Robyn." She nudged, distracting me. I complied.

When I boogie, I'm good. Great even, alive, free, in control, on top of the world.

Donna and I smiled at each other, and I did some twirling when my spinal cord shimmied, stricken by a shrill voice. "By the way!" Methie shouted, having charged at me from behind, "He broke up with you 'cuz of your whining. You're pathetic. Get over yourself!" Methie darted away from me, past the bar, and straight into the women's restroom by the front entrance.

"That does it!"

Esalen, 6/2016:

A memory on replay.

The bright pink cushy beanbag sank a bit as I picked up the phone. A man's voice, stern with a slice of compassion. I didn't want to be right, but I was. He apologized that it took so long, after introducing himself as the coroner. "Your brother's fingers slipped," he explained, but he'd confirmed his identity. His jump from the 14th floor of 19753 Wilshire Boulevard was his final act. I thanked him for the call and hung up.

I immediately called Dad's girlfriend and asked her to take care of him. I never appeased, much less pleased him.

It felt as though it took hours but Dad had rushed home. Dawn ran in. She gave Jonathan a hug and said "I love you." She gave Dad a hug and said "I love you." She ignored me.

They ignored me. It's what they did, the unstated rule.

It's what I learned: invisibility.

It's what I fought, and sometimes still fight, with my all.

Seconds later, I stood facing a scratched, beige bathroom stall door. Seems Methie needed to pee. I let it flow too: "You're an ugly alcoholic drugged-out pothead, and he didn't even have the balls to break up with me. Why would anyone go for you?"

Done. But not really. I marched out to Scorpio—still sitting cluelessly wasted at the booth. "Your new girlfriend is out of control!"

Scorpio grinned proudly, thrilled to defend Methie. "Well uh, yous jush leave uh-er along!"

"You didn't even break up with me, and you go for her? Why would you go for someone so ugly?"

"Oh, well, y-yeah? Why would any-yun go fer someone so"—Scorpio pointed at me—"ugly?"

He capped things off with a correctly articulated "Fuck off and die!"

"Get help!" I snapped.

<u>Esalen, 6/2016, exercise in writing about our deepest shames:</u>

Ann asked for volunteers to share what they'd written. Hint: Ask writers to recite their work, and you best have a lot of time on your hands. I hadn't volunteered at all during the retreat until this point. Now, though, I knew I needed to. Without thinking, I pushed my hand up. After several intense, eloquent confessionals, it was my turn.

Shit. Here goes . . . everything.

I took a seat on stage, next to Ann and facing approximately 120 intensely quiet pairs of eyes. I couldn't look up at all. Reading my own words, and reading them loudly, required my full focus:

"At age six, I wrote in my diary, 'I hate Glenn David. I wish he was never born.' I remember slamming my bedroom window on my brother's fingers when he attempted to climb into my room from the side of the house. He was just being obnoxiously playful. I didn't mean to hurt him. Maybe I did. Yeah, I did. I did want to hurt him. I hated him.

I hated the way he made my life more difficult, the way he stole perhaps another ounce, the only ounce of love I might've gotten from a narcissistic father who doted over his oldest and youngest while dismissing me and Glenn, the middle two.

I hated Glenn's insecurities, his stubbornness, his egotistical 'I know it all and you're pathetic' stance. I hated how he was the second smartest of the Engel kids, inching closer and closer to my academic achievements—threatening to snatch from me the only thing I had going in that family—my only source of praise and pride.

I hated him.

Mostly, I hated what I saw in him. I hated who I saw in him. In my brother, Glenn David Engel, I saw myself. I hated me. I hated me on my 22nd birthday. That day, I watched the young unaffected emergency medical team apply pressure to the straitjacket that interred his body, before they pushed him on a gurney towards the psychiatric treatment unit doors. As they maneuvered my brother past me, he said words that would forever stick to my gut: 'She hates me.' 'She hates me.' I did. I do. I hated him. I hated me. It hurts too much that he said it. I hate me more.

All of my life, since my brother took his life by jumping off of a Wilshire Boulevard high-rise, I've hated myself for hating my brother."

"Oh Robyn—" Ann said. The compassion in her voice, those two words alone, what I needed.

Yet I received so much more. I'd felt the audience's presence, as if they were struggling through each word with me. I heard their gasps when I mentioned Glenn's suicide. I received their warm-loving, accepting applause. They were with me.

For the remainder of the retreat, strangers sought me out to tell me about spouses and partners, friends, cousins who took their lives. About the guilt they've been carrying. That my piece was "beautiful."

This perplexed me. How could my shame, my ugliness, be "beautiful"?

In time, I'd realize that my and our vulnerabilities, those monstrous, shameful, demoralizing things we carry, these are our connecting points to humanity. There's profound beauty in this.

I remain friends with some of these people. They've become cheerleaders, contributors to my efforts with Out of the Darkness, supporters of my other writing projects and life ventures.

All this love, in response to decades-old hatred and shame. Because I was gifted with the opportunity to express it.

"One person's embarrassment is another person's accountability."—Tom Price

Donna danced with a small group of women, and I broke in.

"Are you okay, Robyn?"

"Yeah, a little shaken,"

Breathe, I told myself.

A foot stomping harmonica-vocal beat enticed me the moment I caught sight of a tambourine on a nearby table. (People leave instruments around for others to use.) I picked it up. As I began slapping the tambourine against my upper leg, Methie's hands were locked on it.

"Don't you dare touch my tambourine!" She pried the tambourine from me, placed it on a table behind her, and squeezed my arm with both of her hands. It was a childlike and timid maneuver, despite the vicious expression across her face.

I then instinctively reached out. Palms raised, I shoved Methie away.

Donna jumped between us. "Stop it! Enough!"

A cute young bouncer, not much taller than 5'2",

appeared. "Look, I didn't see what happened, but no more fighting."

Within a minute or two, a semblance of calm returned. But then some words rolled off my tongue rather definitively: "She slept with Charlie!"

Methie, who was now a yard or two away, as Scorpio remained seated in drunken oblivion, defended herself. "That's not true. I don't know why she's saying that."

"The whole town knows!" I added for flair.

I glared at Methie when she pointed me out to a man I'd never seen before.

Next, this black-haired, broad-shouldered angry man blasted: "I understand you were taking other people's property. You need to leave!"

"What? I didn't take anything."

He stepped closer and got louder, "You need to leave! I know about you. You can't act that way in my bar."

"Who are you, and what are you talking about?"

"It doesn't matter!" He extended his arm and pointed at the door. "Out!"

Donna put her hand on my shoulder. "Come on, Robyn."

"What the hell?"

I swung open the door as we departed. "I did nothing wrong!"

"No, you didn't. But it's not worth a fight. This place sucks. It's crazy town."

"Who the hell is that asshole?"

"Just someone who works there, I guess."

I fought back tears and was physically shaken. She held me. "What a night, I'm sorry hon. You'll be alright. We'll never come back here, though."

"Hell no," I patted my eyes.

Methie and Scorpio strode by giddily.

The dark-haired man came out the door, this time with a gorgeous young lady in hand.

"Hey, that wasn't okay to kick me out."

"I work here. I have the right."

"What did you see me do?" I prodded.

"You can't take equipment from the bar."

I inched closer, "What did you see me do?"

"Nothing, but I have friends." He turned to his girlfriend. "Let's go, babe."

"Your boyfriend's a prick!" I shouted as they turned their backs to me.

Damn, I'm relentless. Fierce. No filter when ticked off. It's kinda scary. I'm afraid of myself. That's not right. I'm not right.

I love that I'm feisty, but it's dangerous.

Moreover, to have sunk into all that petty and meanspirited bullshit, oops. Embarrassing.

"Ma'am, are you alright?" This question rose from a man I'd seen on the streets, though he was less disheveled than Scorpio. Definitely more reasonable and kind. He'd apparently overheard the altercation.

"I'm fine. Thanks so much for asking!"

How is it possible that people who have the least are often the most giving?

I'd never return to that bar.

Since then, though, I've encountered that caring man; I've given him food and water on occasion. Always, he's expressed genuine gratitude before sharing with his friends.

Approximately two months later, I learned that Methie had endured a trauma. The trauma. I couldn't *not* break the ice.

9/2016, correspondence between me and Methie:

"First, I'm really ashamed of my past behavior and hope that you'll forgive me. I'm also reaching out to say that I'm deeply sorry for the hole in your heart and life. Know that you are loved. I can put you in touch with parents who've also lost children to suicide, if you'd like.

Much sadness and love. Robyn"

"Thanks for saying this Robyn. I know you hurt too. I am overwrought right now and not ready to talk to other parents. I am sorry if I hurt you. I didn't even want a boyfriend but he is the love of my life. I can only hope you can find peace with that and know we wouldn't intentionally hurt you. I see your beautiful soul and I'm sorry for your hurt. Much sadness for sure! –Methie"

"Thank you. I appreciate your words. It's all behind me. Take good care of yourself. It's a long, tough journey. There's a community of love and support for you here.

I see your beautiful soul too. Of course, it's too early to talk to other parents. Just know that at any point, if you want to make connections with others who know this pain, I can help with that. Love, Robyn"

<u>"Please Believe" by this Author:</u>
Please believe
I know your pain
Your broken soul
That smile you feign
You say "I'm fine"
But it's a lie
You dare not share
Your urge to die
I know your rage
And hate
And shame
I know the burn that set your heart aflame
Consumed by grief
Your life a curse
Cold lonely days
Still nights are worse
Please believe me when I say
Keep holding tight
You'll be okay
Monstrous ills, you cannot halt
Go gentle now
It's not your fault
Mental illness has no cure

You're human with a heart that's pure
I know not how
I know not when
But you'll reclaim your life again
Embrace a faith you never knew
You'll be so glad you wrestled through
Please believe
And hold on tight
As strands of pain fade into light
And tender hues transform your sight
You're not alone
Please know it's true
I'm right here
Holding tight
with you.

Chapter 15: Ruling Lunacy

"In individuals, insanity is rare; but in groups, parties, nations and epochs, it is the rule."—Fredrich Nietzche

Seemed whenever I entered a free-flowing writing zone, my towering wall heater simmering, and my tuchas planted firmly on the brown carpeted living room floor, I was rattled by a loud three-part knock. Next followed "Robyn, it's me!"

Who does that? Who shouts, "It's me!" when they knock on someone's door? Apparently, my neighbor does.

Even though he could easily see my parked car out front, I'd pretend to not be home.

But then a second knock-knock-knock preceded another "Robyn, it's me!"

Sigh. Stomp, stomp, stomp.

I thrust open the door.

"Oh, hi Robyn."

"Hi."

"Yeah you need to know that you have a mailing there." He pointed towards my doormat, on which rested a campaign ad from Jill Stein's Green Party. "I know you like Bernie, because I saw your Bernie Sanders poster on your front window. I think it's good. I like that poster, by the way. Yeah I don't know what time that piece of mail came for you, just to let you know, but I took Harlotta's dogs for a walk at five o'clock, no it was 5:05 p.m., and I saw it there when I got back at 5:21 p.m. or thereabouts. I don't know about Hillary, I mean Killary—" he smirked.

"I think she's corrupt and war mongering. I still think Bernie's the best one. And yeah I thought you should know," he bent over to pick up the mailing and handed it to me, "this was delivered here for you."

"Yep, great, I have to go." I snatched the campaign ad and pushed the door—"Thanks"—closed.

"Sure. Yeah I knew you might need it," he continued. "It's important. I really hope enough people vote for or write in the name Bernie Sanders. Don't forget to vote, Robyn. That's important. Like I said, I don't know exactly what time—"

When he's not focused on my mail, this neighbor ("Geezer") surreptitiously spies on the neighborhood between his front window blinds. He also sits stationed for hours on a sun chair not far from my door.

The highlight of his day, I imagine, is when Geezer walks Harlotta's dogs in the evenings. She, by the way, is his neighbor on the other side of his apartment. Harlotta and I were getting along well, and I'd seen her perform in a few local shows—supporting roles that beg for a hefty, middle aged woman—the exhausted cook or maid, for example.

I'm not sure why she and Geezer have their dog-walking arrangement. The lease clearly states "No pets." Needing to feel important, though, Geezer's happy to comply.

At least the neighbors are on my (left) side, politically.

Politics had suddenly become the single most important make-it-or-break-it factor in relationships. The topic of the day, for years, it would end many relationships (marriages, close friendships, blood relations). Otherwise, it's not ever discussed.

That past summer, Bernie Sanders had visited the Chico State Campus. For hours, Brandi and I waited in 107 degree heat for a glimpse of the man. She eventually found a patch of shade much farther from the stage than was acceptable to me.

Rather, I'd fight for a solid hour to get from the second row of ruthless fans to the first. My best strategy, I figured, was to spout the truth. I thus tapped folks on their backs. They turned around, I looked up and said "As you can see, I won't block your view at all! Would you please let me squeeze in? I can't see anything from behind you." The answer, time after time, was an angry and abrupt "no!" Unacceptable.

"Socialism!" I'd shout, as I merged my way along the second row of folks standing in anticipation of Bernie's arrival. "Social-ism, people! Social-ism! I only need a little room. You have room to spare."

Rejection followed rejection. Never before had I played the short card with such a brutal outcome. Idol worship and mob mentality are strong forces. My determination, even stronger.

By sheer fortitude, I eventually found myself grasping tightly to the sleek metal railing—the barricade between nearly 1,000 of

Bernie's fans and his security posse. They ordered, "Keep it down! Don't push on the railing! Move back!"

"I can't move back. They're pushing on me!" Jesus protect me.

Quote from Josiah, age 10, sans coaching by Auntie Robyn: "I like Bernie. He makes sense."

At the end of his speech, Bernie walked along the front row, shaking each person's hand. I was nearly bulldozed from behind, stormed by the mad crowd trying to get closer to him.

Then, in one remarkable moment, Bernie looked down at me, and his hand met mine. The warmth, firmness, and compassion of Bernie Sanders' palm incited in me a grand need to shout "I love you!"

In turn, Bernie mouthed words back at me. Though roars of idolatry muted his voice, I'm quite certain that my Bernie Sanders said "I love you too, Robyn Alana Engel." Alright, he may've said a thoughtful, "I appreciate that."

I haven't washed my hands* to this day. (*I forget which hand it was. To be safe, I keep both unwashed. No, I'm kidding. It was my right hand. I do wash my left one. Wink.)

Geezer later told me that he saw Bernie at the Italian Cottage. A localized Berniemania had been ignited. Other neighbors on the street displayed Bernie signs and logos on their lawns and cars. I was in good company.

In fact, despite minor irritations, homelife was altogether productive and comfortable.

I was offered a new job too. I'd work with high schoolers—kids who were kicked out of public high school. Graduating from this program offered a final chance for a high school degree. Upon accepting the challenge, I'd imagined classrooms of young punks who attempted to slice me to pieces. Things wouldn't, and didn't, unfold in that manner.

"Do you want to talk outside?" I asked José when he dropped his head onto his desk during a science lesson.

He pushed his chair back and stood tall, "Sure."

"Ooh, it's chilly out here." I zipped up my jacket. "You okay taking a walk around the field while we talk?"

José shrugged. "I'm good."

"You sure? Do you want to grab your jacket or something warmer?"

"I don't got no jacket."

"Oh, I'm sorry."

"Nah, it's alright."

"Would you like me to see if I can find one for you in the donations bin?"

He shrugged again. "I guess."

"'Kay, I'll check for one . . . . So how've you been? You seem distracted today."

"Yeah, worried about my mom and stuff."

"Your mom? Did something happen to her?"

"You could say that." He continued looking down at the grass. "She was raped last night."

"Oh no!" I touched his arm. "I'm so sorry. What happened?"

"I don't even know. I was asleep when she came home crying and then my auntie came over, but she didn't wanna make a police report. I think she got jumped when she was walking home from work or something. She ran out of gas four, five blocks from home. I don't know any more than that, they talked outside. She's alright. I mean, she was crying, but she gave me a hug and said not to worry."

He lifted his face and stared blankly at a clan of tall pines beyond the field.

"It was the one-year anniversary since my dad got shot too."

"José, I'm very sorry. That's too horrible, and a terrible coincidence. No wonder you're distracted."

"Yeah, she said this morning it hurts to walk and stuff, but she'll be okay. My auntie took her to the clinic today."

"That's a lot for you to worry about."

He further unloaded about his tense and challenging homelife, his role as a father figure and caretaker to three young cousins who lived in their one-bedroom, rodent infested Oroville home; drug lords in the extended family; his mother's seemingly impossible battle for citizenship after 19 years in the U.S.

We approached the starting point, near the classroom.

"Thank you for telling me what's been going on. I'll check in with you tomorrow, okay?"

"'Kay."

"You ready to go back to class, hon?"

"Yeah, I'm alright now."

"Sweetie," I reached up and put my hand on his shoulder, "you're brave and caring, and you're going to get through this. Your mom is too."

I gave José a side hug, which he reciprocated.

"Thanks."

"No problem."

Once the students left for the day, I asked the 25-year-old teacher, the one that the administration worshipped as their "most amazing teacher": "Do you think I can find a jacket for José? He said he doesn't have one."

"José? What? He's sooo manipulative! I'm sure he has jackets and warm clothes. He just likes to wear wifebeaters." (I suppose that response isn't as shocking as what I'd heard the other "amazing" teacher say to a student, seemingly but still highly inappropriately, as a joke: "I'm gonna punch you in the face." Really? Really.)

The young Most Amazing Teacher turned her back on me and proceeded to wipe a large eraser board that dominated the classroom's front wall.

I left to dig through donations in a nearby building.

Nothing but old dusty and torn t-shirts for elementary school kids. Wow. People "donate" their trash instead of tossing their trash into a dumpster, and then they feel good about their charitable efforts. Great way to insult the less fortunate. Needless to say, I couldn't find anything for José, not a single sweatshirt or lightweight jacket.

Once in a while, like that night, silent tears prefaced my sleep.

Life is too overwhelmingly sad sometimes. Well, all the time. When we open our eyes to it.

"Evil exists in the part. Perfection exists in the whole. I can choose this broader view—not that I always should—but I always can."— Hugh Prather

My mood switched the next morning from sobered to irritated.

That pimple's the size of Mount Whitney, I thought, as I tried to not stare at my date's forehead. His ad boasted a "heart of gold," and our prior discourse had been lighthearted. Pimples are temporary. I get them too. Don't judge, I told myself. It'll shrink sometime.

We'd ordered at the counter, and Donnie had kindly paid for my pancakes.

"I'm managing his campaign," my date said, biting into a fat piece of French toast. "I always give them great deals. I collect my salary after they win," he bragged. "I got $90,000 after one campaign and she doesn't talk to me anymore. She thinks she's too important."

Donnie spoke in a matter-of-fact, fast-paced arrogance.

I took a sip of water, then poured more syrup on my chocolate chip pancakes. "So you don't care if their politics are opposite yours?"

He reiterated that he earned $90,000 from just one campaign. He has the strategy nailed down. "My people always win!"

Donnie picked up his phone. He tapped its face with his fingertips, studied it endearingly, lovingly even. Very gently, Donnie placed his phone down on the table.

"You have to be somewhere?"

He responded that his boss, who's running for Butte County Assessor, dropped him off. Said boss is six minutes away and will be picking him up. In his forties, and he gets valet service from his boss for breakfast dates? Weird!

Donnie again picked up his phone, eyed it obsessively, then placed it gingerly onto the table. I watched him pat it repeatedly, as I finished my water.

"He's a good guy," he started again. "But I told him that he's going to change. They always do. He said, 'No, I'm not going to change.' I know how it is. I've been doing this for years. I can't be fooled."

Time moved a lot slower than the syrup.

And, my dear reader, you can guess what he did once again. Yep, Donnie swept his phone off the table. Not just that. No, this time Donnie studied its face and announced, "Well it was great seeing you again."

Huh? You never saw me before. Or are you talking to your phone? That's what you're seeing now. That's three fondling sessions in the last twenty minutes. And now you're kicking me out of a public eatery because your ride is arriving curbside momentarily?

<u>Note to self:</u> The chocolate chip pancakes were scrumptious.

<u>Note in response to note to self:</u> They'd have tasted better had I not seen his pimple.

Well, yeah, it was a nice breakfast meal. Maybe it'd be a good workday? Wishful thinking.

The school's long-standing teachers' aide, Molly, fit in nicely with this tightly wound team.

One day I'd forgotten my key. I turned to her, as she was approaching the room directly behind me. "Oh I never give out my key," she proclaimed. "You're a grown-up. I shouldn't have to lend my key to anyone who's not responsible enough to have it on them at all times. It's my principle that I'm very clear about, nothing personal."

"That's fine," I slid to the side. "I'll let you open the door then." Whatever, bitch.

Molly unlocked the door, walked in, and—as I predicted—did not hold the door for me. I caught it in time to see Molly scan a row of desks on which a few students had left their "Caught Ya Being Good!" cards. (These cards were my way of bringing some positivity into an otherwise punitive environment. I'd created bunches of them on colored paper that I found under paper plates and a stash of napkins in the staff lounge.)

She snatched up Christopher's "Caught Ya Being Good" card. "Robyn! Where did you get this paper? You're not supposed to use it. It's not for you. It's cardstock, and cardstock is very expensive! It's the teachers' materials only. This paper costs a lot more than regular paper. I'm going to have to report this."

"Seriously? You're scolding me for that?"

She didn't hear me, wasn't waiting on a response.

Dang, I need to get laid too, I thought, but I don't act like that.

My days left there would be numbered. This now seemed obvious. They'd let me go at the end of the school year, or maybe as early as Christmas break. I didn't fit in with the madness.

Bad, bad Robyn. She recycles neglected cardstock paper to promote the self-esteem of disadvantaged youth! Bad Robyn once forgot her key, nearly gets door slammed in her face for this. Pee in cup, bad girl, then pay big price.

I heated a cup of hot chocolate during my lunch break. "Help yourself to the coffee or anything in the staff lounge," I'd been told. I'd been bringing my lunches, and hot chocolate packets or bottled water, from home. I took advantage of the coffee only, adding meager smidgens to my hot chocolate. In that environment, especially, this kept me going.

Elva, an English teacher who'd been there for years, hovered over me as I poured some coffee.

"You know we all contribute to what's made available here, lady," she reprimanded. "You should be paying for your share of coffee!"

"Um, what?" I imparted a look of confusion. "I just added a few drops." I put the container back in its place.

"Well, it's about boundaries. The entire team is very hard working, except for you apparently." She swung her arms abruptly as she spoke. "You're hardly ever here. But the rest of us invest in the coffee and any leftover items that you're helping yourself to. Courtesy is essential."

Elva gripped the coffee container handle, holding it high, as if to add power to her words. "I don't even know you, but you call yourself a therapist apparently. We're a team here. There's no 'i' in team now, is there, lady?"

Bad, bad Robyn. She pours drops of—gasp--coffee from the— gasp—staff coffee maker in the—gasp--staff lounge, because bad Robyn likes chocolate coffee. Bad, bad girl!

That did it! I placed my mug on the counter by the microwave.

"Look, Elva, I'm 50. I treat others with professionalism, and I expect the same in return. This coffee is made available to all staff here in the staff lounge for all of the staff. I'm a staff member, as much as you dislike that fact. It's coffee. I poured approximately three tablespoons into my hot chocolate, which I paid for and brought from my home, and which I'm drinking out of my own mug that I also paid for and brought from my home."

I was on a roll. Go me! "Furthermore, I'm tired of being scolded about stupid, petty things just because you all seem to be having a bad day, every day. There's no 'i' in team, and there's no 'i' in 'You need to pay for three tablespoons of coffee in the staff lounge.' Finally, Miss Elva, speak to me respectfully or not at all."

I grabbed my lunch bag out of the fridge, picked up my mug, and asked, "Are we clear?"

"Certainly." Welp. The look on her newly pale face informed me that I might have been the first, or first in a long time, to put that sourpuss in her place.

Internet meme: "Is fuck off a real emotion, because I feel it in my soul?"—Unknown

The global scene lifted my spirits, making other things more manageable. As an example of the overriding sentiment, Panty Toot Nation* had garnered millions of followers. (*Name changed to protect this Author from a woman—we'll call her "Fibby"—who turned that warmhearted, inspiring page into huge personal profit. Or tried to and failed miserably.)

Not only was America, but the world (well, minus the former Soviet Union) prepared to welcome our first female President. Little girls can do anything, even become President of the United States! Books were published, classroom instruction imparted, parent-child discourse engaged in, all underscoring this message. Spoken and written words flew prematurely regarding the Republicans' and Trump's failures to secure Presidential appointment.

I'd reluctantly decided to heed Bernie's words and vote for Hillary. My man had no chance, it seemed, due to the Democratic National Committee (money, greed, dishonesty, corruption—politics as usual). We had to defeat Trump, and we would. Hillary was going to win, most were certain. This, the idea of our first female President, consoled me.

<u>11/7/2016:</u>

"Okay, you can only vote for one person." The teacher handed a small stack of ballots to students in the front rows. "Pass these down. So tomorrow are the real elections, and we're having elections here in class."

There was some smirking, some whispering. "Quiet!" she said. "Nobody is allowed to talk in the voting booth. You could be kicked out. Vote quietly and hand your ballots to Molly when you're done."

The count was in. "Okay," the teacher said. "Let's find out who won. Molly, how many votes did Donald Trump get?"

"Four, no wait." Molly flipped through the top two slips of paper.

"Hey, no cheating," Tyler chided. Students giggled.

Molly smirked. "Come on, I'm not cheating." She looked at the Most Amazing Teacher, "It's actually five."

"Okay." Most Amazing Teacher wrote a 5 under "Donald Trump."

"Now how many for Hillary Clinton?"

Without emotion, Molly said, "Hillary got 11 votes."

Students applauded, yet some sneered "Recount! That's messed up!" I couldn't help but notice that Molly appeared to favor a recount too.

The teacher wrote an 11 under "Hillary Clinton."

"But there are two write-in votes," Molly added. "One for Kanye West, and one for Jay-Z."

A group of boys cheered in unison, "Kanye! Kanye! Kanye!" They're a fun group, but Kanye? Could it be worse?

"Who are you voting for, Robyn?" Tyler asked me, on his way out the door.

"Well, let's just say that I'm happy with how this vote turned out."

"You like Hillary?"

"Um, I don't really like Hillary that much, but I think she'd be much better than Trump. I really don't like him."

"Yeah. That's what my uncle says too. See ya."
"See you tomorrow."

Many of us spent the late hours glued to screens of some size and sort. Shock took hold as red after red state appeared. Yet commentators continued to remark on Hillary's victory, the GOP's defeat. They were that rehearsed, that certain, that delusional too. It was as if we'd all been transported onto another planet named The End of Times. I was horrified, tear-stricken, shocked, and very, very scared. I didn't watch to the end. It got too despairing. Sleep didn't come easily that night.

Donnie's candidate won for Assessor too, I learned. Damn. I didn't want that to happen either. I imagined he was celebrating over French toast that would generate more pimples, while he lasciviously salivated over his phone.

November 8. November 8, 2016. November 8, a life-changing day. Especially for my part of the world. 11/8.

I breathed in a heavy morbidity on campus that morning.

José walked into class, more lethargic than ever, and sat in his chair. I approached, "Are you okay, José? I've been thinking about you, especially with the way things went last night."

"Yeah, I mean, no, not really. Mom says we might have to move back to Mexico."

I sighed. "It's really scary. You wanna have a talk?"

"Nah, well, maybe after lunch."

"Okay. I'll find you then."

"'Kay."

It can't get as bad as we think it will, right? I mean, how could someone so inept mess up too much? As soon as he started picking his cabinet, though, we realized—yes, it could and would get very bad. When he opened his mouth or sent a tweet, his official mode of communication, it got worse than bad. Crazy, funny, scary, stupid, horrifyingly bad.

Among Trump's first targets: Sweden and Canada. In time, big corporations, legal and social service entities, media outlets and individual journalists, leftwing celebrity power players, and much of the world—excepting Russia—landed on Trump's hate list.

<u>Trump on (oops, no pun intended) his daughter:</u> "She does have a very nice figure. I've said if Ivanka weren't my daughter, perhaps I'd be dating her."

I got the call the week before Thanksgiving break, totally unexpected. I mean, I figured they'd at least keep me on until the winter break. Nope. My contract would be terminated effective Thanksgiving Day. "Everyone likes you, you're just not a good match."

"Well, actually, I wasn't liked or welcomed," I said, defensive and hurt. "I was scolded for taking some of the staff lounge coffee. And your school is failing its students. One of their moms was raped, and the teacher labels him 'manipulative.' Another teacher threatens to punch kids in the face, I can't even use paper tha—"

"I don't know about any of that, but you can work through Wednesday, if you can be professional." In other words, I needed to shut the fuck up. Which I did need to do, because I had over a handful of students to whom to say "goodbye".

Bad Robyn. Bad, bad, noncompliant girl! She speaks the truth. Bad girl!

"Okay, sure. If you're able, I'd like some clarity on what you'd wanted from me. It would be helpful for my future jobs."

"I'm afraid I don't have anything specific. Like I said, everyone likes you. Nobody had anything bad to say to me. It's not a good fit," he reiterated.

"Okay, thank you." Why the hell was I thanking him? To get a chance for closure with the students.

<u>Trump at a pre-election rally:</u> "If you see somebody getting ready to throw a tomato, knock the crap out of them, would you? I will pay your legal fees. I promise."

<u>Sarah Sanders, Press Secretary:</u> "The President in no way, form or fashion has ever promoted or encouraged violence."

"You're the best one here," José told me, when I said my most difficult "goodbye." "That ain't right."

No, it's not. "I'll be thinking about you. Always remember your strength. I'll miss you, hon."

José bent down and extended his arms to give me a hug. That was a first. He'd never initiated affection with me and wasn't expressive that way. "I'll miss you too."

Chapter 16: Universal Perspectives

"There are two kinds of egotists: Those who admit it, and the rest of us."—Laurence J. Peter

Our planet is an imperceptible speck in an infinite universe. You and I, each but one of approximately 7.7 billion humans who live on this speck. Each resides on one of nearly 200 land masses called "countries."

For a slew of complex reasons that are perhaps as horrifying as they are inspiring, planet Earth spins in an all-but-literal manner, not on its axis, but around one particular country. Even young children throughout the world, if asked, would know that I'm referencing the United States of America.

Woo-hoo! Everybody sing along: *This land is your land. This land is my land.*

While the tune resonates, I've a question: Did you know that the U.S. claims less than 5% of the world's population? This, in a region that spans under 7% of the Earth's crust.

Plus, America is infantile. Other civilizations are traced back hundreds, thousands, even millions of years, yet the U.S. wasn't founded until slightly over two centuries ago.

From California to the New York Island, from

Despite its size and youth, America has become the single most important metric of life on Earth. Moreover, the wellness of humans, animals, and our climate depends primarily upon one person. One and only one individual. Sure, that person has committees and officials, consultants, a posse of security and reporters; a foundation of intricate democratic processes to—in theory—assure fair and equal representation of all; a Vice President who's second-in-command, and more. But his (or, being very hopeful, her) power is undeniable. It's mind-boggling in context, an insane reality.

the Redwood forests

Making matters worse, the current President seems intent on reminding the world of his power, as frequently and as often as possible.

<u>President Trump</u>: "My IQ is one of the highest—and you all know it! Please don't feel so stupid or insecure; it's not your fault."

The man's ego is insatiable. Let's break this down: "Ego" is a concept, not an entity we can study under a microscope. It doesn't actually exist in tangible form.

This concept, however, connotes our need to feel worthy. Children have the most obvious egos, as they should. They're just learning about themselves and their places in their own microworlds.

But adults whose egos are huge enough to wallop the entire McDonalds' chain, for example, well, those people frighten me most. Their power, especially when elevated to a position of leadership, can instantly grow far out of proportion to any semblance of reason or logic.

His ego is Donald Trump's driving force in ruling the country and thus, the planet.

to the Gulf Stream wa-a-ters

Like many, upon Trump's swearing in, I developed a strong urge to leave, to get away somewhere, anywhere else in the world. I'd pretend I was from Canada; everyone loves Canadians. I even managed to dig up a few old t-shirts sporting the Canadian maple leaf.

Next, I went downtown to renew my passport.

As I stood to force a smile, my eyes caught a softly painted ocean scene, displayed on the wall I faced while standing for the all-important, ever-unflattering passport photo. The framed image didn't cite a location, so I created one in my mind. Greece! In movies, magazines, and Internet travel ads, Greece had appeared magical. Greek mythology intrigued me since my teens, when I'd learned about Athena and Zeus. My next travel destination, decision made.

This land was made for you and me.

"It's a harsh world, as everybody knows, and we are like family here." The director spawned a critical expression. "I see that you've been involved with J-, uh, Jewish organizations." She dropped her eyes to my resumé and nodded. "So I just want to make sure you'd be okay with our prayer circles. You should know that you don't have to participate, but it's important that we all support each other." She raised her eyebrows suspiciously.

"Sure. Yes, I am Jewish. I'm fine with optional prayer circles, and if there are opportunities to share my practices here, I'd love to." I smiled.

Her eyelids closed in on each other.

<u>Note to self:</u> You won't get this job.

<u>Note in response to note to self:</u> I got the job.

Thus, I soon found myself working for yet another employer more unhinged than the agency clientele.

"How does it work to take vacation?" I inquired, a few weeks in. "I know I don't have any hours accrued, but can I take unpaid time? It's not until the Fall, but I want to be sure."

This made me nervous—both the expense of such a glorious escape, and getting time off from a new employer.

I was given a half-page form, told that I'd simply need to be caught up with my work. Vacations and breaks were readily approved. Nice.

Even more convenient, this job was walking distance from home.

"So you're working at Chico Family Villa?" Geezer asked me one day at the mailboxes.

"Yes, I am." Do you also know my blood type? Please tell me, because I don't. Oh, and you know the number of days it's been since I got laid. Right? Of course you do. I assume you understand sexual repression quite well. Yeah, it's time to resort to masturbation. Am I right? But that's not a bad thing. I mean, not for me. For you, though? Ooh, yikes.

"Oh um, yeah, I see you walk there and it seems like a good company, but I sometimes hear the kids that go there screaming. Yeah, it's really loud. I almost called the police last week but then it stopped and I realized that yeah, maybe they have mental, you know, mental brain problems. By the way, did you get the telephone book that was on your doormat yesterday at 11:15 a.m.? Yeah I didn't see it there this morning, but I wanted to make sure you got it."

By this time, I was at my door. "Yep. Bye Geezer."
"Okay well yeah, I just"—Slam.
Oy.

"A man wrapped up in himself makes a very small bundle."—
Benjamin Franklin

Imagine the frustrations of not being able to verbally communicate your needs, wants, desires. Is it any wonder that humans who can't express themselves verbally resort to physical means of self-expression? It's an easy outlet for frustrations, a fullproof way to get attention too. The rest of us have a treasure trove of possible tools. Yet we still behave dramatically, if not with overbearing determination, on occasion. In sum, it's understandable that this population might at times behave aggressively.

Danni was a sweet seven year old, whose single mom presented like June Cleaver—the perfectly wise and nurturing mother. But a stroke of misfortune before birth had vexed Danni with the lifelong challenges inherent in what's termed "autism" or "autistic spectrum disorder." She spoke only a handful of words, grunted and otherwise made guttural noises. Of most concern, though, Danni pushed, shoved, hit, and bit—daily and regularly.

When I sat silently next to Danni, creating chalk drawings on the playground asphalt, her sweet side shone through. She smiled, chuckled, even made eye contact to display her purple-winged, orange-spotted giant ladybug with eleven legs (I counted. She giggled as I emphasized each number, 1 through 11.)

Danni's mother reclined on a picnic bench during the session, imparting pleasant smiles when I looked her way. I imagine she was slammed by pure exhaustion, relieved to get a chance to just sit quietly. She eventually took a phone-call and walked away, which she tended to do during our sessions.

President Trump to the 9th District Court: "I'll see you in court!"

Problems arose when Danni discovered a 3-inch round hole in the playground dirt. It looked as though this hole had at some point been intended for piping, but there was nothing set-up for such piping.

Danni poked the top edge of her shoe into it, slowly and curiously.

"Robyn, you can't let her do that!" Jen, a know-it-all intern, snapped. "She could get hurt."

I didn't see a problem. The child was naturally curious. It's not as if she'd get her foot stuck—the hole was too small.

Seconds later, my supervisor Carol, to whom I'd obviously been reported, came darting over. "Take her away, Robyn! It's not okay to let her near this. When Jen gives you input, you can't ignore it. Here,"—she pulled Danni aside by the arm. "Watch," she told me. "You need to stand like this." Carol's peach pedicured toenails (encased by dark brown Birkenstocks) covered the hole.

Seriously? I'm going to spend my afternoon blocking a little hole in the fuckin dirt, because you all have obsessive compulsive disorder and uncontrollable control issues, and nothing better to do but micromanage someone with a master's and clinical license who doesn't get giddy about Christly prayer circles?

Bad Robyn didn't block 3-inch round dirt hole! Pray! Pray for Robyn's soul. Pray hard. Pray often. Hold holy prayer. Pray on the hole, in the hole, about the hole!

When I replaced my foot for Carol's, semi-obedient employee that I am, Carol abruptly disappeared. Danni's mom strolled towards the sidewalk on her phone. It was just me and a very mad girl.

Said mad girl pushed and shoved her body into mine. Danni was my size, though a lot more determined now. Nonetheless, I held my stance and pointed towards a big oak tree that she liked to climb. "Let's climb!" I suggested.

Didn't work. Danni squealed, and then belted me in the belly with her fist. Repeatedly. Shit.

"It's time to go, sweetheart." Her mom returned, and she took her daughter's hand, oblivious to the aggression.

I stepped back.

Carol charged out from her office. She stopped a few feet from Danni. "Look at you! You're ready to go," Carol giggled. "Great work!" She gave Danni a high five.

The mother-child duo departed cheerily.

"How did that go?" Carol turned to me. "Did you keep her away from the hole?"

"I tried to, but she hit me several times." I placed my hand on my belly. "Pretty hard too."

She rolled her eyes. "Yes, Robyn. You have all sorts of experience. You know that's what autistic kids do. Par for the course."

<u>Mike Pence, Vice President</u>: "Despite the hysteria from the political class and the media, smoking doesn't kill. In fact, 2 out of every 3 smokers does not die from a smoking related illness."

A week or so later, Carol called me into her office for a meeting that wasn't on my schedule. Little did I know the director would be there too. For prayer? Jesus.

"We know you like doing this kind of work, Robyn. That is, based on your resumé," she said. "But that doesn't mean that you're actually good at it." Whoa.

"Robyn, I need to interject that I'm really concerned," Carol took over. "You seemed to have an overreaction to being hit. That's just part of the job, you know, working with this population. If it's too hard for you, maybe this isn't the right fit."

Hmm. Apparently, there's more than one hole around here. More than A HOLE. It ain't the little one in the dirt either.

"I understand," I said as calmly as I could. "What would you like from me?"

I was to comply with a Plan of Corrective Action, threatened with job termination if I didn't make changes. Yet this plan had nothing to do with my relationships with the clients. Nothing to do with my job performance. Instead, I had to log an ungodly level of "productivity"—direct contact hours. How I spent this time didn't matter.

See, it's become solely about quantity, not quality in the helping profession. As if quality wasn't already a general problem.

Bad Robyn gets to pray with her clients for hours, quickly. Cover the hole, bad girl, and be productive!

When timesheets were due, I'd worked the numbers such that they got what they wanted. It did involve some more hours than I was paid for, not a huge amount. I didn't care. I had a plan.

When I was called into the next meeting, they handed me a chart that indicated a dramatic increase in my productivity.

"Wow, you really did great, Robyn!"

"We're very pleased," Carol affirmed.

Their smiles, as grotesquely unnatural as Trump's hair.

"Yes, I'm doing my best. Thank you. I'd have preferred to know the expectations from the start, but"—I smiled—"now that I do, I'm fine." I am good. I am productive!

Good, productive Robyn! She works the numbers. Go, Robyn, go! Covered her tuchas and covered the hole. Dishonesty wins. Pray, pray, pray.

We flashed each other cheesy grins, and I departed the office.

"Oh one more thing, Robyn," the Head Honcho stopped me, as my hand reached the door handle.

"Yeah?"

"We're making plans for our annual fundraiser. I'd love to brag about you to the corporate folks and of course, our families. It's going to be the first Saturday in July. Keep that in mind. We don't require staff to be there, but it's strongly encouraged." She imparted another loaded grin.

"Okay. Thank you." No thank you.

Gratefully, I already had plans for that weekend. It's easier to bail when I really do have a time conflict. This year, I was going on the annual camping excursion I'd heard others rave about in years past. Not sure what I did or said, and it certainly didn't involve sleeping with anyone, yet I made the invite list.

I saw above me that endless skyway

How lucky I was to have a handful of days with no work obligations.

We'd reached the designated campsite in the Sierra Nevada basin, and a grandiose Lake Almanor gleamed in our direct line of vision. Incense cedar accented a fresh, sagebrush-scented air.

Approximately thirty of us gathered in a midsize outdoor amphitheater.

Don and Rick strummed their guitars on a patch of cement that served as the stage.

Next, various combinations of musicians took turns, and so on. Music ranged from the Beatles to Sonny and Cher, John Denver, Madonna and just about everything but Skynyrd's "Free Bird."

Several hours had passed when I caught the friendly smile of a man at the other end of my bench. Cute, I thought. He got up to grab a beer, and I noted that he's lanky. Surely, I have more meat on my bones. I'd practically knock him over in one sneeze. And I'm pretty sure he's tall, but my nephew Josiah is taller than me now. What I'm saying is that I don't have a realistic concept of height. Everyone looks tall to me. Nonetheless, "Twig" seems an accurate pseudonym.

Twig was perhaps the only single male in the bunch.

"Hi, I'm Robyn," I broke the ice.

We shared a handshake and pleasantries.

"So how are you connected with this group?" I asked.

"Sheila invited me. We've gone on a few hikes. She kicked my ass every time." He chuckled, as did I. "Oh, but we're not dating. She just invited me, and then she ignored me after she barely even said 'hello' when I got here."

I liked that he specified that they aren't dating.

"Not the friendliest bitch around. Oops, did I say that aloud?" I nudged him with my elbow.

Sheila was the mean girl who made sure to keep the numbers stacked in her favor at every party, such that she had men to choose from. She'd tell my friends, "Robyn's not invited, just because." I assumed that "just because" has to do with my being nicer and younger. (She has an athletic body compared to my Ashkenazi Jewish chub, so I won't go further down the list of adjectives. It wouldn't bode well for me.) This event, though, a huge investment on Meg and Stan's part, was out of her control. So I made the cut.

"True that." He nodded. "How about you? How do you know these people?"

"I'm friendly with Meg. We've seen each other at a lot of live music events, and we have fun dancing. I hardly know Stan, and I don't know a lot of the others here."

Twig and I danced and talked into the night. I learned that he works for a company that installs solar panels, and he rents a room in a small woodsy home in Paradise. He's having some problems with a roommate, but otherwise loves the place.

Twig's a divorced, proud father of two. "They're my whole heart," he said, patting his chest.

"Two kids? Boys, girls?"

"Two girls. Well, I had a son but," his voice quieted, "guess he couldn't hack being in the middle of two sisters."

Shit. I think I know what that means.

Twig guffawed awkwardly then looked towards the lake. "What's there to complain about, right? I'm so blessed right now."

What could I say? I looked down at the full plate by my side; I'd been ignoring it. "Yeah, this is my kind of camping—glamping it up with Chinese chicken salad. I can't believe how much trouble they went to." I twirled noodles around my plastic fork, teasing the food. "I just tossed some fruit and water in a Styrofoam cooler and hit the road."

Sheila bopped in rhythmic motion to the beat. She stopped in front of us, pointed at me and told Twig, "She's an author, you know! It's a good book too. Relationships are tough, don't get me started, Robyn. You wrote the book, lady!"

I was happily surprised by her praise. And damnit, I did write the book. "You read it, Sheila?"

"Yeah I did. I read your *Paradise*-whatever book in one night! It was so good!"

"Well thank you very much, my friend." In this moment, she was a dear friend.

In the next moment, she went prancing across the stage in her usual "Look at me, everyone!" manner.

"You're an author?" Twig turned to me. "That's cool."

"Yeah, I guess. I mean, thank you. I figure I've had so many heartaches, I might as well share them with the world. But my book's motto is to love and respect yourself. I'm good being single." *Like hell I am. Got a cure?*

"Well"—Twig took a swig of his beer—"it's not easy out there." He shook his head from side to side.

"Not at all." I turned to the dancers, "Wanna dance?" *done everything for—*"Sure. Let's do it." *–nothin'. You've done nothing for me!*

7/2017: The number of U.S. states refusing to comply with President Trump's Commission on Election Integrity is reported to have risen to 44.

We watched fireworks sprinkle the night skies over the sleepy lake. Twig rested his closed fist against my leg. Sort of odd. That was it. Until the show was over.

He then escorted me, in the dark, up and down small hills of dirt.

My tent within view, Twig said "Good night. I'll say 'goodbye' to you tomorrow. I've gotta get back and get stuff done."

"Okay. I'm sorry you're leaving early." My luck. "Good night."

When we hugged, he kissed my cheek. I then moved to reciprocate, but Twig spun his head such that his lips landed on mine. His arms dropped abruptly.

"Oh, um, 'kay, well"—he stumbled away—"See ya tomorrow!"

I watched the guy skid down a mound of dirt and fall on his butt.

"Oops, are you okay?"

He popped up. "Yep I'm fine."

"Okay. G'night."

"G, g'night."

Warmed by romantic thoughts during an otherwise chilly night, I faded into a semi-sound sleep.

Morning came. Twig was nowhere to be found. When asking around, I learned that he'd left early "to get real coffee."

Damn. The guy must've darted in fear. I know the routine—the unmanly chicken dance.

Disappointment.

Again.

Back home, I opened my laptop to this message: "I had to leave early, lots stuff to do. Gotta go sell baseball cards on eBay."

Gotta sell baseball cards on eBay? That's a new one. Perhaps the easiest rejection line for me to laugh off.

"Okay. Good luck to you."

"Talk L8R." L8R? Really dude? Well, hope U make fiddy cent on your card sales, Mister Cool.

<u>Ben Carson, Secretary of Housing and Urban Development:</u>
"American people are not as stupid as [the media] think they are. Many of them are stupid, ok. But I'm talking about overall."

My beaming-eyed client was in an especially playful mood. I chased her giddily around the playground. At one point, she "hid" behind a tree trunk—it was the kind of "hiding" that entailed my need to feign an inability to see, well, anything at all. She's a big girl and the tree trunk only hid from view a small vertical slice of her.

"Danni, where are you?" I walked toward the slide. "I don't see you."

She giggled.

"Hmm, are you in here?" I peered at the sandbox, kneeling down to shuffle sand around. "No, you're not in the sand. I wonder where you are."

I strolled towards the tree, then abruptly turned to look behind a large bush. "I bet you're behind"—I looked behind the bush, as she burst into laughter—"No, I don't see you there."

"Robyn!" Jen snapped. Must you ruin all the fun, Miss Know-it-all?

Danni's laughter ceased. She plopped onto the dirt and leaned against the tree.

"I told you, you need to cover the hole!"

Seriously, bitch?

"I feel like you don't respect me." Jen swung around and zipped back into the building, no doubt to tattle on me to Carol.

My young client started to whimper. I approached, sat next to her, and gently applied my hand to her shoulder. "Noo, ahh, waaah!" she wailed. Her flailing arms hit my face and torso.

"What's, what's the matter?" Danni's mom scurried over. "What's wrong Boo Boo?"

Danni clung tightly to her mom's legs while her outburst softened.

"Yeah, I'm sorry, I think it was just too much"—I started explaining to. . . nobody. Danni's mom cradled her as she departed.

I saw below me that golden valley

"It's plenty of notice," I said, handing my resignation to Carol. "I'll be caught up, and I'm taking a vacation anyway, so it's a good time for me to leave."

"Okay." Carol took my letter and tossed it atop a pile of files on her desk.

Okay? No "Hate to see you go"? No "Thrilled to see you go"? No final prayer circle in my honor?

Each of us but one imperceptible speck in but one imperceptible speck of an infinite universe.

This land was made for you and me?

Chapter 17: Almost All Greek

"The single biggest problem in communication is the illusion that it has taken place."—George Bernard Shaw

It felt freeing to have dropped the envelope in the mail—the final piece of paperwork for my trip to Greece. Travel insurance bought. Payment made. Nervousness and excitement simmered, but there he was again.

Damnit. Something in me snapped. I'd had enough.

"Please pick up your chair and move." I pointed north. "Look, Geezer, there's a whole big lawn all the way to the end of the block. I'm tired of you blocking my door. I shouldn't have to maneuver around you to go into my—"

"I, I don't know what you're talking about. This isn't your lawn, Robyn!"

"Quit blocking my door!"

"Don't yell at me, Robyn!"

"Don't yell at me, Geezer! Stop sitting in my walkway!"

He scurried inside, leaving his white plastic chair in my path. I might have knocked it over with my hip, "accidentally." Oops.

As I closed my door, I heard my cellphone going off. Damn. Where is it?

Deep breath. "Oh, hi Carol."

She sounded cheery, unlike the uptight supervisor I'd just quit on. Yet she was that person.

"You're kick-ass," she rambled. "It's just, that place brings out the worst in people. Oh, I was under way too much stress. Between you and me, I have a new job in the works." She giggled. "Anyway, I thought I'd see if you want to meet up for music in the plaza later today. High 'n Bye's playing. It'd be fun to just hang out."

My former boss wants to be besties? Who will cover the hole?

Let us pray. Pray for the hole. Holy hole. Holiest of the most Holy of holes. Pray for said Holy hole and all other Holy holes too. For each is Holy in its own special way. May all be blessed. With no holes barred, we say together: Amen.

Oops. She's awaiting a response.

"Uh, yeah, sure. Thank you for asking, Carol. That'll be fun."

One thing's for sure, Carol's an excellent talker. See, her fiancé Bennett had just finished serving time for drug charges. Or was it drunk driving? She lost track. Their second baby was born autistic. Carol's grandma died yesterday of sudden heart failure, her parents are divorcing after 42 years of marriage, and she's been feeling "on the suicidal side. But that's an every other day thing," she noted, "so don't worry about me. I'm on like three strong meds, and we're upping my Seroquel. It's helping a ton."

Go Big Pharma! Go, go, go, with your big, bad, evil self, Big Pharma! Raking in billions!

"That's good. I mean, that's a lot. Sorry."

I turned my head, looking for a designated exit, but we were outdoors. "The music's starting. Do you want to go closer to the stage?"

"Oh, no, that's okay. I gotta run, Robyn." She shifted her head from left to right. "First, I have to pee. You go ahead."

"Okay. Thanks."

An abrupt hug capped our encounter. So I thought.

"Oh wait, have a great time in Greece. Lucky you! Bennett and I wanted to go there for our honeymoon but of course we can't really afford it and it's too much anxiety for him to do all that traveling, you know? Then again, my therapist keeps asking me, 'Are you sure you want to marry him?' So maybe it'll never happen. I love him though. He saved my life when I OD'd. Twice, actually. Or more? I dunno. Those memories get all murky. I'll tell you about it some other time. See you later, Robyn."

"Take care, Carol. Let's reconnect soon."

Why did I say that? It's not any harder to stop at "Take care." It's easier, in fact. It's six less syllables.

It's hard to be honest, and it's a nice thing to do. But that's mean. I want to simply be mean when it's deserved, and nice when it's deserved. Must I only be honest when I want to be mean, though? Honesty should not complicate human relations. It's the best policy. It's all I know. I think. Err, I thought. But I said "Let's reconnect soon" when I honestly did not want to.

At a loss with myself, I'd dance. It's time, I'd decided. It's always time.

I made my way to a spot in the crowd, just below the stage.
That's when—wait. Is that him? That grin. Twig. He waved me
over. I scooted close for a side hug.

"Good to see you."

"You too." Breaking from the baseball card sales, I see.

"I love this group. They're the best!"

"Yeah, it's fun . . . . Well, good to see you." I did it again. It
wasn't good to see him, but I lied. I gleefully said that it was,
twice.

A bit unsettled, I returned to my original dance spot.

Twig followed up by message the next day. "I was in a bad place
before and want to apologize. I'm wondering if sometime this
weekend you'd like to go for a picnic so I can explain? I think that
would be fun."

They say "First time, shame on you. Second time, shame on me."
Well, shame on me for far too many times. More shame on me
than I can store on this laptop. More shame than could fill this
book.

*Shame, shame. I'm to blame. Can't play the game. With men, I'm
lame. Always the same. I must be insane. I end up in pain. I repeat
the same game, again and–said with a Canadian accent—again.
There will be an encore, and more, or not for shore.*

Thing is, I have a soft spot for what seems to be sincere caring.
It's so soft, I ignore the other traits and all the red or pink flags. I
just want more softness (well, combined with hard). It's a human
need—that combination, I mean.

Added to my defense, we can't really know someone's sincere
and trustworthy until it's too late. Betrayal doesn't fester until after
we've invested our all. Sigh.

I suppose I could look for a pretense of perfection from the get-
go, but how could I trust that? It's never real. Or is it?

I had those feelings with Justin from the start, but he insulted my
height too, and on our first date. Still, he was the love of my life.
Even though things went so horribly wrong.

Twig hadn't insulted me. He just got cold feet. The feelings were
there. All this is to say that I didn't hesitate to accept the date.

He's already two minutes late. A knock at the door interrupted my prelude to despair.

"I was on the wrong street," Twig explained, a bit frazzled.

"No worries. Yeah, it's confusing. We're fine."

Streams of sunlight warmed my back and head, as Twig led me to a peaceful, secluded spot along Bidwell Creek. He'd brought a hearty assortment of snacks (Havarti cheese, pepperoni and sandwich meats, a Pale Ale for himself, bottled water for me). Twig rolled out a large navy blue beach towel across the grass. We sat side by side, and he began to confess.

"I want to explain. So here, the thing is, I'm sorry again being chickenshit after we met. Margie and I used to go to Lake Almanor all the time, so I was in a funk about stuff. But when I saw you at the concert, I was like 'I really had fun with her.' Robyn"—he pointed at his right arm—"I wear my heart here. I'm faithful, I'm a good guy. That wasn't like me."

"I do need to say," I began to lecture, "when you'd left the campgrounds without saying 'goodbye,' I was really disappointed. And then when you ended our messaging to sell baseball cards on eBay, that felt rejecting."

"Yeah, I hear you." He nodded.

I smirked. "Well, I won't completely forget about it. But"—I imparted an elbow nudge—"I'll give you a free pass, since you manned up and we're here. You only get one free pass, though." As if I had only given him one thus far.

He grinned. "Challenge accepted."

"Okay, my turn. Respect is key. Be true to your word and good to me."

"I agree. Friendship first, and I need to gain your trust."

I liked that he realized this.

"And monogamy."

Twig raised an index finger. "Yes! One love! To tell you the truth, I've only been with three women." Wow. He's more innocent than I am. I like that.

Our next stop was a house concert for which he'd agreed to be my date. Donna had invited me.

We warmed lawn chairs, while eating party munchies and enjoying lively music. I felt a good tension between us, all the while sensing Twig's nervousness.

When I tripped over nothing onto concrete, as we walked to thank the party hosts, I picked up on my own nervousness. Then again, I'm klutzy. (On that note, a Facepalm friend wrote this meme: "I wish I wasn't such a cluts." I wish she wasn't either.)

"At least you fell gracefully," Twig said. I abruptly rose to my feet, as he grabbed the baking dish that broke my fall.

"Nah, not at all graceful, but thanks for saying that."

I hugged Donna, before departing. "You didn't tell me about a new man," she whispered.

"First official date," I responded. "I think I really like him."

"Mm, maybe he'll be story-worthy."

I agreed, craving good . . . material.

<u>Trump, pre-Presidential status:</u> "My fingers are long and beautiful as, it has been well documented, are various other parts of my body."

At my place, we reminisced about the fun-filled date. Twig's mother used to love bluegrass music, like the last songs we heard at the party. She introduced him to it, he said. It brought back fond memories.

A few heated milliseconds later, Twig's lips tasted mine. Sparks ignited. Our tongues tangoed. Electricity between us mixed with passion, thoughtfulness, sensitivity. Suddenly, it was two in the morning.

Twig spent the night, but in my living room. Alone.

"I'm not putting out," he'd informed. "It's too soon."

"I agree, too soon. Besides, I'm leaving for Greece on Wednesday. No 'putting out' before then." Strange. I'd never heard a man use that line. He's really innocent, or scared, or both.

When we stood at his car to say "goodbye," Harlotta strolled past us towards the carport.

"Hi Robyn." She smiled.

"Hi. Harlotta, this is Twig. Twig, this is Harlotta."

They shook hands. There was a moment. I don't know what that moment was, exactly. It gave me an odd feeling.

I brushed it off, as she walked away.

"Okay, handsome, I'll be in touch as soon as I get back. If I get an internet connection, I'll keep you posted. There's a huge time difference, though."

"No pressure," he smiled. "Just enjoy yourself."

"I will, thank you."

Twig kissed me caringly before he drove off.

<u>10/2017</u>: President Trump met with Alexis Tsipras, the Prime Minister of Greece, to discuss that country's broken economy, along with U.S.-Greek military ties.

Of note: Tsipras was Greece's first self-proclaimed Atheist leader. What I find truly "democratic"—"progressive" even—is that his wishes to recite a secular oath, and to be sworn in by the President versus the Archbishop, were honored without hesitation.

<u>Per www.Wikipedia.com</u>:

Progressivism is a political philosophy in support of social reform. It is based on the idea of progress in which advancements in science, technology, economic development and social organization are vital to the improvement of the human condition.

I don't care to relive any part of the actual travel to and within Greece. I'll spare those details in favor of sharing a select few highlights, along with fascinations.

If you're fortunate enough like me, you've been to the Greek Isles. If you've seen some cinema, you undoubtedly got a glimpse of their spectacular beauty.

Oh, and the Greek gods, the ones in human form? A delicious feast for the eyes.

So when Greek men served me coffee, or smiled at me, or asked where I'm from, I grabbed my camera. "Can I get a picture of us?" I'd inquire, without room for reply. One, the most gorgeous man of all men throughout all time besides Trevor Noah (Trevor, if you're reading this, you're divine!), proudly raised his chin and scanned a small cluster of tourists after I snapped a selfie. "Anyone else? Does anyone else want a picture with me?" The women did, I could tell, but didn't admit to it.

I guess I have less shame than most. I suppose that deems me less sane than most. And more fun.

Down with shame. Be insane. Don't shun, have fun. Break rules like fools, just the dumb rules though. They're for control and show. Trudeau is hot. I'm sure he gets that a lot.

Despite my fetish for godly sights, Twig routinely entered my mind. Although I saw only one Starbucks during my Greek venture, that one in Athens, there were plenty of places from which to message him.

Me: It was a long, miserable trek to get here, but I'm in Greece now! I'm tired, headachy, out of sorts and I LOVE it here. Athens feels like I'm IN history, even though it's seedy in some parts. There's so much to see and do. The food is fabulous. The people are sweet and friendly. I miss you. xo
Twig: I think about you all the time. Glad you're having fun, can't wait to see you. xo

Heaven. An airy pastry drowned in rich, dark, luscious chocolate. Oh, the chocolate. With a chocoholic reputation to uphold, I had to devour as much as I could.

What could be better? There I sat, in the rooftop bar-restaurant of Saint George's Hotel, able to absorb a full panoramic view of Athens. Shiny silverware, classy white cloth napkins, a plateful of Greek delicacies at the ready.

Within distant eyeshot, a small circle of land—the home of democracy, birthed thousands of years ago. The official meeting spot of the Democratic Assembly. It appeared a mere dirt patch, yet how significant it was and still is. There, the Athenians who rose to leadership by virtue of genuine altruism, discoursed. There, they grappled with the tough issues. There, they made decisions for the good of all, which they expeditiously carried through to completion.

From that speck of earth, we've gleaned worlds of insights into how to behave, how to create, how to love, how to become a full-scale civilized and cooperative society. Communication at its apex.

Athenian Democracy. How far we've regressed.

<u>Per www.merriam-webster.com:</u>
Democracy. 1a. Government by the people, rule of the majority.
1b. Government in which the supreme power is vested in the
people and exercised by them directly or indirectly through a
system of representation usually involving periodically held free
elections.

I elated in torrid stories of Greek gods and goddesses; gawked at
intact structures that date back, not decades or centuries—
millennia; hiked alongside hundreds of camera toting tourists to
the Acropolis. Floated effortlessly in the healing waters of the
Aegean Sea on a crisp sunny afternoon.

Perhaps equally impressive as the sights, I felt calm and safe.
Kindness runs rampant in Greece. People look out for each other. I
could roam the streets freely, day or night, without worry. Of
course, petty theft happens, so I needed to securely guard my
purse, but that was it. Violent crimes and crimes against women
aren't a problem like they are in the U.S. Furthermore, for the most
part, Greece has been at peace for over 3,700 years. What a
remarkable factoid to absorb.

During an afternoon of outdoor leisure shopping through the
picturesque walkways of Mykonos, I paused to get my bearings.
My eyes captured a middle-aged Greek man heading my way.
When he reached me, he handed me a map of the area. "Looks like
this might help you."

I took the map. "Thanks so much," I smiled. "That's very kind."

This man had no ulterior motive. As he drove away, he imparted
a wave and a smile. These kinds of things don't tend to happen in
the U.S.—our land of the free, brave, and filthy rich.
This land that's made for you and me.

<u>Me</u>: Hi! How are you? I'm sad my trip is ending way too soon. It's
like I just got here, but happy I'll be arriving to see you next
Wednesday, 4:30 p.m. your time! Will have lots of photos and
stories. Be well! xo
<u>Twig</u>: Okay. Yeah, I forgot about the time difference. I'll keep it in
mind. See ya soon. x

That was strange. No "Safe travels"? No "o"? He'll keep the time difference "in mind"? What's going on? Shit. Maybe he's distracted by something or worse, someone.

<u>Note to self:</u> Don't go there. Savor Santorini.

<u>Note in response to note to self:</u> Well, since I must. Blissful sigh. Did I mention the gelato? In particular, Viagra gelato. It was so sweet and prettily multicolored, and well I can't vouch for its efficacy. Yep, I didn't score on this trip. But it's all been a climax.

Most jaw-dropping for me was Akrotiri, an underground settlement spanning more than one square mile. This once bustling community functioned at a remarkably high level of sophistication: multistory houses with heating; hot and cold running water; indoor, functioning toilets; and majestic frescoes spanning the towering walls.

Akrotiri remained a flourishing civilization for thousands of years, a population that was suddenly eradicated by one of history's worst natural disasters, Volcano Thera. When Thera erupted around 1500 B.C., nearly 20,000 people were killed. This once life-sustaining stronghold was long later uncovered beneath 200 feet of volcanic ash. I believe excavations continue to date.

It seemed the epitome of cooperative community. All families lived in equitable domiciles; no palaces existed. No hierarchy stifled or controlled the masses. Money hadn't been created. Thus, economic corruption hadn't either.

Imagine a world in which everyone was housed in an equally adequate space that provided for everyone's basic needs. That world existed thousands of years ago, which serves as proof it could re-exist.

"If a man is mad, he shall not be at large in the city, but his family shall keep him in any way they can."—Plato

My clinical hat on, I cornered the guide after we'd finished the tour.

"What about mental illness?" I asked. "Did they see it and treat it?"

The Greeks believed in interdependent mind-body interactive functioning, she informed me. Disorders of the mind were addressed in the same way as those of the body. Hippocrates taught that mental health conditions stemmed from an imbalance of bodily fluids, or humors. An out of sorts brain affects all realms of functioning. Thus, mental illness was viewed, simply, as a brain disorder.

This makes sense. "Did they have problems with psychotic disorders?"

"Absolutely, they did." She explained that when someone behaved in a bizarre or uncontrollable manner, their family was expected to nurture and contain them. This may have involved restraint. Often, though, counseling took place and seemed quite effective.

How cool that my profession is perhaps one of the oldest in history. It's always been valid.

How far we've regressed in terms of our treatment of those with brain disorders who we label "mentally ill" and leave for dead on the streets.

"Obamacare will explode and we will all get together and piece together a great healthcare plan for THE PEOPLE. Do not worry!"—one of Trump's campaign promises

Every night, people swarm the cliff sides of Santorini to view spectacular sunsets. My second to last night in Greece, I joined the audience. We watched as the sun painted a beautiful tapestry of streaming oranges, reds, and yellows woven into a silky cloud-dappled sky. Within seconds, our Star sank softly away, to be replaced by magenta and dark gray hues.

Goodbye, Santorini.

Goodbye, Greece.

Thank you for lifting my heart and challenging my brain in new, beautiful ways.

When this haggard traveler finally made it home, Twig was the first to know. His response: "I thought you were coming back tomorrow. lol. Can't see you today. Maybe tomorrow. Friday for sure."

Shit. Did I do it again? Did I choose another unworthy man? Stupid me. Stupid him. I'm too damn depleted for this. The trip was too damn fuckin good. A quick bout of tears struck, then I wiped them. Calm down. Breathe.

Respond.

<u>Me:</u> Not sure what to make of this, feeling insecure. Trying not to be too disappointed. Friday's good, was hoping for sooner.
<u>Twig:</u> No reason to be insecure. I missed you girl. Can't wait to see you. We'll have a nice weekend together.

Phew! Phew?

Mamma mia, here I go again—
How can I resist you?
Mamma mia, does it show again—
Just how much I've missed you?
<u>Note to self:</u> Stay in Greece. Hold onto our Star's encore performance in the mesmerizing skies above Santorini. That perspective's always accessible.
<u>Note in response to note to self:</u> I will. I'll listen to you more often too.
<u>Note in response to note in response to note to self:</u> You always say that.
<u>Note in response to note in response to note in response to self:</u> I know. Mamma mia times three. But oh, that Santorini sunset. I really am okay either way. Okay? Yes, okay with triple certainty whilst another blissful sigh for that Santorini sunset.

Chapter 18: Backflipping Through Love's Insanity

"Well, love is insanity. The ancient Greeks knew that. It is the taking over of a rational and lucid mind by delusion and self-destruction."—Marilyn French

Bonus. Twig not only showed up on time, he arrived with a bagful of groceries. "I figured let's catch up, and I'm gonna make dinner." His beaming smile both eased and thrilled me. And in something almost too embarrassing to write, sappy Barry Manilow lyrics intruded upon my mental space. *Even now, when I have come so far, I wonder where I can't smile without you but that was thirty years ago when she lost her mind.*

Shit. I thought that only happens in diabetic-coma-inducing Hallmark movies. Apparently not.

After setting the grocery bag onto my kitchen counter, Twig appeared primed for a hug and kiss session. Since I'm not into voyeurism, I participated.

"I missed you."

"I missed you too." Kiss.

"I couldn't wait to see you, and show you"—kiss—"pictures."

We snuggled on my couch as I pulled my camera close to scan several hundred Grecian snapshots. I very rapidly breezed through a bulk of them: my selfies with Greek gods in manly form.

"I won't bore you, honey. I promise. Dang, I took a lot of photos, of . . . food."

Twig showed interest and asked appropriate questions (e.g., the octopus—Was it raw? Answer: It was boiled, in a salad. It was yummy too. I went back for second and third servings.)

After we ate his chicken stir fry, things quickly got heated again. But we'd planned on going out to hear music at the End Zone, a nearby bar. His suggestion. Twig, after all, was the limit-setter between us.

Had I thought clearly, I'd have added the points of his cowardice and . . . well, I wouldn't have pursued a relationship with Twig in the first place. Dodging our "goodbye" at camp, then ditching me to sell baseball cards, now deferring sex again, even after a long-awaited reunion.

But no, I said in a <u>Note to self</u>. *No. Don't be a naughty Robyn! Cover that hole! Nice guys take things slowly. Nice girls too. You love to dance. Pray for the hole! You love to live music. You love, well, yeah, you're starting to love him. Crap.*

Having just returned from the trip of a lifetime, I danced with my new beau at what, for Chico, is an upscale bar. I mean, they clean the counters on occasion. They have intact counters. They have matching stools too. And they even have a small dance floor.

I'd hoped to be seen, to feel extra special, you know, but it was a scant crowd of boozers. Admittedly, that was best. Twig's more like Steve Urkel than Fred Astaire, and I'm more Elaine Benes than Ginger Rogers. I likely needed to not be seen.

Back at home, late into the night, we touched, kissed, and groped. Things felt beautifully surreal. Next and naturally, I suggested we move to my bathroom. Just kidding, we transitioned to the bedroom.

Twig wouldn't leave until the next morning, not that I wanted him to leave at all.

How'd it go?

Well, you know a teenager's giddy, giggly, candy cane sweet feeling when hopped up on a gallon of Pop Rocks-infused Mountain Dew, having just scored front-row tickets to see Taylor Swift in concert? Yeah, me neither. It wasn't like that. It was more an unbelievably calm bliss.

I'd taken a wonderful trip to Greece. Now, a very kind man and I went hopscotching through lovey-dovey land. I was in deep, and (or do I mean "because"?) he was in deep.

Too good to be true? We both know the answer to that one, dear reader.

<u>Note to self</u>: As if you need to ask.

<u>Note in response to note to self:</u> No comment.

<u>Note in response to note in response to note to self</u>: I know. But there's no self-criticism now. That's progress. I don't want marriage again. I'm not looking for "the one." I'm good alone. I'm better alone, in fact.

It's a given that there's always a price to pay for sex and romance. I do and will settle in some ways. I'm more evolved than any man I'd find around here, to keep it real. And I do. So yeah, I require only kindness and respect.

And someone who's not at the extreme end of batshit craziness. Wait, don't we all get batshit crazy sometimes? Especially when we're in love?

Okay, here's the thing: I won't settle for someone who's abusive in any way. How's that? Problem is, you often can't tell a man's potential for abuse, until after you've slept with or (worse) married him. If I want to be with someone, and that's no longer a chronic need, but an intermittent desire, I'll settle in some ways. Or I'll restock the battery stash.

Welp. This note in response to all the other notes could be a boring and tedious book of its own. I just want to feel happy now, so I will. And I love my perfectly quirky and perhaps chronically mildly to moderately insane self. Besides, I'm fortunate enough to be happy now. So I will be.

So I told myself, and I believed myself too.

"Too good to be true usually is. Perfection hides something."
— Henry Cloud

Determined to blend zen into other areas of life, I adopted the motto: "Fuck employers."

They don't like or want to keep me. I'm a good, hard worker, so it's never been a performance issue. They get high-quality work from me. Clients usually click with me.

But I call attention to madness, like the supervisor who's asleep at her desk when I approach with questions, the one who asks me publicly if I'm a dwarf or a midget. The director who writes me up after I complain about said supervisor. The agency that tries to get rid of me when I express myself respectfully, though not cheerily, immediately after being punched in the nose by a client who threatened group homicide. I'm the worker who doesn't believe it's a worthy investment of her time to block a 3-inch round hole while supporting a young child with autism.

Bad, bad Robyn. She's routinely "noncompliant." This does not bode well for job longevity under power-hungry authority figures

in social service systems—many of which are dysfunctional
beyond (my or any) words, despite positive intentions at the core.
Let us pray.

<u>Insane factoid:</u> Christians worship a Jewish God and are taught that
Jews will go to hell because they don't worship the Christian
(Jewish) God, but Jewish people don't believe in hell.

All told, I'd do it now—I'd open my own therapy practice. I thus
signed with billers to navigate the insurance craze. A former
colleague offered me a small office in her building. I acquired a
business license and liability insurance. Within a month, I'd set
things in motion.

Nervousness. I'd never before thought that I'd have the skills or
desire to break free from bosses. How could I possibly make ends
meet?

Well, sometimes there's nothing more enticing than being told
by someone I hate that I can't do something. This practically
amounts to a lifetime guarantee that I'll kick ass with whatever it is
that I'm told I'm incapable of doing. The last boss's words ignited
me. "Just because you like doing therapy doesn't mean you're
good at it." I'd fuckin excel at it.

Funny how we set out to prove certain villains wrong, whether or
not we'll ever see or talk to them again. I mean, they're toxic;
we're best cutting ties altogether. Plus, they don't really give a shit
if we succeed. So why pine for their approval? They'd rather we
fail. They've invested in shredding us down.

Our success threatens their own sense of worth. Which hardly
exists. With every achievement, they feel worse about themselves.
Who's the crazy one? Them for inviting us to play along, or us for
staying in this self-defeating game?

<u>Insane factoid:</u> The smallest size cup at Starbucks is the "tall."

Once I'd furnished my office sparsely, my colleague asked me to
accommodate an office mate, in exchange for reduced rent. Nice.

My colleague's neighbor, Ember, expressed enthusiasm about
securing office space for her therapy practice. Fresh out of school

and not yet licensed, Ember didn't have a therapy practice; she's not a therapist. Interesting.

Why would anyone want to pay rent for a space they don't actually need and might not need in the immediate future? Seemed a bit premature, obsessive-compulsively overambitious, and/or reeking of some type of mental illness.

But I hadn't built a big caseload and was glad to save money. Besides, helpers help each other. It's what we do best. What could possibly go wrong?

Betsy DeVos, Secretary of Education: "I would imagine that there is probably a gun in the schools to protect from potential grizzlies."

Ember and her husband, who wore the biggest black-framed glasses I've seen since I watched *Revenge of the Nerds* circa 1985, met with me to discuss logistics.

"I'm pretty flexible and can make changes so long as it's okay with my clients, of course."

"Totally. Of course." She turned to the nerd, who nodded compliantly.

"Right now, I need it on Monday, Tuesday and Thursday afternoons from 1:30 to 5 in the evenings, and Wednesdays from 2 until 7 p.m.," I clarified. "Things can change quickly, though, so let's stay in close communication. Are you good with that?"

"Yes. We'll use it in the mornings from like 7 a.m. until 10 a.m., and on Friday nights." She smiled, then turned to her husband, who conferred another passive nod.

Friday nights? For trysts? Ew. I should've put a plastic cover on the sofa.

Tuesday came, and I placed my heavy file box by the office door. But damnit, light streamed through the door crack. Someone was in there, and I had a session in 10 minutes.

Knock, knock, knock.

Ember abruptly slid her bra strap under her tank top, as she flung open the door. "You said I could have the office at 1:30 today!"

Whoa. "No. I NEED it at 1:30 today and on Thur—"

"Oh yes you did! You said 1:30 today!"

"No, Ember, I was clear, I—"

"Okay but you need to"—huff. "Fuck." She turned to her husband, on the couch, tightening his belt. Then as if on cue, he rose to his feet, dropped his head, and trailed Ember who departed angrily.

I scurried to disinfect the sofa.

Odd. My traveler's clock had been moved from an end table to a far corner of the room, with its face against the wall. My blue-green floor rug had been rotated from a horizontal to vertical position, and a large coffee mug with the words "Just Relax!" rested on my chair. Yikes. Another lunatic in this field.

Me: "How was your day, babe? Mine was ok, but new office mate is cray cray."
Twig: "Lol. They always are. Hey, its too windy. We won't be hiking!" He's making decisions for us now?
Me: "K."
Twig: "Are you mad? You seem mad. Getting a weird vibe here."
Me: "No. I'm just not going to argue. I prefer you not make decisions for us. Was looking forward to getting out with you like we planned. Stressful day. We'll talk about it when you come over, ok?"
Twig: "Yes, we need to talk. I feel like your mad at me and I haven't done anything wrong. I'll be honest, I might not come over."
Me: "What just happened? I haven't said anything blaming. I explained why I'm being brief. I can't make you come over. But I'll be extremely upset if you don't. I'm already in deep. You have my heart. If you are going to run away when we have problems, this can't work."
Twig: "We'll be fine. I want you and your heart. I'll be over at 6 p.m."

Nervously, Twig sat next to me on my sofa. "Look," he fingered my shirt buttons, "I'm the first person to admit when I did something wrong at work."
"That's differ—"
"It's differ—"
We finished the word simultaneously: "—ent."
"You're nervous," I put my hand on his thigh.

"No, I'm just saying that, okay, I went back and read our messages. Okay, I sounded like a dick. I was still pissed off at my roommates. That situation is really getting under my skin. I shouldn't have taken it out on you."

Wow. A man who admits to his dick sounds, and the source of his frustrations. I like—no, I love—that. It's like a seventh inning grand slam to clinch the world championship (in baseball, I think).

"Thank you for saying that. I understand. I'm not going to fight with you. I just don't want to be told what we're going to do—"

"Then why didn't you—"

I extended my arm to cover his mouth, giggling nervously. "Your statement left no room for discussion. So I said 'k.'"

I freed him to talk.

Twig chuckled. "All I wanted to ask is, 'Why didn't you ask me why I said 'no hiking'?"

"Because 'why' is judgmental, and you'd already said that it was too windy."

He nodded, "I did that."

We took hands when I got more personal regarding my anxiety in intimate relationships, my abandonment issues and past traumas. Twig claimed to understand.

Eventually, we found ourselves in a seductive position.

"I think that makeup sex is in order now, right?" I stroked Twig's forearm. "And I mean, we need some exercise too since we didn't go hiking."

"Your smile is naughty," he teased.

After a bout of "exercise," we added some more steps. See, we walked to his car, and into the gas station mart where Twig grabbed a six pack of ale.

Note to reader: This is another pattern I noticed but refused to notice, as I do. Or as I don't do. Twig drank in the morning, afternoon and evening, every single day. It wasn't just a single beer. He took down beer after beer. How could he be so skinny? I don't know but it's not fair that I (a nondrinker) am the one with the beer belly. Hell, it's as though my muffin top expanded into a beer-filled donut shop at some point, and it's doing a great business.

Harlotta stood by the carport, upon our return. Weird timing. Was she stalking us?

"Hi, Twig." Excuse me lady, I'm here too.

"Hey," he responded, then "how you doing?" How Joey Tribbiani of my beau.

"Great. Uh, Robyn, I'm here to ask you if you want to perform in a show with me. I do it every year." She put extra emphasis on "every," glancing towards Twig.

"Cool," Twig chimed.

"Yeah, I've starred in shows since I was only 4 years old. I'm asking Robyn because we just need someone really short." She chortled, and Twig guffawed.

"Hey, hey, now. Be nice!" I interjected. "We littles are fierce."

"Ha! Sorry Robyn," Harlotta got back on topic. "We need someone to play Annie Bidwell[5] for the Christmas show at the Mansion. Annie was super short like you. It's really fun. There's a big reception afterwards. Are you up for it? I'll help you learn your lines. I know all the tricks of the trade."

"I haven't done any acting, but it sounds like an honor, actually."

"Don't worry. Like I said, I'll coach you. You'll be fine."

I looked at Twig. "It sounds fun, huh?"

"Do it, girl" he nudged.

"Well, sure," I told Harlotta. "Please just get me the script as soon as possible."

"Oh I will. Coolio!" she exclaimed, grinning at Twig.

I took Twig's hand, during "Goodbyes," and she sauntered away.

Insane anecdote:

I was told that I could not order a "medium" iced almond milk boba tea at a drive-through today, because they only have "regular" or "large" size drinks. So I ordered a "regular" iced almond milk boba tea. My "regular" and not "medium" iced almond milk boba tea was handed to me in a small size cup stickered with "small cup."

---

[5]Nineteenth century suffragette, wife of statesman John Bidwell. Annie played a key role in growing Chico, CA.

I knew he'd lost his son. I guessed it was by suicide. I wanted Twig to know he could confide in me, that I felt for the depth of pain and guilt he'd likely been tortured by. It made me think of Dad. Dad lost his child to suicide. God, I can't imagine how he survived and survived for almost thirty years after burying his older son.

"Are the holidays extra hard, with missing your son?" I broached the subject during dinner that night. Incidentally, we were eating chicken stir fry. That's all we ate together. Not that I'm complaining about a man who cooked for me, but variety would've been nice. I'd have preferred he'd toss in a tomato or a mushroom or a potato chip or anything edible. I was tired of his one and only specialty: white onion, brown rice, and unseasoned chicken mix.

"I guess." Twig slapped his free hand against the table. "Why do you ask? I want to just enjoy dinner, okay?"

He dropped his fork onto the plate. Teardrops strolled slowly down his face.

I eased my hands onto his. "Honey—"

"No, don't go there!" He pounded his now fisted hands against the table. "I didn't even notice. I should've saved him. I didn't even know he was fucking depressed."

"Honey," I whispered, "I'm so sorry."

"What? You're a therapist, so you have to talk about everything? Robyn, you have no idea. This is going to be my fifth holiday season without him, and you have to go and make me talk about it!"

Twig yanked his hands back from under mine, stood up, and shoved his plate to the center of the table. He proceeded to pace back and forth from one side of my dining room to the other.

"You ruined dinner. It's tearing me up. He's dead because of me. Congratulations! You pushed me away because you just had to go there!"

I slowly, stiffly took my dishes to the kitchen sink.

Twig shadowed me. "Where is this coming from, Robyn? We were having a great time until you forced me to talk about something I don't want to talk about! Why do I have to keep saying that? Why can't you just respect me?"

My heartbeat hastened. "Okay." I lifted my hands from the sink and chose words cautiously. "Sweetie, I won't ever bring it up again." I stepped closer to Twig and glanced directly into his eyes. "I love you, babe."

"I love you too, but you keep poking and poking. You make me talk about something I keep telling you I don't want to talk about!"

His tirade reminded me of Justin's ruthless paranoia. I began to see Jekyll's Hyde or Hyde's Jekyll. Nah, it was definitely Jekyll's Hyde, and it was ugly.

"You're scaring me, Twig. I've never seen you so angry."

"Oh, honey, if you think this is angry, you ain't seen nothin'." In place of Twig's face, I now saw Justin's. Instead of lovey-dovey bliss, I now experienced a sharp blade-through-the-marrow fright.

Self-care. Self-love. Protect self. Charmed by another mentally ill hothead with no clue how to manage, much less acknowledge, the male "f" word: Feelings.

"I'm gonna go die now," Twig said. "I'm not kidding."

"What? Are you telling me you're suicidal?"

"Are you crazy?! There you go again! I need you to respect my wishes when I say I don't want to talk about something. The one time I ask for privacy, here we are." How utterly twisted. "You turned this into a whole big production, like you're the victim."

<u>Note of noteworthy note:</u> Perhaps the most notable trait of all types of mental illness is a rigid inflexibility.

"I'd like a hug before you leave."

"No. You're just going to manipulate me into staying. You'd say 'just stay 15 more minutes,' and then more time, and more time."

"I don't play games like that, Twig."

"I'm going." He walked to the door and slid it open. "Come here and give me a kiss."

Knowing it was the end, I approached to give Twig a quick (final) peck.

The next day, we exchanged a few messages. First, I told him I needed space.

He responded, "Okay, I'll leave you alone" and then, two

minutes later, "Why do I feel like were done." [Yeah, he doesn't always use proper punctuation. Nor is patience his virtue.]

"I won't be censored. I won't be worried about what I say or don't say from one moment to the next. I've been through this before and it ended in divorce. I need to feel safe in a relationship. I woke up at 2:30 in the morning last night, I was so anxious. I can't do this. I won't do this. I love you, and this is breaking my heart."

I went on to say everything I appreciated about him and our time together.

"This hurts so fuckin much," Twig wrote.

"I know. I'm sorry."

The breakup was painful, as are breakups. Every time I go through it, I remember and cannot believe how much it hurts. It's like your insides are ruthlessly suctioned out of your body, sent through the world's most powerful supersize, razor-sharp sawmill, then tossed out for ravenous vultures to gleefully feast upon for dinner, dessert, and an after-dinner snack. The cycle repeats itself for far too many hours, days, months, and sometimes years.

Yet I'm glad I did it and did it fairly swiftly.

With Twig out of my life, perhaps I'd restart a semblance of imperfect perfection; of jagged bliss; of battery-operated entertainment that didn't drink, cook bland chicken stir fry every single evening, or yell at me for promoting intimacy. Thankfully, adult toys behave differently. Smiles.

I missed him, though. I cried a lot.

I did the right thing.

Twig was out of my life.

So I believed.

Chapter 19: Neighborly Love

"It is easier to love humanity than to love your neighbor."
—Eric Hoffer

Knock, knock, knock.

Harlotta wrapped strands of her greasy black hair around her fingers, as I opened my front door.

"Hi there. Come on in."

"Hi Robyn, thanks."

She headed straight for my couch and sank into it. "I'm so fuckin tired," her fingers now pressed to her brow. "I had way too much to drink last night."

Oy. I faked a semi-giggle and closed the door. I mean, if one can fake giggle, that's impressive. But if one can fake a semi-giggle, and I'm not sure this one can, that's halfway impressive, and that's what I fully did.

I picked up the script, which I'd printed off and placed on my coffee table that morning. "Ready to practice?"

"Oh yeah. Gimme a min." She pulled her phone to her face. "Lemme find it. It'll be fine, no worries."

"Well, I'm grateful for this distraction. I've kinda been having a hard time, and I hate the holidays to begin with."

"Oh yeah?"

"Yeah, I mean, I don't do Christmas and would rather just skip the whole thing. But Twig and I just broke up and that was pretty sudden."

"Hm, oh here it is." She kept her eyes on her screen. "I know, I have bad luck with men."

"Me too. I really fell for him, but he's got a bad temper. I'm so over angry, unstable men."

"Oh, lemme read this to you, Robyn. Talk about bad luck." She hit a few things, then moved her fingers up and down her phone screen.

"This is my last message to a man who's been trying to date me for like six months. This is what I told him. 'You say you're always truthful and love everybody. Well that's not true if you call liberals *libtardians*. You say I shouldn't rule out men who have different politics. Lemme tell you, it isn't only politics,' Harlotta nodded in agreement with her own words. 'It's what kind of person you are in your soul and if you're honest. Anybody who loves the President like you is a pig of the worst kind. I don't ever pretend to be somebody I'm not. Leave me the fuck alone!'"

She cackled and glanced at me proudly.

"That's pretty clear," I nodded. "Did you hear back?"

"Not yet, but he usually takes a couple days. I just sent it. There's someone else anyway." She looked up at me for a split second, then abruptly shot her head down. "Okay. Are you ready? We can keep reading from the script until we have it memorized."

"Was everybody seeing this stuff and acting as though they weren't? Was insanity just a matter of dropping the act?"
—Susanna Kaysen

"Sure, let's do it."

"Oh, one more thing, Robyn, we get to dress up in period costumes. You get to get all fancy to play Annie. I wear an old-fashioned flowery long dress and bonnet and stuff. That's my favorite part. Anyway, okay"—she finagled her phone again—"I got it."

Period costumes. Period pieces. Periods. The period. A period. Justin and I used to joke about it. Like, what's a "period piece," if not a pad or tampon? Imagine having to hold up your skirt, then your petticoat, remove your corset, bustle, panties, and then your period piece when you're on your period and have to go potty.

Ricky goes potty without a period piece! Go Ricky! Bad Robyn, mocks the period piece. Pee in cup, pay big price. Bad girl. Pray for hole and keep it covered.

We used to read from Justin's vast assortment of encyclopedias, sharing facts about the petticoat, for example, which isn't a coat at all. It's a skirt. Well, it started as one. Whence Americans turned it into a slip, though, we termed it a—insert immature giggle "dickey."

Justin did an impeccable Alex Trebek impersonation. "It's another term for a dickey," he'd say.

"What is a 'detachable bosom', Alex." I'd reply, and we'd both giggle in juvenile elation.

"For bonus money, Alex, I'd like to underscore that dickeys had tabs to prevent them from popping up unexpectedly."

My laughter, in synchronicity with Justin's, got so out of control, it turned to tears.

Sigh.

It's hard to reconcile that with his terribly troubled, sinister side. I don't understand it. Was he performing for me? Was that his real self before he took a serious drop into the dank recesses of mental illness?

It's probably all real: his and our madness, our love and hatred, sanity and insanity.

It's probably also unreal. That type of freely uninhibited loving connection—that good of a man with whom I'd share exuberantly playful, lasting love. A fantasy.

Especially beyond the thirties, it seems near impossible to find a single man who isn't a jerk or lunatic or self-serving dumbass upon first encounter. In fairness, women are batshit crazy. (I'm only man-bashing for the moment because I'm a straight woman. Thankfully, though, I'm not involved with another highly charged, overcomplicated female. I can't imagine.)

If I played for the other team, would I even be drawn to an empowered woman like myself? Probably not. It's the seemingly sweet, woefully wounded man that yanks pathetically on my heartstrings time and again. Like now with Paul Revere. Well, that's my nickname for him.

When I danced in a big crowd to live Dead music—or Dead live music—this past Saturday night, I found myself smiling at a man inches from me on the crowded floor. His glass lenses, thicker than the high-powered telescope at our local observatory. That, added to the fact that he called himself an "urban camper when not a couch surfer," accentuated by a giggle-snort, seemingly attracted me so much that I found myself in a lip-lock with him as the night progressed. I enjoyed this rush of unexpected fun.

The performers cleared their equipment from the stage, and Revere put my number in his phone. He even tossed out a possible New Year's date, to confirm his interest.

As it goes, there was no next-day phone call.

Two days later, correspondence ensued.

"I tried to text you. Bad signal. I don't think you got it."

"Drats. No worries. It was fun to meet you. I hope to see you again soon."

"Are you free this weekend?"

"Not Friday. Saturday, yes."

No message until Sunday from Revere.

"Sorry to keep you hanging. I couldn't make it. Brunch now to talk about the logistics of a proper date?"

"Right now? No, I can't, catching up on lots of things. Need some notice, but thanks for asking."

"How about Wed?" Wait, 'Wed?' You want to marry me? You can't even manage to call me!

He then sent a blurb about a music event the next Wednesday.

"Well, I've other things planned that night, but maybe we can connect to meet afterwards, since I'll be a few doors down from the show."

"Keep in mind Western Union works in a pinch."

"Ha! I'll send smoke signals."

After I wrote this, I realized that perhaps Revere was serious. I did a bit of googling to investigate. Who knew, besides him? The telegraph method of communication still exists.

The man was serious. He doesn't use his phone to actually contact me, yet he expects I'll send him telegrams? I just—no words.

"I thought you were kidding about Western Union," I wrote. "This is taking too much work. Best of luck to you."

Sigh.

Thing is, Mr. Revere, I'm afraid you want someone from a different period. Keep that dickey tabbed. That detachable bosom shalt ne'er pop up. Those nasty impetuous period pieces. Period costumes. Oh shit, I needed to make sure I had my lines memorized. Tomorrow I'd perform.

<u>Ben Carson, Trump's Secretary of Housing and Urban Development</u>: "The doors of the world are open to dose who can read."

Showtime loomed, as a few sweet female thespians helped me with the many buttons, snaps, and fasteners of my exquisite costume. Clothes had been tailored to fit me perfectly; it's an impressively dedicated crew.

I felt like royalty in an evergreen silk and dark green velvet gown. My hair curled and pinned up, I may've even done Annie justice.

The show went very smoothly. Most fun for me, the adorable young girls who gawked and wanted to get pictures with me afterwards.

Thank goodness I didn't have to wear a corset, the garb that prevents a lady from slouching at the price of suffocation and a crunched rib cage.

But I did wear a bustle to add tush to my tush. My tush is much smaller than my bust. But it's not flat. Still, it's not nearly enough to lift the skirt. Why it's called a bustle, when it lifts the butt and not the bust? I don't know. That's probably America's fault.

<u>President Trump, 12/24/17</u>: People are proud to be saying Merry Christmas again. I am proud to have led the charge against the assault of our cherished and beautiful phrase. MERRY CHRISTMAS!!!!!

With the show behind me days earlier, I decided to push myself to work on this book. A change of setting, wherein I'd be more focused, was needed.

My office? Ember couldn't possibly be there on Christmas Day. At any rate, it was after 2 p.m. on a Monday, and thus my designated time—if worst came to worst, I could kick her out.

It would. Worst met worst, that is. The front door was unlocked, all lights on. Seriously, on Christmas Day?

I opened my office door to find Ember sitting alone on the loveseat, face dropped towards her lap and phone on her knees. She abruptly looked up, horrified. "Oh my God, don't you ever knock?"

"Sorry to startle you, Ember, but it's almost 2:30," I looked at my watch. "It's my time to have the space."

"I pay my portion of rent, Robyn! I just need to finish something, and my home is too loud right now. My folks are in town, and there's a neighborhood Christmas Festival."

"Okay, well, take whatever time you need. I'll wait in the waiting room."

"Oh, how kind of you!" She rolled her eyes.

"Yep," I strolled to the waiting room, laptop in hand, sat on a well cushioned chair, closed my eyes and breathed deeply.

"Yeah, the bitch kicked me out again. I can't believe how rude she is!" Ember stormed by me, phone to her ear, then out the front door, which she slammed shut.

"Merry Christmas to you too, sweetie!"

She popped her head back in. "What did you say?"

"Oh, I said Merry Christmas."

Ember emitted a subtle, definitive "Fuck off" and shut the door with a bit less steam this time.

Geeze. God bless her clients-to-be.

The afternoon traded itself down from shitty to much shittier. I couldn't focus.

Within an hour, I headed back home.

There, I opened my Facepalm page to a shocking sight. At the top of a stream of posts, Harlotta stood hand in hand with—wait!—he's tall and skinny, wearing a cap and holding a beer bottle—Whoa, it's, I think it's, it looks like Twig.

Her post headline: "Christmas announcement, this is my new man!!"

My heartbeat spun into overdrive. I felt as though my jaw dropped miles below sea level. What the hell? I couldn't believe it.

Yeah, I broke up with him. But yeah, this really bites. A friend? Were they fucking all along?

Although tempted to respond to the post itself, I didn't. I refused to be seen as connected to either of them. They looked like juvenile dorks. I'd rather pretend my relationship with Twig never happened.

I thus messaged Harlotta privately: "You're dating my ex? I would NEVER date a friend's ex. That's wrong. I've had you in my home, and I confided in you about our breakup, all the while with you two starting something? I feel betrayed and disrespected by both of you."

No response for several days.

"So, what, you're just going to just ignore me, when I live a few doors down from you? How will you keep that up?"

"Nobody's ignoring you," she replied the next day. "I've been extra busy rehearsing for another show and hiking with Twig and things. We didn't get together to hurt you, and we hope you can find a way to heal through this trying time."

Could you be more patronizing?

Why is the standard response to a situation like this, "We didn't do it to hurt you"? Of course you didn't. You don't give a shit about my feelings. That's the damn point. And having to find out on Facepalm—that just adds a hearty dose of toxic salt to an open wound.

"I only have one thing left to say," I concluded: "Karma. It's real. Ciao, neighbor."

"Be the bigger person," my beloved blog readers and close friends advised. "It won't last, Robyn," they consoled.

As far as being the bigger person, well, I can't help my diminutive stature. And have you seen Harlotta? She's extra thick and wide. Given Twig's obvious affinity for the large edition, it's odd that he wanted to date economy sized me.

She's a hell of a lot less independent. Perhaps there's a happily dysfunctional codependence going on.

Would they stick? I thought and feared they might.

Regardless, what still irks most is the serrated knife she left to bleed out my backside. Until this happened, I didn't realize how aggressive some women can be when they target a particular man. Not that a woman is fully accountable for affairs, of course. I simply didn't realize that "girl code" means nothing to some or many.

It all caused fury. It's as if I meant nothing to him, and I can't imagine doing this to someone I loved. I also can't imagine doing that to a friend, neighbor, acquaintance. Shit, I just wanted a peaceful place post-Twig, not this dose of drama.

I'd taken a solo excursion to Wilbur Hot Springs when 2017 shifted into 2018. I had to get away. I'm glad I did. It helped relax and rejuvenate me.

Back home, I walked to the mailboxes and there she was, retrieving her mail.

<u>Note to self:</u> Don't continue this awkward silence.

"Hello," I said matter-of-factly.

"Hi Robyn. Happy New Year."

I hesitated.

<u>Note in response to note to self:</u> Say "Karmic New Year."

<u>Note in response to response to note to self:</u> Don't say "Karmic New year."

<u>Note in infinite response to self:</u> What the fuck do I do?

And then, a "k" sound tried to slip through my lips, but "Hh, Happy New Year" made it out instead.

I did good. I was the bigger person, the better woman, neighbor, and friend.

Did I feel better? Not a damn bit.

Thing is, I care greatly for the world. I've created change in too many ways to mention. I believe that lives across the globe are precious, especially young lives. Everyone deserves housing and food, water, medical care and all of the things that are needed for survival.

Except my neighbors. I hate them with every ounce of my being.

Karma, please be real. And real bitchy.

Chapter 20: Disorderly Conduct

"The Edge . . . There is no honest way to explain it because the only people who really know where it is are the ones who have gone over."—Hunter S. Thompson

As days crept into weeks, then months, it stuck. Meaning, they stuck. And from the looks of things, Twig had even moved in with Harlotta. My ex became my neighbor.

I'd loathe seeing his car daily. I'd hate parking next to her clunky sedan in the carport. My innards twisted into an embittered knot at the sight of either of them.

All she had to do was apologize, and things would've been less awkward. She broke "girl code" instead. She pretended nothing was going on between them. Her desire for a man eclipsed any thoughts about someone else's feelings, or any consequences whatsoever. What would it be like dating my neighbor's ex? Checking the mailbox from the same spot? Doing laundry at the same time? I doubt she considered any of it.

Like many women, she bases her worth on whether or not she has a man. Harlotta went so far as to snag a friend-neighbor's guy, think nothing of it, and post a boastful photo for all to see. Including said friend-neighbor.

Well, we weren't really friends. Yet we live in such close proximity, you'd think she'd have paused. But that insatiable yearning for a man, her sole drive.

As for Twig, the dweeb wanted to escape a tense housing situation. He found someone with much lower standards than me, and with whom to get drunk on the regular. They're perhaps a solid match.

They're similar in lacking self-respect. He chose her, a few doors down from me and a lot less appealing in various ways. Who's next—the leaf blower who does community service for reduced jail time?

I'm certain he's feeling proudly vindicated too. I ended things after I dared to poke a tender wound. You shouldn't communicate about hard stuff in a relationship. Especially not about suicide. Don't address that. Ignore it. It goes away.

Bad Robyn—she tries to talk about relatable and devastating mental health traumas. How dare she!

But I get it.

What man wants to engage in dark discourse with his partner, when he can instead live in substance-induced oblivion with her all day, every day? And she houses him too? Twig made the lazy choice.

Point of fact, dear reader: As I wrote "Twig" in the above sentence, he walked by my front window. It's strange to see more of my ex than I did when we dated.

Don't worry, though. I've remained mature, unless she starts something. He never does.

That's a lie, that part about my maturity. A few times, I intentionally parked a bit too close for comfort, making it difficult for her to pull her car out.

Damn Tourette's. Those motor tics have minds of their own, you know?

It seems I'm also prone to verbal tics too, because I've shouted "Skank!" as she walked by my front window, once or twelve times.

But I knew I should stop. It's a new year. I don't want things to get worse. I need to be the bigger, stable one here.

<u>President Trump, 1/2018</u>: "[I was elected] to President of the United States (on my first try). I think that would qualify as not smart, but genius and a very stable genius at that!"

"She's talking shit about you again, Robyn," Morty informed me. Morty's a friend from NorCal Dems4Peace. He forwarded Harlotta's Facepalm post:

"Robyns the worse person in the world! She talks smack about people, she's a child psykiatryst and she acts like one!"

I emitted a laugh-snort.

If only I was paid a Big Pharma six-digit psychiatric salary. Twig and Harlotta both knew that I'm a therapist, I thought. Strange, yet flattering.

"I don't care what she says about you, Robyn. You need a break. Can I take you out for drinks this weekend?"

Shit.

Morty likes me. Morty's a grandpa. Not a modern-day youthful grandpa. More, a there-are-some-white-hairs-sprouting-from-his-nostrils-and-you're-creepy grandpa.

"Thank you," I wrote, "I'm really strapped for time these days, and I don't drink. I'll take a rain check."

That's fine, right? A polite rejection that's not a real rejection. Besides, it rarely ever rains in Chico; I'd be safe.

"You bet. Take care."

"Take care, Morty."

I don't understand it. I've seen Morty flirt with much younger women too. One couldn't have been older than 30. I've been called close-minded by men who, at 60+, said I should be open to dating them. They're fit, after all, and great catches.

Dudes, look, I designated my age range in my dating profile. Read it. Accept it. Respect it. You're not going to endear yourself by degrading a gal.

Men can go younger, but a woman can't? Or she has to accept a date by any man, no matter his age? That's not only misogynistic, it's delusional. Not until I'm a senior citizen will I consider dating one. If he's a good one.

That said, celibacy seemed fine. I was good with it. In fact, life generally calmed down as the New Year approached.

Weeks after my verbal and motor tics subsided—without medication too!—I stepped out to put a few items in my car. I froze in hesitation. Harlotta was by the mailboxes, a handful of steps from the carport. Today's parking job on her part was much worse than my taunts. This time, her car was so dangerously close that I wouldn't be able to open my car door without hitting her crap-on-wheels.

Enough time had passed. I'd be the bigger person.

I moved towards her, cautiously confident.

"Would you please not park so close to my car?"

Harlotta raised her head from her mailbox, beaming eyes and tightened facial muscles.

She stormed to the carport. "Look! This is halfway! See this line!" Note: There were and are no lines in the carport. "I'm not over the line! Geezer lets me park here! I'm not in your sp—!"

I opened my car door to prove my point. "I can't even open this without hitting your—"! My door tapped her car.

Her eyelids shot wide open. Harlotta grabbed her front door handle, swung her door open viciously and slammed it against my car. Then again. And again.

Fuck.

A long vertical streak of red paint now decorated my black Prius.

Her sturdy chest met my face as Harlotta forced her way past me. I felt as though I'd been rammed by a wall of pure brick-lard, but I managed to maintain my footing.

She then spun to face me, her phone in hand. "I'm taking pictures! Oh and my therapist Ember says she knows you and you're the worse person in the world!"

I heard noise that I can best describe as wicked cackling, as she darted away towards her apartment.

"Touch me or my car again, and I'll call the police!"

"You're just jealous," she yelled from her front lawn, "because Twig wants me, not you."

"Be his sugar mama. I don't care. Ask about his son too. He loves that!"

Her face turned a darker shade of angry flesh pink. Oh shit, she might want to end me now. I scurried into my apartment and heard "Fuck you!"

With shaky hands, I turned the dead bolt.

From my side window, I watched Geezer enter the scene. Rather, he made his appearance known. Apparently he'd been spying, and he took her side. He scrambled over to Harlotta. They stood in front of her door, pointed and glanced my way, gossiping.

What the hell? Fuck them both.

Damn.

Calm down. Breathe, breathe.

I called Brandi.

"Don't wait. You have to call the police, Robyn."

I saw my hands shaking as tears shot down my cheeks. "Shit. I can't believe this."

"I know, Robyn, but these things are why people go ballistic these days. Does she own guns?"

"No, I doubt it. She's actually liberal. A liberal fuckin crazy bully! I think they're, we're, the worst!"

"Yeah, there's crazy ass shit going down all around. You need to make a police report, Robyn."

Brandi was right.

A pleasant and factual officer took my phone call report. I requested an in-person visit, to have a cop with me when I draw clear lines with Harlotta. I refused to live in fear like this.

They couldn't send someone out until the following day, I was told.

Waiting and waiting. Do I call the emergency line? The nonemergency line? I tried both. Again and again. "Ms. Engel, is this you again?" they asked.

Shit. "Yes, I'm sorry. I got confused and have been waiting for hours for someone to come by. I don't know how long she'll be home for. Her car's there now."

"This is the emergency line. You can't abuse it."

Sigh. I guess fear makes me feel impatient, needy and seemingly crazy. Or plain crazy. Is fear the root of insanity? Seems feasible. Now it was.

Needing to do something with my angst, I drove to my car dealer. An hour later, I walked away with a written estimate for the damage: $154.83, to be exact.

Back at home, I got busy with the rest. My insurance would send written indication that this was entirely her fault, they told me, after they received photos of the damage. I took and sent several pictures.

Then came the knock at my door. The officer was nice looking, mind you, but very haggard—bags under his eyes bigger than any carry-ons I've taken through the airport. Okay, not quite, but they stood out.

I explained the scenario thoroughly.

"She didn't actually hurt you, so what's the problem, ma'am?"

Really? "I'm frightened to have to live by her now. She still parks right next to me, and it's not even her spot. I have the estimate for the car damage. Can I show you?"

"I don't need to see that. I'm just trying to understand what you want me to do."

"I was hoping you would talk with her, with me there. She's really big." I extended my arms to indicate a width the size of Oprah Winfrey's waist every other month.

"Look at me. Please understand. I'm very small, and I'm scared of her. I need you to talk with her because you have a uniform and you're a man with guns." Oops.

"Guns? Now I'm concerned about you, ma'am. Honestly, you're the one who's threatening."

"Please, please let me explain. I'm honest. I'm a good person. I'm a social worker and therapist and author. I mentioned guns only because my friend said that these incidents lead to gunfire sometimes in this crazy world and she doesn't want me to get hurt or killed and she told me I had to call the cops so I did. Harlotta's intimidating and you could intimidate her with your guns." What the fuck am I saying? Buy my books?

"You want me to threaten her, I see."

"No, no. I said that wrong." Can I give you free copies? Autographed.

"You want me to shoot her?" He shook his head. "Ma'am, I really question your mental stability."

"I'm sorry. I say the wrong things sometimes when I'm really scared. I'm only four foot, eight." If only I was crying, that would help. It didn't happen. "It's just that I had a roommate call the police on me before, and—"

"So you've been reported for this type of volatility before?"

"No, no. Please. You can read that report, if there was one, and both officers—"

"It took two officers?"

"I, I don't know why they sent out two for domestic violence. No, I mean, Carrie was a real nut. I took her blow-dryer, that's all. I didn't steal it, though. She left it in the bathroom by my side of the sink and I was raging mad about it because she left her hair all over the bathroom."

<u>Note to self:</u> Robyn, shut up already.

<u>Note in response to note to self:</u> Noted.

The officer scratched his forehead, then covered his mouth to conceal a yawn. Thank goodness he wasn't fully alert.

"Alright, look. I'll go talk to her, but I don't see how this is going to solve anything. You need to stay here and calm yourself down. Don't come with me."

"I won't, I won't." I raised both hands, palms towards him, surrender style.

What the hell? I'm not the criminal. Am I? I did nothing wrong. Right?

Harlotta stepped out to show the cop photos of our cars in the carport. She indicated to him that she hadn't parked across the (imaginary) line in the carport. It looked to me as though he also saw that imaginary line. Was it not imaginary?

Dude, tell her to never damage my car again. Tell her to leave me alone. Can't you see how big and wide she is?

I watched her shake the officer's hand. "If she gives you any more problems," he said as he handed her his card.

The officer returned to me.

"Look ma'am, she seems to be the reasonable one here. I suggest you stay away from each other. I told her that too. Don't provoke her, and you clearly won't have anything to worry about. The landlord can deal with the parking situation. That's not my job. Like I said, just don't provoke her."

Play nice. He thinks I'm crazy. He might be right.

"One must be sane to think clearly, but one can think deeply and be quite insane."—Nikola Tesla

"Okay," I told the depleted cop. "Thank you very much. I do appreciate your time and help."

"You're welcome."

"Oh, um, one more question. Can I get a written report about the incident?"

"Yes. You should be able to get that at the station on Monday."

"Great. Thanks again."

He nodded and disappeared.

Exhausted too, I got ready for bed.

"I'm trying to mellow out, finally," I told Brandi, just before she sprang new information on me.

"When I went to review *The Tumpeter's New Clothes,* I saw that Harlotta wrote some shit about you."

"Oh damnit. What the hell? She's trying to bring me down any way she can."

With Brandi on the phone, I signed into my book reviews and read aloud in a stupidly whiny, pathetic tone:

Robyn Engel is the worse writter in the world and terrible women. What ever you do do not bye her books! I'm pretty sure she stoled the idea for this stupid book. It seems too familiar. Don't bye it!

"Um, yeah, that's why it's called a parody. Ya think I stole-d-ed the idea from Hans Christian Andersen, Brandi?" I chortled. "Holy shit. I guess you can't unglue stupid from crazy these days."

"No kidding."

"I mean, bad publicity is good. But I'm still hoping Trump will sue me, not this bitch."

Brandi laughed.

"This is just too good to not blog about it."

That I did. Meaning, I posted a summary about my altercation with Harlotta, including Geezer's allegiance to her. It's too good of a story. My readers deserve to know.

They were incredibly supportive too, told me to be the bigger person and all. I could only reply that I'm less than half her size, but I'd try.

Thing is, I had no idea she'd see my blog. But she did. Perhaps Geezer was an anonymous follower, having nothing else to do but intrude on every aspect of my life. So he tipped her off.

"Hello this is the Skank," she commented on the blog post. "I have all the evidents I need on you. I'm ready to film you any time. You lying terrible women. You assaulted me and called the police. Watch your back! Your horrible!"

Damn, okay. I'm officially scared again.

It's a lousy status—feeling unsafe in your own domain. I didn't step outside at all that day, except to check my mail, and that was only when I saw nobody around.

Wish I hadn't done that.

One business envelope rested in the box. I ripped it open to find a letter from Geezer:

I hereby request that you cease and desist from writing about us on your blog on the grounds that it is detrimental and hurtful. I will seek legal representation should you continue this behavior.

Seriously? You're threatening to sue me for my freedom of speech and of the press and even when I used a fake name for you and Harlotta? I could've used your real names, and you'd still have no grounds for a lawsuit.

Get a fuckin life!

Over the next few days, I wrote various versions of response letters to Geezer and Harlotta. Still, I need to be the level-headed one. I didn't deliver any of them. I'd let it die for now.

Geezer and Harlotta get plenty of attention in *InSanity*, but they'll have to purchase it. Heck, I'm still hoping for a real lawsuit, one to take my books into skyrocketing sales. I should probably expedite things by using their real names, but who wants to hear about my neighbors with boring names like—oops. You almost got me good, there. Silly, sneaky reader.

Months later now, I'm still perplexed by Harlotta's reactionary flip of reality. I was the oppressor, in her mind. Yet she moved in on Twig and then Twig moved in with her. As if I don't exist, she boasted publicly about it. She crazily damaged my car and then technically assaulted me when she pushed past me. In the meantime, she was all over social media in attempts to bring me down. How do people flip reality for delusion so shamelessly, readily, bizarrely?

My brain reminds me of the term, "projection." I learned Freud's paradigm of ego-defense mechanisms as a Psychology student at UCLA. None of it seemed relevant. Until nowadays, I hardly ever noticed projection. Now, though, it's hurled all over the place. Levels of projection are ever-rising, in sync with cyber mockery and bullying.

<u>Per Wikipedia.com</u>:

Projection - Psychological projection is a defense mechanism in which the human ego defends itself against unconscious impulses or qualities (both positive and negative) by denying their existence in themselves while attributing them to others. For example, a bully may project their own feelings of vulnerability onto the target.

As far as my housing status, the officer must've been too exhausted to amend the report I gave by phone. Phew. Harlotta was clearly at fault in writing, as in reality.

With that and my car estimate, added to the insurance note indicating my innocence, I made a trip to property management.

I asked to speak with CEO Richie Evole.

Surprisingly, Richie was in. "You're fortunate, I was about to run out," he told me, "but I can give you two minutes of my time." He walked me to a private conference room and shut the door.

"Thank you so much, Mr. Evole. I was assaulted by my neighbor, and there's evidence that she also damaged my car. I'd like management to do something, so it doesn't happen again. There could be an easy solution, since there's an open parking space for apartment twelve."

"I see," he flipped through the papers I'd provided. "Well, Krissy's the manager of that building. I'll talk with her about this. She'll get back with you as soon as possible."

"Okay. Please do follow up. As things are now, I don't feel safe."

Richie looked at his watch. "Hm mm, I need to run." He extended his hand.

"Thanks so much for your time, Mr. Evole."

Stupid formalities. Lip service. Posers, me included.

Per usual, Geezer sat close to my front door, upon my return home.

"Not again! What do I have to do to get you to stop sitting here? Call the cops on you too? I'm so sick of this! There's plenty of lawn. Stop blocking my fuckin door! What will it take?"

"You don't, I'm not—." He jumped up, grabbed his chair, skirted inside, and slammed his door.

5/2018: First Lady Melania Trump launched an anti-bullying campaign called "Be Best."

KNOCK, KNOCK, KNOCK.

Shit. What now?

It was Krissy, the apartment manager, in a formal business suit, nylons, and heels, as if she has the world's most important job.

"This is for you." Krissy handed me a sealed, business-sized envelope, then turned and walked away.

"What? What is this?" I shouted. "Is there something I should know?"

As she opened the door of her snazzy sports car, Krissy said "It speaks for itself!"

I slumped on my couch and tore open the envelope:

Dear Ms. Engel,

You are hereby issued a 3-day notice of eviction due to threatening your neighbor with physical assault.

Whoa, what?

I called Richie Evole, in tears. "I don't understand. I gave you all that information, and you're evicting me?"

"Well, you threatened a dear elderly man, Miss Engel."

"I don't know what you're talking about."

"Geezer's been a reliable tenant for almost 10 years. We take his word for it. He said you threatened him with violence when he was just sitting outside."

"That's not true! You're telling me I have to leave? Within three days?" I can't believe this.

"Not necessarily. But you need to stop that behavior or we'll be forced to proceed with the evictions process."

I ended the call, highly panicked.

"Find a lawyer," I said out loud.

That took, naturally, more work than I'd hoped for. Apparently my property management has been sued before, and the only local housing firm in town was defending them. I had to find out-of-town counsel.

"I'm hearing a lot of complaints about them," my soon-to-be-retained attorney reported. I liked her too, and the fact that she's a wicked sharp *her*. It doesn't escape me how fortunate I am to have been able to afford legal counsel, or how ridiculous it is that this is what it took to be able to keep my rental.

Of course, everything took longer than it seems to you, dear reader. It wasn't until my attorney wrote a stellar letter or two to the management that I started to feel comfortable at home. By this time, it was the summer of 2018.

I also started progressing with work, this book, and re-establishing a semblance of zen.

As things go, an unwanted man disturbed my tranquility.

"You have a birthday coming up," Morty messaged. "I need to redeem my rain check and take you out for dinner. How's next Friday night?"

Shit.

I got myself into this mess by not being clear. "Okay, but I have a lot going on, so can you do a quick bite at the taqueria across from the plaza? Say 6 p.m.?"

Come Friday, Morty paid six dollars for my taco. In front of the cashier, he then asked casually, "Do I get to spank you for your birthday?"

"No! Now you're pushing it!" I guarded my taco and moved my tuchas out of his arms' range.

I mean, if a man pays (only) six dollars for my taco, he isn't entitled to spanking rights too.

As we sat across from each other—Morty with a fat burrito, me with a small, moist taco, he asked about my weekend plans. "I'm free all weekend, if you happen to be too." Oy.

I told Morty that I don't wish to date. I'm happily single.

"That's too bad," he lowered his head, dejected.

"I have too much I'm focused on, lots of writing and political advocacy and stuff. Work too, of course."

"Well, I'm not necessarily talking about a relationship, Robyn. I was simply hoping we could have some fun together this weekend. See where it goes from there." He raised his gray bushy eyebrows.

Gross. "I'm really too stressed these days, sorry."

He leaned in closer to me, a sour cream-salsa-guacamole mixture dripping from his mouth, "I could help relax you."

Barf.

Paul Revere, wherefore art thou now? I'd rather have you. Or Scorpio, or George, Jeff, anyone else. Or nobody else. Please. Make it stop.

"Sorry. I'm best alone. Really. I don't want to date, Morty. And I'm still anxious about the neighbor problems."

"With Harlotta? Is it that bad?"

"Yeah, it got really bad."

"I do know a good lawyer in town."

"Thanks. Actually, I have one. I'm good."

"I see."

"I'm just kinda still frazzled by the whole thing, and I'm good being single."

"Okay, well, I'm done, and it looks like you're about finished too."

Morty dabbed his chin with a napkin, stood up and turned his back to me. "If you change your mind about some fun," he pushed the exit door before finishing, "you know how to find me."

Okay then. I'm being ghosted because I rejected Morty.

"Okay. Thanks for dinner." But not really. My taco is worth more than six dollars, old man. Fuck you, but not really. Just no. Not ever. I can take care of myself. Me and my taco, we'll be just fine.

<u>President Trump</u> described Canadian Prime Minister Justin Trudeau as "very dishonest and meek."

When I saw Morty last weekend at a Dems4Peace event, he said that he'd noticed I was a very small girl in a 1970s photo I'd posted on Facepalm. Um, yes. I was very small. Perceptive grandpa.

"You know now, medically speaking," Morty continued, "you'd qualify as a mi—".

I know, right!?

Distracted by a phone call, Morty walked a few steps away to talk on his phone.

He returned, "Well, I'm going swimming with the grandkids. See ya."

Okay, Morty. Are you trying to tell me you're striving for shrinkage so you can date and spank a medical midget?

I thought I'd heard the worst of it. But this one, sigh.

Could it get worse? Of course.

Driving home I spotted Harlotta standing on her lawn, seemingly stepping out for air.

Upon noticing me, she shouted "Fuckin jealous little bully bitch!" whilst wildly waving both of her third fingers at me.

Sweet.

"Fuck you, skank!"

Damn vocal tics.

Chapter 21: In the Balance

"I am interested in imperfections, quirkiness, insanity. We don't talk about planes flying. We talk about them crashing."
—Tibor Kalman

We're all about self-preservation; sometimes, some people, to an insane extent.

Take, for example, the unfaithful.

Too many people have experienced the shocking misfortune of walking in on one's lover in bed with someone else. What a jolt to the brain. How could this not send a person into insane rage? Only the insane would remain sane upon such a discovery.

Your domicile, your safe place, your own laundered bed sheets. Add to this, all the hormones that swirl, twirl, hurl and act crazy when our lover moves onto someone else—and you see it happening.

Even in this extreme scenario, however, culprits remain masterful at the art of manipulative blame. "How dare you invade my privacy. You said you were going to work! Do you even have a job? I'm sick of your lies!" Caught naked with another lover, the cheater turns themself into an innocent victim.

I can't comprehend this type of projection, when all the evidence is stacked against the perpetrator. It's as if there's no conscience in there whatsoever.

In the past five decades, <u>President Trump has been accused of</u> rape, sexual assault, groping, and other sex crimes by at least 25 females (minors included). He's claimed innocence to all counts: "This is a conspiracy against you, the American people."

For a victim to be completely negated, adds trauma to trauma. Who wouldn't be ready to kill the guilty party?

I mean, I'm not justifying murder under these circumstances. Well, not in writing. Not here on this page. And if accused of doing so, I'll deny it. I might even blame it on you for twisting things against me, dear reader. Devious grin.

All I'm saying is that I understand the emotional homicidal rage that anyone would likely feel in this scenario.

Let's hope that weaponry isn't within their reach.

The **insanity defense** is used in only about 1% of felony cases in the U.S. and is successful less than 25% of the time. Thus, it wins

I'm certain my ego couldn't handle it. I'm a confident, self-

fewer than 25 of every 10,000 felony cases per year.

respecting woman. Not so much that infidelity alone wouldn't temporarily destroy me, however. It would. Undoubtedly.

And if my man wants someone else, or if he already found someone else, he needs to break up with me before banging someone else. It's that simple.

I know my worth.

Well, not consistently. I don't always know it. I often question it. Heck, if I walked in on my guy screwing somebody else, I'd feel like shit. And that feeling wouldn't likely dissipate anytime soon. It's a potentially permanent ego scar.

The ego: the centerpiece of it all. We fight to the depth of our beings to develop, restore, strengthen, and preserve our fragile egos. At infancy, the nubile ego's demoralized by adults who never fully developed their own egos, because, well, who has? I mean, besides Nelson Mandela and Buddha.

"If you want the cooperation of humans around you, you must make them feel they are important, and you do that by being genuine and humble."—Nelson Mandela

Generations back were hard pressed to access compassionate resources. Nobody spoke about mental health issues. It's no wonder we're not healthy. We're completely off-balance and prone to insanity.

Well, I say "we," when I mean "those other people." Probably not you, dear. Not me either. I think I'm sane, stable, fairly reasonable, and reliable. Anyone who likes me and my writing is too. There's no crazy wackadoodle between us. Am I right?

<u>Note to self:</u> You do and would lose your mind in certain circumstances.

<u>Note in response to note to self:</u> Sure, but everyone deserves a free pass now and then. It's a fuckin crazy world in which it's abnormal to always be normal. I'm normal because I'm abnormal about some abnormal things during otherwise normal times, normally. We'll go with this premise, for self-preservation.

My biggest ego sting now was the neighborly situation. I stayed glued to it. And when I hadn't seen Twig's car for a full week, I checked Facepalm.

Harlotta's relationship status: "Single."

Whoa. They're done? Really?

It seemed so. What a relief! Karma, sweet karma. Thank you, bitch.

I don't care how or why, I'm just glad to not have that relationship flaunted in my face anymore.

"Sweet, crazy conversations full of half sentences, daydreams and misunderstandings more thrilling than understanding could ever be."—Toni Morrison

Admittedly, I'm not good enough to want the best for people who hurt me like that. Karma's my bud, while I still hate my neighbors. I'll leave "Love thy neighbor" to thine religious vile folks who spout gospel. Thoughts and prayers to the lot.

Meanwhile, things seemed overall better in my neighborhood. Perhaps because of my legal intervention, property management spoke with Geezer. The past few days he'd positioned his chair approximately 15 feet further from my doorway, no longer blocking it.

Ah, small victories—not enough, but significant nonetheless.

I'm still not motivated to converse with Geezer. Plus, I'm beyond injured to talk to Harlotta or Twig. I sure hope I get a decent new neighbor. (I recently noticed a vacancy sign at the apartment between their respective units.)

Anyway, I advise you not to worry about "Love thy neighbor." We don't have to love the mean-spirited or disrespectful. Sure, I respect those who are genuinely that openhearted. But that's not me, and I'm okay with that.

As I'd conveyed in *Woman on the Verge of Paradise*, my divorce and its aftermath took me to a new place. I truly don't want to remarry. I'm also not seeking a prince.

The warm-blooded, womanly part of me, though, had consistently craved coupledom with someone who's at least respectful and kind. That part kept me open, maybe too open (pun intended?).

Heck, I want a sex life throughout my life. Sex has gotten better, not worse, over time. Maybe there's something to be said for experience. And perhaps I'm attracting less uptight men, being so open (no pun intended this time?)

Let's face it, good sex is good for stress. It's good for the ego. It's good for its own sake. Good sex is just really good or even better—like no other earthly, unearthly experience.

Thus, I'd continue dating, or trying to date. Trying to have sex with a decent man, I mean. (The bar's been low, incorporating wiggle room regarding the definition of "decent".)

Along the way, I'd still fall for sappy pickup lines and very strange men. I'd end up feeling foolish, but I also know that you never know until you know, and then you still don't know. You know?

Meet Saul, because I did. Cute, cleancut, and playful. He delivered charming lines. "A pretty person like you often has a beautiful soul." That's all it took. I needed to meet him, even though I'd told Kevin not to set us up.

"No. I'm good being single, Kevin." I'd said. "Please don't but thanks."

We were at Studio Inn, both trying stand-up comedy as newbies. Kevin's married, though he doesn't seem at all happy about this and thus regularly warms barstools.

Without my knowing, Kevin told Saul, "Robyn's great. You should reach out to her."

Upon perusing Saul's page, I saw picture after picture of his arms around an exotic, sultry woman.

"Who's the gorgeous lady in your photos?" I inquired. Things had been going well. We'd been "chatting" online for nearly an hour. I really liked Saul. He'd said he was looking for a girlfriend too, so I naturally assumed he's single.

"What are you talking about?"

"The beautiful lady, Maritza? Is she a friend or a relative, or—emoji wink—?"

He barked, "She's only a friend! Please calm down!"

Whoa. "Okay, it's fine. A woman needs to be careful, that's all." You're telling _me_ to calm down, dude?

"No, no. It's not a thing to worry over. She wanted more but I don't. She is just a FRIEND! I still want to take you to dinner. I believe that friendship is the best start."

My mistake, my insanity perhaps, was NOT in asking that simple question. Nor did I err in asking Twig about his son. Nor in trying to calm Justin down every damn time he yelled at and criticized me. Nor was it in trying to convince George that my anger towards him for being too cowardly to drive in the rain was justified. Nor in giving Jeff a chance at friendship postbreakup—even though it didn't feel right. Nor in having dismissed my brother on his last day on earth because I had no other abilities, insight, or strength at that time.

A depleted martyr can't save anyone.

My mistake and perhaps my insanity was in _not_ prioritizing myself. In giving Saul a chance after that off-the-rails response. In wanting to be the one to love him "better" or "differently" than anyone else ever had, even though he'd caused me discomfort and pause.

In agreeing to every date that I didn't want to agree to.

In being nice every time I'm treated shabbily.

I should've listened to my instincts and said "No thank you" to dinner. I didn't put myself first. I don't do that with men. I still need to make this change and make it consistently.

Sometimes it works out. Temporarily. at least. Our brain tricks us into believing that it's good to put others before ourselves. Ultimately, it's not.

Saul and I were pleased upon meeting inperson. Dinner was great. We had friendly discourse about work, his family, my writing. Unlike most other dates, he picked up the bill without hesitation.

And then, better still, he invited me to his place. "I'll play music for you," Saul pointed at his guitar that stood upright against a brick fireplace.

His shiny black guitar across his lap, my suitor sang soft familiar tunes.

I sat entranced, falling for him a bit more with each note.

After a handful of John Denver, Celine Dion, and others' music, Saul played Josh Groban's "You Raise Me Up."

I envisioned Saul and I walking across stormy seas hand in hand.

Then the song abruptly ended.

Wearily, he set his guitar faceup on the floor.

"I'm done."

Saul dabbed his eyes with the back of his hands. "I feel too sad now. That song was for my ex-girlfriend Lydia. She died of a drug overdose last year. I don't think she really wanted to live anymore."

He stood up. "This"—Saul pointed at his guitar—"this is my priority. And I don't want a bad reputation."

Say what? Dating me would demote your social ranking? No dude, I raise them up. Never had a problem with that. Well, yeah I have. I mean, they did. It was their problem, not mine. They had, um, big issues. Well, not that big. Shit. You know what I mean.

Micromatters aside, I took Saul's macabre hint.

While slipping my jacket on, I grabbed my purse. Only twenty minutes after Saul had begun to serenade me, err, his dead ex-girlfriend, the date ended.

He gestured towards the front door.

"You have a GPS to get home, right?"

"Yeah, I have a GPS." But Lydia could raise me up and drop me at home faster, over stormy seas and stuff. She has that kind of power. Right?

At my car door, with Saul on the opposite side of my car, I said "Thank you."

Why'd I say that? I didn't know what else to say. I certainly wasn't grateful. My mistake.

Of course, now I have all sorts of words for him. For example: May you never raise it up again.

Sigh.

I get it. Grief is tough. There's no user manual. And what I term "passive suicide," trying or hoping to die without actively killing oneself—that's even more stigmatized and less talked about. So much so, no (other) professionals have given it a term, to my knowledge.

I understand all of this. But how could anyone think serenading a date with a song to their dead ex-lover is appropriate?

"We're just not a match," Saul told Kevin that night. He said nothing else about our date.

"Oh my God, Kevin. First, he fuckin sang a song to me, I mean for me, no, it was for his ex-girlfriend Lydia. Number two, she's dead. Fuckin dead. What the hell? I don't think I'm the problem."

"Wh,what?" Kevin looked slightly stunned and very much amused. "Oh, I remember once he mentioned an ex who died. I thought he'd moved on, though."

"No, he hasn't."

My hurt blocked any sense of compassion. "Tell him that I told you that he serenaded his dead ex-girlfriend," I smirked.

Kevin shook his head curtly. "I'm gonna leave this one alone, Robyn."

"Okay."

What could I say? I'm left unsettled. "Just please don't set me up again against my will."

"Hey, Robyn," he defended, "I was trying to be nice. Sorry it didn't work out."

"Yeah well, have a nice night."

"You too."

Kevin picked up his glass of whiskey—a bit on edge, he took a swig.

"In the war of Ego, the loser always wins."—Buddha

Chapter 22: Burnt Offerings

"Sometimes there's no cure for the crazy." Dale sighed, stroking my hair. "I think we all just have to keep loving through it. Maybe that's the cure."—Emme Rollins

Since his election, each day under the Trump Presidency seemed even worse than the last. We didn't think it would or could corrode, but it did. He did.

My view, however, was like watching a horror movie from a nicely cushioned seat in the back of a theater. I'm privileged in so many ways. None of President Trump's asinine and callous acts directly injured me.

Things would hit close to home, though, literally.

Two years to the day after his election, on November 8, 2018, my community was rocked in a horrifying way. Lost in the minutiae of my daily grind, I'd heard murmurs about a fire in Paradise but thought nothing of it.

Over the proceeding hours, though, word broke about the Camp Fire. Within one day, godawful flames had incinerated the entire town of Paradise—our lovingly gritty extended family that grew generation after generation of steadfast roots throughout its pine-infused annex.

Like most of Chico, I wanted to help.

As the weekend rolled around, buzz caught my ear regarding volunteer forces at the Walmart lot. With pen and paper, a face mask, and a quickly scribbled list of resources, I headed for Walmart.

Definitive folds on my left index finger marked my car door handle, as I prepared to step out.

<u>Note to self:</u> What do I do?

<u>Note in response to note to self:</u> Don't ask me. You know what to do.

I lied to myself. Nothing prepares a person for this kind of catastrophe, not even as a prospective helper. There's no time for truth. It was a good lie, I figured, shutting the car door with faux confidence.

My body propelled itself in a navigational manner through a patchwork of cars, trucks, motorbikes, humans. One by one, faces conveyed hollowed perseverance. When eyes met mine, I asked "Are you okay?" Every time, and remarkably, they said, "Yes, thank you."

I soon found myself amid vendors offering food and clothes. At a bench beyond the scurried activity, a woman gripped with one hand both a flier and a dog leash handle. I then eyed her lanky greyhound a few feet away.

I stepped around the loyal canine and approached.

"Hi, are you okay?"

"Well, I guess so. We're here somehow," she chuckled.

She showed me the flier and pointed at the third listing, one for a housing site in Yuba City—approximately 40 minutes away.

"Do you know if they have space? I don't mind Chico, but I wanna get a new start somewhere farther, lost it all anyway two days ago." She shrugged. "Again."

"Again?"

"Yeah, we were burned out in '08. This was way worse. These flames were 100 feet tall. Scariest thing I ever saw. Thought we were gonna die for sure. Now we gotta get somewhere and most places don't take pets. My boy, he's here"—she pulled her dog closer and ran her hand along his frail spine. "He needs to come with me." She kissed his head.

"Of course he does." I looked at her dog's heavy eyes, and then at the flier. "I don't know about this one. Would you like me to call?"

"Yes please."

"Sure." I pulled my phone out of my purse.

"I'm Robyn. What's your name?"

"Maggie."

"Lemme see what I can find out for you, Maggie."

It rang three times before I could leave a message.

"Nobody picked up," I told her. "I'll be back when I find out anything. Okay?"

She nodded. "We'll be here."

My body shifted towards an expansive stretch of faded grass, several football fields in size and spotted by rows of tents. Small groups of people clustered together between tents to share coffee, sandwiches, blankets, jackets.

A few yards beyond the activity, a man had positioned himself on the ground in front of his tent door. In statuesque manner, he sat with legs crossed. His hands encased his kneecaps, as if to keep them from popping off.

Check on him, I told myself. You know what to do. Ugh. Liar, liar, pants on—oops, probably shouldn't use that word now.

"I mean as, as big as they look on the tube [he gestures to form a square] you don't see it until they come here and what we saw at Pleasure, what a name, right now, wha, what we just saw, we just left Pleasure."—President Trump in Paradise, upon touring its burnt remains

The grass crunched beneath my sneakers, as I closed in on the angry man.

My ringer went off.

I looked at the stern-faced man. He looked at me. I raised my index finger to relay that I'd be right back. Great. Lousy way to win him over.

"Hello . . . . Yes, this is Robyn. Walmart, yeah . . . . Hundreds of people, but even more volunteers than Fire victims I think. It's amazing really . . . . I know, it's already getting super cold at night . . . Can they bring pets? . . . . Sounds great. I'll keep your number and get back when I can . . . . Thanks so much."

After that call from James, the CEO in Sacramento contacted me. Another very kind man. He emphasized that the space is in very good condition. It's 22,000 square feet. They'll provide food, clothing donations, whatever's needed.

I rushed back to Maggie. "Good news! That place has plenty of bathrooms and shower stalls. It's nice, large, and clean. They take pets. They'll have counselors there too."

Her face brightened. "Okay, that sounds good."

"So you should look out for a white van that's going to be transporting people there at 1 p.m. I'll try to get back here before then. Okay?"

"What time is it now?"

"It's, let's see," I pulled up my sleeve to check my watch. "It's 12:15. You have forty-five minutes."

"Okay, thank you."

I next found the booth with red-vested volunteers.

"Hi, I have info on a very nice shelter space in Yuba City," I told a middle-aged, red-vested man.

"Oh, not unless it's ours—is it Red Cr—"

"Well, no, but it's a viable option."

"I don't know. Who's in charge?"

I heard these words slip out of my mouth: "I'm in charge." Over fifty years as a human being on this planet, I'm not going to let a petty power play get in the way of doing the right thing.

"You're in charge?" He sounded skeptical. (How rude.)

"Yes, I'm the Site Director," I offered a handshake.

And hey, if you're going to lie about your job, give yourself a well-earned title.

"Okay, can I give out your number?"

"Yes, please do."

With my name and phone number in hand, he agreed to spread the word. Now to get back to angry man.

"I have a strong opinion, I want great climate, we're going to have that, and we're gonna have forests that are very safe . . . and we're gonna have safe forests."—President Trump

Angry man hadn't budged. "Hi, I'm sorry about that. I got interrupted there."

He shrugged. "I'm not fuckin important."

What do I say now? "Are you okay?" Dumb question.

Angry man pushed himself to a standing position.

His face reddened as he took two even steps towards me, then stopped.

"Am I doing okay? Am I okay? What the hell do you think, lady? What are you, some do-gooder who's about to tell me I have to leave, right?"

"Well, I do worry about folks being out here when the rains start."

"You're fuckin kidding me! I'm not budging."

I see that.

"Do you have any idea? Any idea what I've been through? I stayed. I stayed for 18 fuckin hours. I stayed to protect my home in Concow. Not just for me, for my neighbors, for my friends. I stayed and kept hosing it down, the lawns, the roofs, the trucks, everything. Only me and my buddy Dan stayed. And what do I get for that? It's all fuckin burned! The whole town."

He turned his head to his side and spit out a wad of saliva.

"My only home. My mama's home. Now you're telling me to leave. These people are feeding us and being nice to us. It's like family here. But I can't even get FEMA help because I lost my ID in the Fire. And you're telling me to leave. Fuck that!"

"You can't get FEMA help?"

"Nope, no ID. You have to have an ID."

That didn't seem right. "Can I make a phone call for you?"

His demeanor shifted. "Yeah."

"Okay," I extended my hand. "I'm Robyn."

"I'm Joseph. Hey, I'm sorry. I'm just," he huffed, "It's been one hell of a year."

Joseph's eyes welled.

"I'm really sorry."

I plopped down on the ground, pulled out my resource list, and called FEMA. Someone answered. She was helpful too. I wrote step-by-step instructions for Joseph, along with my name and number.

Joseph said he'd be fine taking it from there.

"I said, you gotta clean your floors, you gotta clean your forests."—President Trump

My ringer went off again. Katie wanted to help transport folks to Yuba City. She had two friends to help too. I'd meet them at the Walmart entrance in 20 minutes.

My ringer went off again. Matt has a truck. He's driving around looking for anyone in need of help with transport. I'd find him, then Katie. Hopefully, Maggie's okay. Joseph's on his way to the FEMA drop-in center, it appears. Need to call James back.

I soon coordinated rides for 10 people (two singles and one family) plus three pets. This included Maggie and her greyhound. I'd met seven volunteers, two of whom lost their homes in the Fire themselves. Yet the first thing they set out to do? Save lives.

"Three things in human life are important. The first is to be kind. The second is to be kind. And the third is to be kind."
—Henry James

Two months had passed when his call shook me.

"I'm at the Fairgrounds now," Joseph informed me. "They keep stealing my stuff. I can't even take a piss without my things getting stolen. I lost more since the Fire than I did because of it. I can't sleep at all, it's like—" his voice cracked. "The post-traumatic stress, it's real, Robyn. We have a curfew. We're cooped up like prisoners. I can't, I think, I hate to say it, but I think my cousin's been stealing my checks. I was gonna leave here. I dunno what to—I don't, I don't know, I dunno if I can make it."

I heard Joseph's tears.

"Listen, honey. Listen, okay?"

"Okay."

"You're not alone. I'm here. You're going to be okay, I promise." I lied; I couldn't guarantee a damn thing. "How can I help you now?"

"Can you take me to the drop-in center? I need to get it all started again."

"Sure. I'll meet you at the Fairgrounds tomorrow, but I can't get there until two o'clock. Okay?"

"Two?"

"Yes. That's as soon as I can. I have some appointments before then. Will you be there then?"

"I'll be here. I just . . ." his insides spilled out of him like the yolk of a freshly cracked egg, "Please, Robyn. Please," he begged. "Be a good person! Don't let me down."

"I won't, Joseph. I am." I hope. "I promise." Shit, I have no choice.

<u>President Trump said this about climate change:</u> "I don't think science knows actually."

I couldn't get there quickly enough. The Chabad Jewish Student Center had given me a warm jacket and the last of the cash they had on hand for Fire victims. "I'm sorry that we don't have more." She handed me an envelope with $300.

"We've just given away our eighth car. We're getting more donated too."

At the Fairgrounds' main entrance, I'm told Joseph's gone. "They took him by ambulance a couple hours ago. They said he might've had a heart attack."

"Oh my God. Do you know where he is?"

"I don't know. That's all I know."

At home, I studied my laptop screen, finding and recording numbers for the few local emergency rooms. My tears moved faster than the rest of me. Damnit, Joseph. I was supposed to save you. I can't do that if you drop dead on me.

Four nervous hours passed before my ringer went off.

Phew, his number. "Joseph?"

"Yeah, it's me, Robyn. It wasn't a heart attack. They said it was just anxiety."

"Oh thank goodness, Joseph."

"Yeah. Hey, you can call me Joey, by the way. It's what my close friends call me."

"I was so worried about you, Joey."

"I'm sorry."

"No, don't be sorry. I'm just so glad you're okay. Where are you now?"

We proceeded to make plans for the next day.

I don't remember our discourse as much as I do the sense of full-fledged genuine humanness.

Joey's eyes welled when I handed him the donated money. Moreso, my presence seemed to instill a newfound calm. As I drove him to the Camp Fire relief center, I realized that Joey and I had formed a relationship unlike any other.

There were no layers of complication, no unspoken agendas, no diagnostic labels, no shyness or bravado, no artificial pretenses or power plays—just two human beings, being human together.

Practically speaking, I didn't help much at all. In fact, Joey spoke competently to FEMA and other support representatives.

He could've gotten there on his own or with someone else. He'd still have to wait weeks for a new license plus word from FEMA.

"Someday, I've gotta write my story," he shared on the ride back to the Fairgrounds.

"That's great. Writing's my thing, Joey. I'll help you with it."

"Heck yeah. You can publish it for me."

"I will." I nodded. "I'll publish your story."

Note to you, dear reader: If you're reading this, I told the truth. If you're not reading this, you and I are both liars.

"Perfect," he nodded.

Back at the Fairgrounds, we stepped out of my car.

"Now you gotta let me give you a big hug," he said.

Joey and I exchanged a warm, grateful hug.

"You keep fighting, Robyn. I'll never forget you."

"Much better days are ahead, Joey. You're strong and brave. I'll be cheering for you all the way."

He nodded. "We'll stay in touch."

At that, Joey imparted a military style salute and walked off.

As I watched Joey fade away, I realized that I hadn't literally saved his life. My path's been cushioned in ways that I've routinely taken for granted.

Still, I did hold the world within view for one man who couldn't otherwise see a thing.

How I did that, I don't know.

I was simply a good enough person, who told a few good lies.

FACTS ABOUT THE CAMP FIRE:
It lasted from 11/8 to 11/25/18.
It incinerated an area the size of Chicago, of Indianapolis, an area the size of all these cities combined: San Francisco, Oakland, Berkeley, and Alameda.
153,335 acres burned
13,972 single-family homes burned
18,793 structures lost
85-88 identified dead bodies
296 or more unaccounted for; may likely never be identified. This number dropped quickly from public view and news streams. Locals have overheard emergency responders comment quietly about spots wherein "hundreds of bodies, huddled together, perished."

Chapter 23: MenNoPause

"I used to think I would never find someone who loved me as much as my ex did. Then I remembered, he hated me."
—Jennifer Hall

As friends do, Brandi had faded into the vague periphery of my mind. There comes a point at which you choose between a simple gratitude for the good times of the past, or a relentless struggle to resuscitate what's already dead.

When I saw her name on my phone one evening, I grinned. She didn't forget me.
"So great to hear from you, Brandi. It's been too long."
She spilled: "Robyn, I have big news! I actually have a boyfriend now."
"Woo-hoo. That is big news. You haven't had a relationship in years. You weren't look—"
"I know, it's crazy. It just happened for us, Robyn. We've been working together for four years and after things ended with you and Jeff, I started looking at him differently."
Whoa!
"Wait, you're with Jeff now? I mean, you set me up with him in the first place. You said you had no hormones, no urges, Brandi. You helped support me through that breakup. Jeff's not well. He'll cheat on you. I don't—"
She cackled. "Well, he rekindled my urges, Robyn. We were like brother and sister, but then things changed. What can I say? You told me the sex was so good, I started to see him differently." She guffawed.
"Wow Brandi, I'd never do this to a friend. I thought you wouldn't either."
"Oh my God, seriously, Robyn? It's not like we talk about you or ever even think about you. Not everything's about you Rob—"
"Okay, well good luck then. You deserve each other."
"Really, Robyn?" she chortled. "You're just jealous. I just hope you'll re-evaluate someday and realize how dramatic and selfish you're being. A real friend would be happy for me."
"Get help, Brandi."

Ugh, the twisted projectile of cheerily incised dismissal. Rejection. Betrayal. Dumped by a friend. Lonesome pain.

At times like these, all hurts and wounds from relationship breakups spiral through my mind, as if one seamless sequential array of disarray.

Yet, my dear reader, this chapter represents many years of dating interspersed with lengthy stints of celibacy.

I'm grateful that menopause, or premenopause, or whatever state my female body sans female body parts takes (at 47, I had a full hysterectomy), didn't affect my libido. I mean, it did. It improved it.

Thus, without pause, henceforth, musings of men traverse my brain waves.

A spike in loneliness propelled me to a comedy show, and I was invited to its after-party.

The man who bestowed the invite is a hysterical, charming comic.

"Sounds fun, but I don't do drugs or drink at all," I told him.

"It doesn't matter, Robyn. Come anyway."

I sat in the corner of a dark brown leather couch, amid a surreal drug trip, sober.

A man to my right, someone from that circuit who'd intrigued me, struck up discourse.

Huey, we'll call him, is approximately three times my size—with a humongous belly.

"Hey, what's your situation, pretty lady?"

"I'm single, divorced, but yeah, single."

Huey stroked my arm as we talked. It felt nice. Human touch— sigh. I reciprocated.

He moved in for a kiss, and then more kissing. That felt nicer. I went with it.

Partiers came in and out of the room: "You guys are cute!"

"You can go outside for privacy."

Thank God for molly! I got the benefits without having to touch that stuff.

I awoke the next morning to a message from Huey, "So sorry for last night hope I didn't make you feel uncomfortable."

"No apologies needed. I had fun."

We proceeded to hang out. Err, he hung out and got me up and down and sideways and backwards and all around. Huey's strong and flexible that way.

I had severe performance anxiety, though. He's a man of girth. I was astounded and scared by its sight. We worked it out eventually, though, every time.

Huey and I took walks and went to shows and stuff too, but you don't care about that. You just want the excitement. I did too.

A few months into our courtship, he said, "I don't feel like you're the one for me. I'm not breaking up with you, but if you're open to dating other people?"

I thought about it. No, I didn't think about it. "That won't work for me."

Damn tears.

We're still cordial. I was hurt and sad, of course. But there was no malice.

Plus, it's a relief to not feel the pressures of having so much to take in. You know?

Alas, a nerd like me who doesn't do drugs. We'll call him PeeWee.

Someone to really communicate with about what we want in a relationship, about life and dating, stress, friendships, all of it.

"Can I just vent to you?" I'd asked—amid computer frustrations, fiscal worries, having lost my laundry room key, and other miscellany. He listened. He's sweet, the nice man I'd been seeking.

PeeWee and I met on a crowded dance floor, partying to welcome 2019. He awkwardly said that he didn't know how to dance, stepping painstakingly to Maroon 5's "Girls Like You"—with his hand positioned comfortably on my ass.

There were a few kisses on the dance floor, and then "Can I take you home?" Man's not too shy. "We can just cuddle." I fell for the line. By that, I mean, I believed he truly meant it.

"No, this is too fast, but I am interested. I'd like to see you again."

We kissed more at my car after the place shut down.

I arrived home to a text thanking me for a wonderful night.

Sweet messages periodically flowed in, "Good morning, beautiful. Have a great day."

"I was about to make dinner for myself, but I'd rather share with you." PeeWee cooked me meals—soups, pasta salads, homemade pizza.

These preceded make-out sessions, and after a couple of weeks, sex.

The sex was questionable. I questioned whether or not it happened. He's that peewee. Honestly, I felt nothing. Never had such questionable sex before. Bad sign. Still, I liked him.

We tried without a condom, once we'd been tested and cleared. That helped, slightly. I felt a tinge of something, a faint but meager sensation, as if someone burped in Paradise.

"I understand your problems with men," he told me. "I'm bisexual and have issues with men too." PeeWee disclosed this casually as we shared a meal. Gulp. Say what?

I could date someone who's bisexual. Afterall, he's a caring, nurturing, liberal that cooks for me. He listens to me too. How awesome is that? Maybe I'm the one on the wrong team, or maybe I need to be on several teams. There are plenty of options.

On the way to see a movie, he blurted: "I got a dress that I was waiting for. I'll show you later tonight."

Say what? "A dress? You didn't tell me you cross-dress."

"Oh, yeah, I like dresses. This one has bright colors. That's the only reason I ordered it. Why, is that a problem?"

Gulp. "I just, give me time to adjust." We can exchange clothes, maybe? But he's bigger, so that won't work.

This one, though, this sealed the deal: "My ex-wife has a new boyfriend, so I have to cancel our hike for this weekend. She's going out Saturday night, and I need to watch the kid."

"Oh-kay. Well, I'm disappointed. I'd prefer you check in with me first."

"My kid comes first. You have to understand that."

"I mean, he's 14, and he treats you like crap. It's not unreasonable that I'm not okay being dumped at the drop of a hat."

"It is unreasonable! My kid's always my priority. There might be times when I need to cancel because Sandy has a date, or my kid has problems, or whatever family stuff goes on. She's wonderful woman who does most of the childcare. I need to be flexible."

"You're letting her keep you under her thumb. Either you make time for me or you don't. I'm not disposable."

"Come on, Robyn. You're making this about your problems with other men. You need to give me space to be a father and husband. I mean, ex-husband."

The argument repeated itself three or four times.

Been there, done that. "I'll really miss you. Good luck."

No response.

I won't miss the questionable sex.

Standup comedy became—without doubt—a lifesaving force. My performances improved too.

I was in my zone, riding the onstage high that my comedic routines unexpectedly and occasionally deliver. My lines about, well, length and inches and stuff—e.g., "In penis math, one inch equals two" reaped laughter. To my left, an attractive man and his lovely brunette friend cheered giddily.

While performing, I commented on her good fortune, assuming they were a couple. Her expression told me "We're just friends, but you just gave me an idea."

After the show, as I chatted with other comics by the bar, this sweet lady approached.

"Hi, I'm Marla." We shook hands. "You were hilarious! Can I introduce you to my friend?"

"Thanks, sure."

Marla walked me to Clark, at a nearby table.

"Oh, I assumed you were together."

"No. We both teach at Chico Middle School."

He's a teacher. Cool.

Clark, with chest pressed out, said: "I can give you nine inches." His smile, intoxicated and intoxicating. "But it'll be in three installments."

"Hey, nine is nine."

So naturally or not, I ended up driving Clark home. I mean, I couldn't let him drive drunk. This followed more chatter, and Marla's assurance that he's not a creep. I could trust a lovely woman who's a teacher, with her drunken male teacher friend, right?

Turned out, hours later, yeah, I could trust him. Myself? Not so much.

It was very fun and naughty but not to-the-full-extent-of naughty. Clark had repeatedly requested that I spend the night.

"My bed is really big, so our bodies won't touch at all," he bargained.

The night ended with Clark telling me it was up to me to contact him "since you're rejecting me," but I got the most flirtatious, drunkenly cute smile from him and meager wave "goodbye".

I called the next day.

We made plans for the evening.

Clark brought over dinner and drinks. We talked about past relationships and what we're looking for. A seductive tension thickened.

He turned to me, "What do you want to do now?"

"I want to kiss you."

Things heated up blissfully smoothly. "Are you okay with this?" Clark asked.

"Yes."

It was a wonderfully pleasurable night. He gave me one installment. (I suspect it was approximately 5 inches. I didn't take out my tape measure.)

Clark texted the following afternoon.

I went to his place for a salmon dinner that upcoming Friday night.

He asked me questions, didn't interrupt my responses to tell me tediously boring factoids about himself. I really, really liked him.

As soon as Clark bit into the salmon, though, he felt sick. A few minutes later, I was politely, apologetically asked to leave.

What a disappointment.

"How about if I bring you some homemade matzo ball soup?" I offered. Good move. I'd win him over for sure.

My soup turned out great. Clark appreciated it so much that he bargained for potato latkes next. I agreed, with a playful (but serious) disclaimer, "That's going to be it for my Jewish dishes, though."

The night arrived.

Dinner time: "These are great. Thanks for making them."

"Well, truthfully, I used a mix. It's easy," I grinned. "And I *had to* taste-test plenty of latkes in the process."

We moved to the couch after dinner.

He took my hand. "I planned for you to stay the night," Clark said stoically, "but you like me more than I like you."

Um, Okay? Shit, what's going on?

"I hate hurting people, so I want to keep dating you, but without the sex."

Huh? "What would that look like? We already crossed the line."

"Yes, and it was wonderful. But I potentially want to see other people."

You're hurting me so as to not hurt me by refusing to have sex again with me because although the sex was wonderful, you've decided that I have more feelings for you than you do for me, and you therefore want to continue to date me without having sex, but you'll simultaneously date and have sex with other people?

"I think you're projecting stuff onto me," I shrugged. "Okay, then."

I got up to retrieve my purse and the leftover latkes.

"Why are you—? That's it, you're NOT staying the night. Now I regret having had sex with you." Dipshit.

He walked to his kitchen, retrieved a roll of aluminum foil from a drawer, and tore off a large piece. Clark meticulously wrapped the leftover latkes in foil, then handed them to me.

Damn straight, you don't get these!

I took my other belongings and walked to the door. What do I say now? I looked at him.

"Well, have a good night," is all I could muster, because I'm foolishly nice like that.

His expression, sad and patronizing.

Another end, another less than super man.

This time, in the aftermath, I weakened. Badly. Very badly. I went back into the weird, soul sucking world of online dating.

There, Eldee S. stated that he's looking for someone "emotionally available." I assume when someone's looking for emotional availability, they're emotionally available. We made a nice connection in writing and by phone, so we met in person.

Eldee and I had a pleasant day together. We talked openly about a variety of topics. He said he rejected Mormonism, so I asked about that.

"I don't want to talk about it." Welp, okay.

Back at my place, we fooled around a bit. Eldee took his shirt off. He was wearing an undershirt.

"Is that the Mormon underwear?"

"Yes. I can't talk about it."

"Oh, but I thought you rejected your faith."

"I did. I guess, not fully yet."

"It must be difficult."

"The undergarment has inscriptions on it, but I can't tell you what it says."

"Alright." I didn't ask. What, you'd have to kill me if you did?

Apparently so, I've learned. There's all sorts of required secrecy to the religion.

I don't mean to mock any particular faith. I simply don't trust any person, group, or entity that keeps secrets from the world outside of its members. There's a cultish vibe to that, and cults cause damage. Cults can't be trusted. If there's nothing to hide, what are you hiding? It's strange.

Speaking of strangeness, Jackson appeared to be a cute, hip, 34 year old who allured me with risqué lingo about wanting to please me. When I pushed back a bit in specifying that I want a supportive friend and lover, he said all the right things. He's only been with two women and doesn't want to move too fast either. Thus I gave Jackson my number.

He texted me a picture, one that highlighted a big bulge. No, not that. His belly. And his face, not so cute, kinda fat. That'd be okay with me, were he honest. But he self-described as "slim."

I'd already suggested we meet for coffee, though. To that, he'd said "coffee isn't close enough."

What? You're not even willing to sit and talk for a few minutes, so that I'd feel comfortable first?

I reread our thread as I was about to go to bed that night.

I awoke alarmed at 4 a.m. I messaged Jackson to tell him that something felt wrong.

"You don't look slim, as you describe yourself. With sex as your selling point, we have different priorities."

"You caught me on a fat day, what can I say! I thought you're not into superficials. I don't sell or buy sex. Your words don't earn respect. You could of just asked to meet for coffee. It's not close enough but I like coffee. It could've been great sex. I don't know what book you read but my God is loving. No wonder men hate woman and blah blah blah."

Jackson sent message after message, 27 or so of them, thereby depicting the boundlessness of true insanity.

But then I met Sven. We very quickly created a meaningful, quality connection. Sven and I corresponded for four hours on the day we met. This culminated in a phone call to hear each other's voices. He cleared all my red flags and dealbreakers. He's liberal in all ways. He's from Sweden, then based in France, now in Northern California, where he plans to stay.

Following a marital breakdown, he adopted a child as a single dad. Sven's very intelligent and ambitious. We were in touch sporadically the following day until—wham! Nothing.

He disappeared on me; I was "ghosted." Ouch. For the first time since Justin, I thought I'd possibly found someone to have lasting love with. Then he was gone. I had no clue what to make of it.

Not only that, his profile was taken down. What the hell. I messaged him three times, and he kept not responding. Last night,

I put it all out there that, having read through our correspondences, I know I wasn't imagining the meaningful relationship that had begun. I'm left sad, confused, worried, and (damnit) I deserve at least an explanation.

No response.

So it goes. It appears that no older man has the desire or skills for meaningful intimacy. This one, though, seemed intent on a serious, lasting relationship. I guess not, not at all. Sigh.

I'm spending way too many wasted hours online to fight my loneliness, resulting in increased loneliness.

Then loneliness stopped, unexpectedly, thanks to the man with long nostril hairs and a poly lifestyle, Paul E.

We reconnected at a concert in the park. A mutual friend asked if we know each other, to which we said "yes" and got caught up.

I admit to being attracted more than I was in the past. He must've plucked his nose hairs because I didn't see any. I think we're both a bit less stressed than we were back then. We agreed to be "friends, at least."

Paul invited me for dinner at his place. A home cooked meal? How could I turn that down? I didn't.

Tasty food and genuine discourse ensued. We owned being unsure about pursuing more than a friendship. We sat outside, while he barbequed chicken and veggies, served with salad and rice. He had a little fire going.

My host escorted me to my car and kissed me. On the lips. With tongue. In a way that friends don't. Suddenly, we were dating again.

Paul slowed down sexually, due to age, and I think that he's convincing himself that monogamy is his choice. I told him I don't want to try to talk another man into something that's not his natural inclination or mindset.

I also realize that I can be mean. Unfairly so. He's sweet and pretty all-loving plus more on the passive side with women. Thus, he felt my meanness.

Paul came to see me perform comedy.

We laughed and sat together on a bench, snuggly.

To my shock, Brandi showed up with Jeff. Crazily, she acted as if we're fine.

"Hi, Robyn. Are you guys dating?"

"We're just friends," we said in unison, as if planned. Paul tightened his grip around my waist, and I rested my head on his shoulder.

Brandi and Jeff slipped away, all the while I felt entirely victorious.

The sex between Paul and I was, like with PeeWee, questionable. He's puny. That's fine. I mean, not his fault. But I think he's delusional, given the extent to which he boasts about his successes with ladies. He could barely get it moving.

"You scare me," Paul confessed out of the blue. "You're complicated."

"Why? How so?"

"I don't know. You, you have a particular way of saying things." Wha,at? "What if I don't fall in love with you?"

"What if I don't fall in love with you?" I retorted.

"Then we'll be great friends."

"We already crossed that line."

"You, you, you—" he paused and sat stupefied.

"I don't understand this. What did I do? Do you want me to leave?"

"No."

"Do you want me to stay?"

No response.

Paul slouched over, appearing pained and constipated. "I don't know. You're too complicated. I don't know what else to say."

Oy vey. Nor did I.

It was different with Vincent. We had two in-depth phone conversations, at the end of which he said he'd call to make a plan to take me to a club that upcoming Saturday night.

He never called. I went anyway. Vincent showed up with a buddy at the club. What the hell?

The music stopped between songs, all eyes on him, all ears on me. So I crossed the floor to confront him.

"I lost your number," he defended himself.

"What is wrong with you? You can't hold onto a phone number for three days? And you have the nerve to show up here anyway?"

Vincent lowered his head. "I'm very sorry," he walked away meekly.

I exchanged fist bumps with a male friend, who happened to be sitting nearby.

"What is wrong with men? Why can't I find one?"

"Well, Robyn, you're pretty intimidating."

"I am?"

He nodded.

Therein I realized that I'm not insane. I just have an angry temper when my ego's been squished, squeezed, chomped on, and spit out.

Then again, it's insane how much power I've given others to impact my ego.

Speaking of the ego, and weirdness, anger, and my poor choices and all, remember Revere? The one who told me to contact him via Western Union?

Yeah, I went on a getaway to Ashland, Oregon for my 53rd birthday. He was there, at a pub where I chatted flirtatiously with a young hottie approximately 22 years old. Total ego boost.

Next thing I knew, there was Revere, standing behind the lad, staring at me while holding a glass of beer, which he drank from a straw. Who the hell drinks beer from a straw?

I gave him a "You're cramping my style" expression.

He disappeared. Revere wanted me to see him. Drinking beer from a straw. Oy vey.

Please, please, please, make it stop. Pause, please. Permanently. And for the untold time, I declared myself done with men.

Chapter 24: Wherein There's a Will

"Love is the only sane and satisfactory answer to the problem of human existence."—Erich Fromm

Toxins vexed the air at my destination that day, so I stuffed a cloth mask into the front pocket of my jeans.

"GOD morning, Geezer!" This high-pitched, crackling vocalization from my newest neighbor startled me, despite its familiarity.

In a world of 7.8 billion humans, the most unwelcome ones keep finding us, just when we've put them completely out of mind. That is, my former roommate returned to close proximity: Carrie. She took occupancy of the unit that was up for rent, as Geezer's other next-door neighbor.

You're right, reader. It's the same Carrie that needed to know our home dress code when she interviewed for the spare room in Stephen's home; the one who called the police when I held her blow-dryer hostage, after she'd placed her hair all over our shared bathroom and rearranged my hygiene products; whose diet consisted of kale smoothies for every meal.

Now she's lost her mind and we're going hoppin' people say happiness takes so very beaches and you can't smile without the diamond yellow feathers who could ask for more?

Perhaps the mainstream notion of insanity is flipped on its head, I'm thinking. What if insanity is changing your behaviors and getting the same results? Makes a lot more sense. Destigmatizes that bitch. It means we're all insane or prone to it.

And if you stood next to me at the large window on the north side of my living room, you'd notice a certain car parked behind the white truck. I don't know if you'd recognize it, but I sure do. It's Twig's. He's back too.

Per Morty's unsolicited report, Twig begged Harlotta to take him back after the Camp Fire. She did.

In fact, she took his last name too. They're married. Yep, he locked in that new housing arrangement.

Thus, while it broke and killed more lives than we'll ever know, the Camp Fire also brought some people together. Beautiful, right?

I'm all for that. Everyone deserves comfort and love. Everyone who's nice to me, that is.

These neighbors aren't, so fuck 'em. I already fucked one of 'em, and it was pretty good but then he went for Harlotta who I taunted, after she nabbed Twig and bullied me. Now it seems we're one insane grouping in my little speck of this crumbling planet that, as far as I'm concerned, should revolve around me.

"A long time ago I stopped wondering why there are so many crazy people. What surprises me now is that there are so many sane ones."—Rachel Khong

Enough pontification. It's time to move on to the task of the day; I walked from the window to my purse, which I dug into for my car keys.

A mixture of obligation and curiosity occupied the passenger seat. Courage too, I suppose, though I didn't think about that. Before and during that half-hour drive, I avoided deep thought altogether.

White sprinklings of makeshift shelters in which emergency workers were stationed caught my eye. Caution tape had been stretched about with seemingly no rhyme or reason, as if protecting already incinerated patches of earth that supported rusted fragments of vehicles.

What I remember as Jack in the Box—now, a flimsy wooden frame of an eatery in which I'd sipped a pumpkin something-or-other weeks earlier.

My favorite two-story antique shop, a delightful treasure trove, mere dirt and ash.

Charred tree trunks, stop signs, faded panels of fencing—vast, surreal ghost town.

Yet as I drove alongside the Terry Ashe Recreations Center, my eyes caught this message on a display panel: "#Paradise Strong!" Signs of resilience had stubbornly, remarkably, taken the fore.

Then, a rather unexpected sight—waving affectionately at passersby, Santa Claus! The skinniest, most perseverant and spirited Santa ever to grace this region. I couldn't help but blow him a kiss. Claus glared at me in response, suspect and troubled.

Did he know I'm Jewish or naughty or both? Oh, well. I still adored this Santa—regardless of his frigidity.

This land is your land.

Yards further along Skyway, I pulled into a parking lot. It was time to meander by foot.

I trekked through fledgling blades of grass towards Skyway, then stopped. With eyes closed intently, I inhaled sweet pine. The scent, faint and nostalgic.

Upon opening my eyes, an inspirational message eclipsed the scene. Inscribed in children's writing on a hand-cut cardboard heart that was strung to a signpost by purple yarn, "Love is stronger than fire!" Sweet words.

Youth, our most innocent of unsung heroes.

I thought about my trips to a Chico elementary school. That campus had seamlessly integrated a former Paradise elementary school. With almost no time to prepare for the expansion, the kids and staff had frenetically posted murals and artistic creations to warmly welcome their new peers. Two schools in one, voilà.

This land is my land.

When there, I'd see smiling faces in all directions. There's no indication of an "us" versus "them" dynamic. Kids seem to get it in a way adults never will.

Insane Factoid: It costs 2.06 cents to make each penny and 7.53 cents to make each nickel.

My client's schedule shifted such that I arrived during recess. I give my young clients autonomy to choose therapy activities. This one chose tetherball. During my typically agonizing attempt to compete in tetherball against my client, a girl approximately my height approached to declare, "I'm in first grade." She eyed me up and down.

I surmised that her point is that she's my height at age six. I provided a smile and a diminutive life lesson: "We all come in different sizes, right?" She nodded and spryly dashed away. Meanwhile, the ball hit me smack dab on the nose. Ouch.

Mere seconds later, it seemed many kids had noticed my lack of tetherball savvy. "Maybe you should just hit it, you know like, hard," I was advised. "Want me to help?"

"I'm okay, honey." Sweet punks.

I tried. My client ultimately and proudly defeated me by 15 (to zero) games.

By the way, did you know that a "cheap shot" amounts to one's opponent hitting the other's body with the ball, the result of which is that the person hit by the ball loses? And this is perfectly legitimate. Yeah, I'm no fan.

Perhaps dodgeball would be a less vicious option. God I hated dodgeball. Talk about a violent "game."

Oh yeah, I ran into Ember at that school. Well, we crossed paths. I thought I'd rid my life of her too, since she went to start her own practice elsewhere. But it seems she also took one of the volunteer counseling positions for Camp Fire victims. How generous of that selfish bitch.

Passing through the quad, Ember and I faced off squarely. I conferred an unenthused "hi." She conferred a glare. That was it. Fuck that. It's hurtful, rejecting. Ignoring a person, treating them as though they're nonexistent.

How mean.

But I've been similarly mean. I ignored Glenn on campus, in class, sometimes and often at home. I didn't know better. It's not the same, right? I was a kid—though not really, or almost not really. I was over 18 when we'd see each other on the UCLA campus and even had one class together.

Nothing had been modeled for me. Intimacy scared me to a point of paralysis—I just didn't know how to relate to him. I guess he didn't know either, because he said nothing. But it was on me, the older, healthy one, to break the ice. To be more stable.

It's like living with someone who's severely depressed or anxious or struggling with bipolar disorder, any intense mental illness. It's damn hard. There's really no right thing to do, and it's too easy to go wrong, or to feel as though you've failed. Because none of us can fix mental illness. There's no cure.

Besides, how do you talk to someone who has psychosis? The same way you talk to anyone else, I guess. But at the time, I couldn't. Well, I literally could. I could make words and express coherent thoughts. Yet something stronger than strong held me back.

My own severe depression, deep sense of worthlessness, fears, probably a mixture of many emotions. Guilt, a biggie. But not malice. Perhaps it looked that way. And he looked that way when he was at his worst—malicious, destructive. Even that's understandable. He was robbed of control over his mind.

I gripped my own hand, centering myself on the grass, reminding myself I'm still here for me. Through my tears, I noted another kid-written slogan, this one on a cutout star blowing slightly with the wind behind the other: "Stay strong!"

I heard myself release a heavy exhale. I then looked around and decided to walk to the ice rink. They'd excitedly announced the reopening of it this week.

Leaning against the thick, sturdy ice rink wall, I watched a precious toddler in a puffy yellow jacket and pink mittens, holding her mom's right hand and dad's left. They glided along proudly. Her face, though, indicated extreme fear. I giggled.

"Robyn, is that you?"

I turned to see who'd made the inquiry.

Methie. "Oh, it is you. Going skating? Robyn, you know I've—"

"Yeah I'm not—"

"—been wanting to see you and are you going skating because I heard it opened so I told my sister-in-law since I was gonna check on the house I'd get the details on skating. We're gonna bring my nieces and nephews here 'cuz we all love it, and I've been wanting to say sorry more personally for all that with Scorpio, can I give you a hug?"

"Of course."

We hugged.

"No, Methie, I'm sorry. I wish I hadn't—"

"I still adore him Robyn but he can't love anyone like he knows, because of his issues and problems you know, and he told me that and I was really hurt in my heart but I had no idea you were dating Robyn. He didn't tell me that I swear. We just have so much in common and we still hang out you know. I still really love him."

I don't remember you talking quite so much, girlfriend.

"I came to see the damage at my grandmama's house and we're going to rebuild and go ice skating and make an even bigger house with a 25 square foot loft and tree house with a swing for the kids and we're so excited"—she beamed.

"That's grea—"

"Yeah Scorpio is going to help but he needs new tools, of course I'll pay him and he's charging about half of what he should charge so I told him he shouldn't do that because it's not good for our friendship and we value that more than anything, but he doesn't want to take more than that from me so I'm glad we're okay and my grief is heavy for my daughter the one that committed suicide—"

God I hate when people say "committed." How about "died by suicide?" Or possibly more accurately: "died due to extreme mental illness"? Take the damn stigma and blame out of it, people.

"—miss her too much but Scorpio has been a really good support, really really good, and she was really tortured I loved her so much she was my whole heart. She's not in pain thank Jesus, and we can be friends now and it was great to see you Robyn!"

"You too, Methie. Thank you."

Patterns. Repetition. Beginnings. Endings. Middles. Musings. God mornings. Saintly afternoons. Tortured minutes. Crazy nights, if you're lucky. Weirdnesses, frequently and unexpectedly. Bad Robyn. Gets mean when ego hurts. Her writing's irrelevant because Ricky goes potty. Go Ricky, go! Rejected Robyn. Keep the hole covered. Bad girl.

Methie's sincerity took me down a notch. I can't believe I was so mad-jealous that I called her "ugly." I let my anger get the best of me. I've an angry temper. Into my fifties, I'm just now acknowledging this. But it's not too late. And I am acknowledging it.

Most of the time when I've thought myself crazy, I was mean instead. Mean isn't necessarily crazy. It's an immature, stunted state of existence, that's all.

True insanity is truly insanely illogical. The truly insane need, above all, patience and kindness. That is, when they're able to receive it, which is most of the time.

All told, I'm not sane or insane, just imperfectly human—the kind of person I hate at times, one that easily slips into bouts of instability, especially when sex or love are in the mix. I'm the kind of sassy, passionate, forthright and forceful person that I love at times too.

Loneliness makes me feel crazy.

Ego damage sets off cascades of intense emotions.

Sex cures and causes insanity.

Love does the same.

This land was made for you and me. Even now, here I go again.

On the drive back home from Paradise, I contemplated my brother's final mindset. His darkest of depressive episodes. They don't compare to mine, but I understand the urge to die. I know the invisibility, feeling a burden, the desperate need to terminate this weight.

Yet I can't compare my much healthier brain to a diseased or psychotic brain.

Sans unhinged schizophrenic demons, sans a debilitated mind, I've survived. It's luck, pure luck. I didn't and don't have a schizophrenic brain. It could've too easily been me.

I do still need antidepressants for a lifetime. But I can mostly manage my depression.

Psychosis doesn't allow for any sense of control. A person experiencing psychosis has an understandably meager will to live. It's incredibly tragic. Love is the only answer, while it's not an answer.

Perhaps there's no simple way to navigate any of this.

I'm here. I breathed and kept surviving.

I breathed and tended to me.

Glenn chose death. I hate it. I accept it.

Justin made that choice. Twig's son did. Methie's daughter, a loved one or more of yours too, dear reader.

It's not my fault or yours.

I've chosen life—however lucky I've been to perceive it as my best option. However lucky I've been to have a lot less to worry about than the torment my brother faced.

I need to keep choosing life. There's no other way to give and
take acts of kindness. No other way to ease anyone else's journey.
You have to choose life, in order to inspire others to do the same.
You have to choose life, to experience gratitude.

I choose life, and I intend to give my best to the whole of it.
I arrive home, in sanity.

Conclusion: It's Not Just Me

"Sometimes you climb out of bed in the morning and you think, I'm not going to make it, but you laugh inside--remembering all the times you've felt that way."—Charles Bukowski

<u>Late 2019</u>: Word broke of a highly contagious virus that originated at a public market in Wuhan, China. "Don't touch your face," experts advised. You know the rest, and it continues, tragically.

<u>On work</u>: There are few drawbacks and many rewards to having my own practice. No holes to cover. I'm not harassed for setting a reasonable limit with unreasonable people. No boss asks publicly "Are you a midget?". Let's not pray. Shall we not?

<u>On the neighbors</u>: They're still here. Geezer's on his sun chair a few feet from my front entrance as I type. My best guess regarding Carrie, who's been quiet, is that she's currently blow-drying her hair while blending a kale smoothie on her kitchen counter. Harlotta and Twig have been shut-ins since the pandemic hit our region. She doesn't park in the carport at all. Their windows are covered in aluminum foil. So, yeah, things are back to normal abnormalcy.

<u>Amen for A Man, Justin Two</u>:

   A distinguished looking man caught my eye from across the table.
   "Hi, I'm Robyn."
   "I'm Justin. Nice to meet you." A friendly handshake ensued.
   Defined cheekbones, thoughtful demeanor. Wait, Justin. Justin? Yikes. I'd vowed to never date another Justin. How could I?

   We talked after the show in the Lab's front parking lot, but Jesus—a hippie comic who looks like the Western world's version of the Lord—interrupted. "Robyn, sorry, can I get a ride home? I'm drunk."
   I couldn't let Jesus take the wheel.

"Sure, in a minute." I turned to Justin, "Sorry, but I'm performing on Saturday night here, 8 p.m."

"Okay, I'll be here."

I dropped Jesus off in front of a dark alley. "My place is down that walkway," he told me casually. What Jesus refers to as a "walkway," I call a sketchy dark alley. But thou shall not judge.

Saturday night, as I got my notes together in the outdoor patio, Justin Two ("JT") stepped through the gate. I approached him, arms outstretched.

"I'm a hugger. I hope that's—" JT's embrace conveyed firm assurance.

After the show, free-flowing chatter ensued at a small wicker table in front of JT's house.

I watched him light a candle to illuminate the tranquil setting. Tulips graced a tall thin glass that centered the table.

"Pretty flowers," I noted, and JT told me that they're plastic.

We learned of various commonalities. Neither of us drinks or smokes. Neither owns a television. Each opens the passenger's side car door first, when serving as the designated driver. Like me, he's divorced with no kids.

"I'm not looking for an open relationship," I clarified. "That seems to be what all the men I've been dating want."

"No, that isn't a real relationship."

"I agree."

Time flew. It was 1 a.m.

JT pulled one of the tulips from the glass and handed it to me. "You'll get real ones later."

At my car, there was a brief moment of glancing into each other's eyes under a bed of stars, and then his two lips were on my two lips. And then, a second sweet kiss.

"I didn't expect that," he said.

I was hoping. But not hoping too much, because you know how I've been very disappointed again and again and again, and then highly disappointed again, by men? Yeah. I hoped a lot, while trying not to hope at all.

<u>Three months later (Time slips by when trying to finally publish a book):</u>

My entire narrative was flipped on its head by a man who's more grounded than I am.

It's not our similarities that impress me most. It's JT's stating that he shouldn't expect me to react to things the same way he does, that we have different views and priorities based on vastly different life experiences. That's to be respected and appreciated, not fought against.

I've tried too hard to get the guy to see it my way, instead of simply evolving into a better, more open-minded human.

We each know we're good alone. Self-love matters most.

Yet we like and love each other, so we're madly invested in our relationship.

I signed off from online dating. Forever. Fingers crossed. Toes crossed. Breath held. May it be so.

Please, Jesus, I did you a solid. I didn't let you take the wheel.

<u>Final Musings:</u>

I'm amused by a musing. It canoes while it's snoozing, in a fuchsia canoe through polka dot stew. Inspire kindness not pride. Proud is too loud. At the showy fraught spot, hot to trot, you are not.

Blues, blue's clues tattooed on suede shoes. One for the money, two for the crockodile rock show at the copa, co, co, puhhhh, cuh, cuh, cut it out. Without a doubt. Sauerkraut. Who likes that shit anyway?

He views me. Canoodling's due. His grin bestows beauty. Those alpha arms, too. My muse. I can't refuse.

I smile at him. I mean, I can't smile without him. I write the songs because I've been alive forever, but I only wrote six songs and I repeat them over and over and over throughout the decades. Oh, Barry. Heartthrob. Does forever ever end? Don't phone a friend.

He's coming over to sit with me, as he should.

Wait, I'm attached.

Shit. I can't be flirting with another man. I forgot. I mean, I've been in flirt mode most of my life. I just forgot JT. It means nothing, right? Wrong. It makes me a skank. Tourette's. Skank. I'm the damn skank. Skanky harlot, that's me. I'm all about being better than this, but I'm another floozy like the rest. What the hell. Is this for real?

Charlotte? Wow. I haven't seen you in ages. But you're so small. You must be Charlotte's grandbaby.

What do I do now? He's sitting next to me, getting cozy. He's striking up a convo. Fuck. He's dark and so cute and I brought this on myself.

JT went to buy me a ginger ale, he's thoughtful like that, and here I go seducing another man.

I love JT. He's so good and kind and would never even think about cheating on me. I don't deserve such a solid man. I'm very bad. I'm crazy. Damnit. Now I understand how easily these things happen. You know? You do know, right? Because I know you know. I know you know that I know I'm the damn skank all along.

Popcorn. It's not even a popcorn ceiling anymore. It's got all sorts of shades and shadows and mountains and peaks and valleys, and grays and blacks and whites and yellows and weird patterns and shapes and all. Like a penis. Or a vagina. Or anything else for that matter.

What the fuck do I do?

My eyes shoot open. JT's by my side, laying on his tummy. As usual, we've awoken simultaneously.

"Good morning, my sweetie." I lean over to kiss his cheek.

"Good morning, honey." He rubs my back.

"Um, I need to confess. I didn't do anything but I almost did, babe. Because I love you so much and I don't ever want anyone else but you but well, he was cute too and I kinda like young men and stuff so I just, I just smiled, and he sat next to me, and then the guilt woke me up. I'm sorry sweetheart. I'm, I'm very sorry."

JT imparted a silly, loving grin. "Really?"

I giggled. "Yeah, it's true. I mean, as true as any dream could ever be true. I'm sorry, but I mean, it was a dream and I even remembered you in my dream. After I forgot about you altogether."

I rolled onto my back. "What are you thinking, my love?"

"Coffee. Gonna make coffee. Want some?"

"Sure."

<u>Alternative Titles (for fun):</u>

1. Coca-Cola Cabana Boy
2. Greek Gods and Viagra Ice Cream
3. Be Good Girl, Cover the Hole
4. Please Don't Be My Neighbor!
5. Grand Granny Under Panties
6. Big Ego, Small Man Part
7. An Analysis of Shrinkage
8. Pee in Cup, Pay Big Price
9. Drunk Jesus Doesn't Drive
10. Damn Vocal Tics!
11. BJ's and Blow-dryer Buffoonery
12. Straws Aren't for Beer
13. Ricky Goes Potty!
14. Pesky Little Musings
15. This Land Is Our Land
16. Please Believe
17. It's Not Your Fault
18. Keep Loving Through It

<u>Thank You Notes:</u>

It took a village. I'm very fortunate for a team that's as kindhearted as it is talented. My folks didn't just say "Good luck." They readily poured their time and skills into this book. Their contributions helped me make *InSanity* both a source of pride, and a worthy contribution to the literary world.

Bryan Pedas, your constant support and care, your ability to know precisely what I need to hear in the exact moment that I need to hear it, your skills in offering the most palatable of feedback, your loving friendship—this all keeps you at the top of my list. You are the best.

Debra She Who Seeks, Canadian Goddess of all Goddesses, I remain humbled by your generosity, patience, clarity, wit, and keen eye for every single hyphen—those damn sonsabitches!

Friends who happily set their lives aside to focus on *InSanity*: Sue Goldberg, Ken Lynch, and Silona Lynne Reyman, I treasure you.

When I cried out desperately for assistance with graphics, Steven
Kistler responded. And he responded by knocking this cover into a
more spectacular universe.

Thank you, my dear readers. May you take from *InSanity*
whatever challenges you to be your best self as often as possible.
May it inspire new thoughts about humanity, about "mental
wellness" versus "mental illness," about tendencies to judge and
categorize members of the human family.

Most of all, may it provide you with enhanced self-love and
inner peace.

Love, Robyn

9 798773 385127